CHAPPAQUIDDICK REVEALED

What Really Happened

Kenneth R. Kappel

Shapolsky Publishers, Inc.
New York

10 9 8 7 6 5 4 3 2 1

Library of Congress Cataloging-in-Publication Data:

Kappel, Kenneth R. 1941-

Chappaquiddick Revealed

Bibliography, p. 301
Includes Index

1. Kennedy, Edward Moore, 1932- .   2. Kopechne, Mary Jo, 1941-69.
3. Chappaquiddick Island, (Mass.) History.   1. Title.

ISBN 0-944007-64-3

Photo Credits p. 303
Excerpts from *The Bridge at Chappaquiddick*, by Jack Olsen
reprinted by permission from the author.
Column from Mike Royko which appeared in
The Chicago Daily News, permission by Tribune Media Services.

Published in the U.S. by Shapolsky Publishers, Inc.
136 West 22nd Street, New York, NY   10011

Distributed to the trade by Carol Communications

Introduction
by John H. Davis

When I was in the early stages of researching my 1984 book, *The Kennedys: Dynasty & Disaster*, I followed Senator Edward M. Kennedy's 1980 campaign for the democratic presidential nomination with more than a special interest. For, if Edward Kennedy succeeded in winning the nomination and then went on to attain the Presidency his victory would have colored my entire book. Instead of the book being, as I had originally envisioned it, a tale of overweening dynastic ambition followed by disaster after disaster, the book would have ended upon a ringing note of final redemption: the restoration of the Kennedys to national power after a series of unprecedented family calamities.

But, alas this consummation was not to be. It was not to be chiefly because Senator Kennedy's 1969 automobile accident on Chappaquiddick Island, which resulted in the death of a young woman, Mary Jo Kopechne, would not as Kennedy and his political aides had vainly hoped, eventually wash out of the public consciousness. As a result of this intractability the Chappaquiddick accident became, in the long perspective, the most consequential automobile accident in American history.

I had always suspected that Ted Kennedy's accident on Chappaquiddick had destroyed his chances of ever attaining the presidency. I was surprised, therefore, to note from informal conversations with some of Kennedy's campaign workers, early on in the Senator's quest for the nomination, that many in Kennedy's entourage had deluded themselves into believing that Chappaquiddick would not be a factor in the struggle against Jimmy Carter for the nomination. "No, they're not going to dredge *that* up again," was their constant refrain. Or, they would say something like: "Chappaquiddick happened over ten years ago. It's ancient history. Everybody's forgotten about it by now."

As it turned out, Chappaquiddick was *not* forgotten in 1980. Both the media and the public were aware there were still too many unanswered questions pertaining to the case to allow it to be so readily forgotten. What was Senator Kennedy, a married man with a pregnant wife at home, doing cruising around Chappaquiddick Island in his car late at night in the company of an unmarried twenty-nine-year-old woman? Why, after his automobile accident caused the young woman's death did Kennedy wait ten hours before he reported the accident to the police? So perpetually nagging were these still unanswered questions that no sooner did Ted Kennedy's campaign start gathering momentum than the accident *was* dredged up again, and dredged up again, it seemed, with a renewed fervor, and with equal fervor flung into the Senator's face.

In February, 1980, no less a trustworthy family publication than the *Readers' Digest*, a magazine boasting the largest circulation of any monthly in the world, came out with a major cover story on Chappaquiddick, the result of a lengthy and meticulous investigation of the accident by a team of *Digest* researchers and hired experts. This, in turn, was followed in March by a page one expose in the *New York Times* of Senator Kennedy's hitherto unknown telephone calls, made during the early morning hours before he reported the accident to the police, and an account of how the existence of those calls had been successfully covered up at the official Inquest into the accident ten years before. Soon the *New York Post* was flinging Chappaquiddick mud and dirt into Kennedy's face in huge front page headlines. And so it went throughout the rest of the campaign until the Senator went down in bitter defeat in November, at the hands of a beaming Jimmy Carter, thus dashing the hope of a restoration for the Kennedys to national power in the foreseeable future.

The curse of Chappaquiddick had exerted its force once again. For Kennedy the name of the little island off Martha's Vineyard had taken on the same weight and significance as had the little Belgium village of Waterloo for Napoleon.

No, Chappaquiddick would not wash out of people's minds. Nearly a decade after the accident had plagued Edward Kennedy's 1980 campaign, a book on the calamity, *Senatorial Privilege: The Chappaquiddick Cover-up*, by Leo Damore, became, after attempts to squelch it, a national best seller. In fact by July of 1989, it was the *New York Times'* No. 1 best seller.

As the twentieth anniversary of the death of Mary Jo Kopechne approached in the spring of 1989, Chappaquiddick was once more in the media wind. Since I had written extensively about the accident at Poucha Pond in my book on the Kennedys, major television talk show producers began phoning me asking if, in my opinion, there was anything new on the case.

I was at the time doubtful whether anything new would develop twenty years after the fact, other than that which Leo Damore had recently published, but then I read the manuscript of Ken Kappel's book, *Chappaquiddick Revealed*, and was immediately persuaded that there might indeed be something new on the accident.

It is the special merit of Ken Kappel's detailed and carefully researched investigation of the accident that he was able to discern the importance of certain previously overlooked and undervalued physical evidence of circumstances surrounding the cover-up. By combining that evidence with the new material that he unearthed he was able to construct a fresh new interpretation of what actually did happen on Chappaquiddick Island the night of July 18-19, 1969.

What, in brief, has Ken Kappel focused on in the way of significant, previously overlooked evidence in his book?

For one, evidence of widespread blood stains on the back of Mary Jo Kopechne's blouse that could not have been caused by blood oozing from her nose, mouth, and ears while underwater (since such a blood flow would have been too diluted by the water to cause deep stains on her clothing), but may have come instead, as Ken Kappel theorizes, from an accidental blow to the back of her head *before* the Senator's Oldsmobile hit the waters of Poucha Pond.

For another, evidence that Mary Jo's body did not sink, that it retained its buoyancy when it was retrieved from the sunken car at 8:55 A.M., the morning after the accident by scuba diver John N. Farrar, indicating that Mary Jo did not immediately drown after Kennedy's car sunk into Poucha Pond, that instead she suffocated in an air void and so could have been saved within a half hour of the accident had Kennedy sounded the alarm.

Even more significant, is overlooked evidence uncovered by Ken Kappel consisting of a series of photographs of the Senator's car just after it had been hauled out of the water that revealed the existence of massive vertical dents running from top to bottom on both passenger side doors of Kennedy's four-door Oldsmobile sedan, dents that could not have been caused by the car's impact on water but suggest collision with trees before the vehicle hurtled into Poucha Pond.

Finally, Mr. Kappel has focused his attention on another item of previously overlooked evidence that demands an explanation; photographs of the loose, unhinged, askew side-view mirror on the driver's side of the car when all the observable damage done to the vehicle by the accident appears on the roof and passenger side. Why was the side-view mirror knocked askew?

And what has Ken Kappel noted in the way of previously overlooked instances of cover-up?

That Senator Kennedy's chief counsel at the official Inquest, Edward P. Hanify, purchased the Senator's Oldsmobile from the insurance company that had impounded it after the accident and then had the car crushed in a compactor, thereby destroying evidence of the strange vertical dents in the passenger side doors and the askew side-view mirror on the driver's side.

What new interpretation of the accident has Mr. Kappel arrived at in the light of the foregoing previously overlooked physical evidence and further evidence of cover-up?

In a conjectural hypothesis that I do not necessarily endorse, but believe is worthy of serious further investigation, Ken Kappel theorizes that a possibly drunken Senator Edward Kennedy driving out-of-control with Mary Jo Kopechne down one of Chappaquiddick's dark, wooded, dirt lanes, after he left the party at the Lawrence cottage, at one point may have skidded off the road and struck trees, severely denting the car's doors on the passenger side. And injuring the back of Mary Jo's head on impact, knocking her deeply unconscious and causing the staining of the back of her blouse with blood. That subsequently Kennedy left the car and went back to the party to find two of his most trusted companions, his cousin Joe Gargan and long time family friend, attorney Paul Markham. And that the Senator's Oldsmobile containing Mary Jo's unconscious form (assumed to be dead by the three distraught and medically untrained men) may have been pushed down Dyke Road by another car and into Poucha Pond to make it appear that Mary Jo had been driving the car alone, and had caused her own accidental death.

Take this startling interpretation into willing suspension of disbelief and consider the examples of previously overlooked evidence that Ken Kappel has assembled to sustain it, and the reader may well come to the conclusion, as I did, that there might be something new in the Chappaquiddick case after all, something that makes the accident into a crime more serious than it was originally determined to have been. Especially since it is now reasonably certain, according to recent testimony of Kennedy's cousin, Joe Gargan, to author Leo Damore, that Kennedy did not report the accident until ten hours after it had occurred because he wanted it to appear to the police that Mary Jo had been driving the car alone. (Gargan was supposed to have reported this version of the accident but had backed out of doing so.) If alcohol were a factor, they would naturally not be able to report an accident that would certainly have led to a manslaughter charge against the Senator.

As authors Leo Damore and Ken Kappel have shown, the accident at Chappaquiddick stubbornly refuses to wash out of the public mind. Far too many unanswered questions still remain. Questions such as now that we have been told by Joe Gargan through Leo Damore that Kennedy wanted the accident to appear to have been caused by Mary Jo Kopechne herself, driving alone, how did Kennedy expect to convince the police of this scenario and cover up his own role in it? By getting good old Joe Gargan to tell the authorities the crucial lie? The lie that would mask Ken Kappel's scenario?

Ironically, it has been the maddeningly effective cover-up of the true facts surrounding the death of Mary Jo Kopechne, perpetrated by Senator Kennedy and his loyalists, that has contributed to public interest in the Chappaquiddick accident and caused it to remain a permanent roadblock to the higher political ambitions of Senator Edward M. Kennedy.

JOHN H. DAVIS

John H. Davis is the author of a number of books chronicling famous and powerful families in modern American History, including *The Guggenheims, The Bouviers,* and *Mafia Kingfish.* Mr. Davis wrote on Chappaquiddick in his national best selling book, *The Kennedys: Dynasty & Disaster.* A *cum laude* graduate of Princeton, he studied in Italy on a Fulbright Scholarship and served as a naval officer with the sixth fleet. He resides in New York City.

Writing may have been a game in other ages, in times of equilibrium. Today it is a grave duty. It's purpose is not to entertain the mind with fairy tales and make it forget, but to proclaim a state of mobilization to all the luminous forces still surviving in our age of transition, and to urge men to their utmost to surpass the beast.

Nikos Kazantzakis, *Report to Greco*

Foreword

Beyond an idealistic belief that truth should be told in order to both inform and serve history — unfortunately, this thing, *truth*, an essential component of true democracy is all too often ignored, even ridiculed or denigrated by *conventional wisdom* as not the way of the *real* world — I have labored with conflicting thoughts regarding the question:

Why write a book on Chappaquiddick?

There is simply no easy answer or single reason. Looming large is the legitimate case to be made regarding the fact that Edward M. Kennedy continues to hold a seat in the United States Senate. A poll which was reported on CBS radio in March, 1989, indicated that Kennedy is the leading candidate for the 1992 Democratic Party Presidential Nomination. Yet, opinion polls over the years have shown that a majority of the public does not believe his version of what really happened that tragic night. He chooses to flout public opinion, and consequently sets a bad moral example for all of us, especially for our youth. Both the press and the Democratic party continually legitimize a claim to high moral ground for Edward Kennedy, by considering him a spokesman for the liberal standard of decency and for the party itself.[1]

Finally, it is time to speak for Mary Jo Kopechne, who was virtually ignored as this matter wound its way through the courts without justice being achieved. Kennedy did plead guilty to leaving the scene of an accident which caused bodily injury to Mary Jo. In other words he pleaded guilty merely to a lapse of judgment. It will be shown herein, and it is the opinion of the

---

[1] At the 1988 Democratic Convention, the Senator's rhetorical question: "Where was George?" was righteously returned at the Republican Convention with T-shirts adorned with a bridge and which stated "Where was Ted?" From my vantage point it seems the appropriate question is: "Where was Mary Jo?"

author that the proper charge should have been manslaughter, which, had he been found guilty, would not only have prevented him from holding elected office, but could indeed have placed him in prison.

As a former *LIFE* magazine staff member, I was drawn into this project as a result of inadvertently discovering new material, new evidence, *new hard demonstrable facts* that were missed, ignored or somehow not brought into the public eye by either the previous authors on the subject or those many hundreds (if not thousands) of reporters, analysts and armchair theorists who were early on the case.

At the outset, I unequivocally state to the reader that the bones to the truth about Chappaquiddick are contained herein. Further, that the final conclusions, which are merely this author's opinion and theory based on the facts, have not been publicly published elsewhere. I do not claim omniscience; yet there is no doubt that Kennedy family spokesmen, retainers and hangers-on will claim that a weak branch or a flawed thread was followed in reaching the final conclusions posited herein. I challenge them to first come forward and explain how the *new material* presented below can fit into the Senator's version of that tragic night before they dissemble and criticize. Careful reader, you decide.

To be fair, there is no doubt that, at least on his better days, Edward Kennedy has attempted to lead the way, even to set an example in his public life. And that he has shouldered a large burden regarding the families of his fallen brothers. His good deeds and intentions aside, Senator Kennedy has become part of the problem. His personal ambition is overreaching, and ultimately he succumbed to a fantasy based on his father's dream of family destiny. What is worse is that he became blind to the deeper laws that determine civilization, that govern even the appearance of deeds for a statesmen; in short he has developed hubris.

I did not consciously seek to research, investigate or write about Chappaquiddick. While doing research on another project, it became clear that the truth about Chappaquiddick, which is to be found in the *complete* public record, had never been properly analyzed, its fragments never adequately linked to show *how*, which leads to *why*, the tragedy occurred that night on Chappaquiddick Island.

This horrible event has remained an unsolved mystery largely because the myriad of complex — and obscured — facts were brilliantly covered-up by a state-managed (that's Massachusetts) endgame.

My work has benefited by: the early research work of others; the perspective of time; and, some luck with a magnifying glass. By piecing together certain key facts, not particularly volatile when considered separately, I became the passive observer of a theory that emerged on its own, synergistically. The result is an entirely new interpretation of the probable events that night.

It has been written, by no less a source than Burton Hersh, an authorized biographer of Ted Kennedy, that family, friends and associates were alarmed about the Senator's alcohol consumption combined with his driving, following the tragic murder of his brother, Robert. Hersh stated:[2]

> If alcohol helped, alcohol would have to.
> Throughout all of which serious Kennedy advisors watched. "If you get drunk regularly in public with various important personalities," one of them ventured privately, thoughtfully, of Ted, "there has to be an element of self-humiliation present doesn't there?" It was a question worth asking about a man who was generally regarded that spring as very probably the oncoming President of the United States.

They were right to be concerned. It appears, and will be shown below, that a heretofore unreported automobile accident

2 Burton Hersh, *The Education of Edward Kennedy*, New York: William Morrow & Co., Inc., 1972. p. 489.

which took place earlier in the evening, on the narrow roads of Chappaquiddick, led to a secondary chain of events and actions completely ignored until now — culminating in a tragic and unnecessary death.

Unfortunately for Mary Jo Kopechne, and in the opinion of the author, it may have been these secondary actions which took her life. While the original and and heretofore unreported accident was without intent, it is the purpose of this book to prove that the later actions were premeditated, wanton and willful. Such conduct legally constitutes manslaughter, if not negligent homicide! Yet, in all fairness, it must be clearly stated at the outset that one of the theses of this book is that Senator Kennedy and his associates had no evil intent, no thought of committing murder or causing a death, and in fact became victims themselves as a result of their need to cover-up, to hopefully save the career of a future President, and, most important, keep him and themselves out of prison after certain actions had been set in action. Attorneys all, they are living in a self-created hell, and may never tell the American people what really happened. Paul Markham, who ably assisted Kennedy that night and the following morning by writing out Kennedy's statement to the police, stated, "I see no prospect of talking about it. Not today, not tomorrow and not the next day. I see no necessity of talking about it ever!"[3]

Their foremost purpose was to keep the Senator out of prison. Steven Smith, (married to Ted's sister Jean), had been anointed by patriarch Joseph Kennedy to manage the family business. As has been widely reported, Smith assumed the role of executive producer of the cover-up at the Kennedy compound at Hyannis. Smith stated clearly:[4]

[3] *NY Times,* 7-21-69.
[4] Robert Sherrill, *The Last Kennedy,* New York: The Dial Press, 1976. p. 125.

Our prime concern was whether or not the guy survived the thing, whether he rode out the still possible charge of man-slaughter.

The conclusion reached herein is that, underlying what passes for public knowledge on the subject we have come to call "Chappaquiddick," is a horrible truth. The truth is that Mary Jo Kopechne died inadvertently and unnecessarily, but not in the manner we have been asked to believe by Senator Kennedy and his associates.

This grim information has been most forcefully asserted by an individual in a position to know. Trained scuba and life-saving professional, John Farrar, the longtime Captain of the Martha's Vineyard, Edgartown Fire Department Emergency Rescue Squad, discovered and recovered Mary Jo's body from Ted Kennedy's automobile which was found upside down in Poucha Pond, just off Chappaquiddick Island. In my meeting with Farrar he seemed to be a rigidly moral man who has no love for the Kennedys. Like the members of the Kennedy family, he was raised with money and privilege. Educated among the elite at Milton Academy and Brown University, he became a very conservative Republican. Some people do not contain a capacity for deceit. I found John Farrar to be one of these people. He possesses a spirit zealous for truth and righteousness.

Even after twenty years Farrar feels stymied and frustrated that his word, his professional and informed expert opinion, has been ignored because it is at cross purposes with the enormous power and needs of the Kennedy family. He has attempted to tell the world the truth about the accident: that Mary Jo Kopechne *did not drown*, nor was she dead when the car entered the water. On the contrary, Farrar asserts that when he found the body she was in a position with her head held up in what may have been an air pocket at the top of the overturned submerged vehicle. And, that she ultimately suffocated, rather than drowned, some time after the car was submerged. Farrar finds it difficult to believe that any rescue attempts were made by Kennedy and his associates (as their testimony indicates) in the early morning hours, He stated:[5]

> Her hands were still holding the back seat in what I should say was an attempt to keep her head in this [air] pocket. I must say that there remained a chance that the girl's life could have been saved if rescuers had got into the car earlier.

Kennedy's prominent appearance on the national stage indicates a continual flirtation with the American people regarding a hope — now a mere fantasy — to be president one day. In fact, his presence occasionally fuels the rhetoric of pundits from both the Left and Right.

It is not inappropriate to imagine that, in his heart of hearts, he had hoped that the young Turks might tie themselves up early in the 1988 primaries, leaving the possibility for a brokered convention; as Alexander Cockburn wrote so tellingly:[6]

> The most imposing rhetorical presence was Teddy Kennedy, who made just enough jokes about his future to leave those dismayed at the candidates on view [at the 1983 Democrat Party mid-term convention] with the faintest of hints that come deadlock, come low water, the chariots will roll again.

No less a personage than John McLaughlin of the network show "The McLaughlin Group," himself formerly the Washington editor for *The National Review,* speculated on national television that Kennedy's name would be bandied about in 1988 as a nominee, but that revelations from a forthcoming book would then halt the process. The present author assumes that the reference was to Leo Damore's 1988 book, *Senatorial Privilege.*[7]

---

[5] Zad Rust, *TEDDY BARE: The Last of the Kennedy Clan,* Belmont, Massachusetts: Western Islands, 1971. p. 41.

[6] *Village Voice,* 4/19/83.

[7] See Appendix F.

As recently as, December 10, 1988, the *New York Times* mentioned that Senator Kennedy's name was being mentioned, if not privately proposed, as Chairman of the Democratic National Committee. In that his former aide, Paul Kirk, had just stepped down as Chairman, and the charter would have to be changed to allow an elected official to head the party, one wonders whether or not Senator Kennedy, since he has no White House in his future, is still attempting to claim a major power broker's role.

In fact, on a more immediate level, Chappaquiddick forces Kennedy into self-censorship and causing him to continue to limit the national debate on substantive issues. What we see is an uncomfortable man merely heaping scorn on himself when he calls out, "Where was George?"

> ...even though **I knew Mary Jo Kopechne was dead** and believed firmly that she was *in the back* of that car, I willed that she remained alive. [Emphasis Added.]

Thus spoke Edward Kennedy under oath at the Inquest into Mary Jo Kopechne's death.[8] This statement attributes too much information to have been known by the individual who claimed not to have been aware of how he got out of the sinking car. How could he have "*known*" that she "was dead" and "*believed firmly*" that she was in the back" if, in fact, he had not been either informed by others, supervised others, or placed her there himself before the car entered the water? It is likely that his statement given under pressure as sworn testimony contained a classic Freudian Slip; and the truth emerged under stress even though the Senator had an urgent need to suppress that truth.

Some say we should give the truth about Chappaquiddick a "wink and a shrug"; Teddy Kennedy is owed the Presidency or at least "a walk" in view of the fact that his three older brothers gave their lives in service to our country. I do not agree.

---

[8]   Inquest, January 10, 1970, Edgartown, Massachusetts.

Mary Jo Kopechne was an innocent, a true believer. She had formerly been a Kennedy family employee on a professional career track.[9] She gave her life. Rather, it was taken from her. She deserved more; and now her tormented spirit deserves a champion.

Robert Sherrill,[10] who wrote decisively on Chappaquiddick, put the issue of Kennedy's fitness for the Presidency (even for the Senate) into perspective simply and accurately in his *Inquest* magazine review of Garry Wills' 1983 book about the Kennedys, *The Kennedy Imprisonment*. "Can you think," he asked, "of anything politically significant, politically impressive, that Edward Kennedy has done in the twenty years he has been in the U.S. Senate?" Every time I repeat this question, whether to a neutral party, Kennedy foe or friend, or even a past Kennedy staff member, I am nearly always met with an initial silence.

I wish to make it clear that this is not a "Kennedy" book. It is not a dynasty book, not even a book on the whole Edward M. Kennedy. The scholars, the enchanted, and other writers will never cease to concoct the tales, perpetuating the legendary myth of Camelot, of America's near-royalty. For this author, the irony is that for Royalty: Jackie was the one.

The purpose of this book, then, is to dissolve the shrouds of secrecy that were professionally draped over this mystery. As the facts began to fall into place and I sat down to write, it was essential to seek a tone for the book which would adequately speak to the new evidence. Evolving from the role of an impartial researcher *cum* investigator, I frankly became outraged as the salient facts fell into place, and found myself becoming a self-appointed public prosecutor. While I have been urged by many, and have attempted, to relax the tone of this book, the

---

[9] Regarding the other women who attended the party that night at Chappaquiddick: one is now a housewife in the Washington, D.C. area, another is an "important" book agent who helped bring forward Geraldine Ferraro's post-election book, and the other three are partners in Boston area law firms.

[10] See Appendix C.

facts as presented below leave an angry taste. A real prosecutor attempting to convince a jury would use stronger language than you will find here. The prosecutor in this case, Edmund Dinis, had become quiet for reasons we will see later. I believe that this work lives up to the responsibility I have undertaken.

It has been said that Chappaquiddick is the most mentioned unsolved mystery in contemporary times. Jack Anderson called it "one of the great political stories of all time."[11] Kennedy's own attorney in this matter, Edward Hanify, had stated that Mary Jo Kopechne's death had generated "more publicity than any other fatal accident in the history of the United States and perhaps, the world."[12]

It is my intent that this book which presents the first new theory in many years, and which is based on new hard evidence previously overlooked, will shed new light on *what may have really happened* that night. With no desire to be a ghoul or self-aggrandizing hack careerist, I put work on this book on the shelf when Senator Kennedy withdrew from seeking the Presidency in 1982. When he started up again in 1984-85, so did I, and when he stopped, so did I. But now I can simply no longer believe that he has really stopped, that he *can* stop; neither can I.[13] He seems unable to realize what has gone on before in his life, and seems to want to erase the past by attempting to do what he considers as good deeds. All attempts at rehabilitation aside, justice remains unserved.

As for myself, in order to let go, you must finish what you start. To paraphrase an influential liberal who has written on the

[11] Leo Damore, *SENATORIAL PRIVILEGE, The Chappaquiddick Cover-Up*, Washington D.C.: Regnery Gateway, 1988. Interview with Jack Anderson, 3-15-84, p. 262.

[12] Damore, interview with Richard McCarron, 7-29-83, p. 290.

[13] [Author's Note: Unless otherwise cited, all footnotes contained in official documents and transcripts presented below are editorial, the opinion of this author. There has been a difference of opinion of how to spell the word Dyke, as in *Dyke Bridge* where the car entered the water. On Martha's Vineyard they write Dyke, *not Dike*, consequently *all* mentions below of the bridge and road are presented as *Dyke*.]

Kennedys: "Even if it is only a footnote, history should reflect the accumulated record — should show the truth."

Postscript: from the *New York Post*, April 15, 1986

> Sen. Ted Kennedy was fined $75.00 for speeding last week in Duxbury Mass., it was learned yesterday.
>
> Kennedy, 55, driving alone in the 1981 white Cadillac owned by his mother, Rose, was clocked doing 80 miles an hour at 11:50 a.m. by state police.
>
> He has already paid his fine $50 for speeding and $25 for driving without a license.
>
> In 1969, a car driven by Kennedy, plunged off Chappaquiddick bridge, killing Mary Jo Kopechne.

PART ONE

THE RECORD

"He who controls the past, controls the future."

George Orwell, *1984*

1

WHO, WHEN, WHERE

On Friday afternoon, July 18, 1969, at approximately 1:00 P.M., Senator Edward M. Kennedy, 39 years of age, arrived at Martha's Vineyard, Massachusetts on a small airplane. Martha's Vineyard, an island only ten minutes flying time from Hyannis Port, on Cape Cod, is a quaint and historic part of America. During high summer season, the Eastern seaboard's liberal elite gather to partake of the sea, sun, air — and mutual considerations. The late James Cagney, Walter Cronkite, James "Scotty" Reston and Jackie Onassis have all been regular seasonal residents. Carly Simon is a leading light among the younger set. Even the late star John Belushi maintained a get-away home on Martha's Vineyard. For some it is a welcome, if not more wholesome, summer respite from the oddly "chic" Hamptons on Long Island, New York.

Historically, the Island has been home to whalers and commercial fishermen. Martha's Vineyard once shared with Nantucket, a few miles due south, a reputation as producers of legendary ship captains, who sailed the seven seas.

Senator Kennedy had arrived to take part in the annual Edgartown Regatta, as members of his family had been doing for some thirty years. An added attraction, that Kennedy later indicated was a social/political *obligation*, was a party to be held at a cottage on Chappaquiddick Island. The Indian name Chappaquiddick means "separate island" and it sits a scant 220 yards from Edgartown, the main township of Martha's Vineyard.

Chappaquiddick is reached by a ferry which runs regularly and often during the summer months. The open-decked ferry, while small, could handle two automobiles and up to twenty passengers.

The ferry's name, *On Time*, is ironic in relation to the record which is about to unfold, might have been more suitably entitled *Out of Time* which is certainly thematic with the events which conspired to tragically end the life of Mary Jo Kopechne. Miss Kopechne was an invited guest at the party that was held Friday night at the Lawrence Cottage on Chappaquiddick. Mary Jo had worked for Robert Kennedy when he was in the Senate. She was an election specialist, and, after Bobby's death, she had gone to work for Matt Reese Associates. Her expertise in electoral politics qualified her for this company, which set up campaigns and field organizations for political candidates.

Mary Jo had graduated from Caldwell College for Women in 1962. She had been a business major and worked in the Civil Rights movement in Alabama before joining the staff of Senator George Smathers of Florida. She lived in Georgetown with Nance Lyons (also at the party) and two other girls.

There are varying reports as to why the party in fact took place. The *New York Times*, July 20, 1969, stated some 36 hours after the tragic accident, "According to Kennedy staff members in Washington, there had been a party on Chappaquiddick Island... for David Hackett, a friend of Robert Kennedy." The *Chicago Daily News* weighed in with a report that Senator Kennedy's attorneys would soon produce a list to local Police Chief James Arena: of six men, in addition to Senator Kennedy, who were at the party. These six named were: Joseph Gargan, Paul Markham, Charles Tretter, Ray LaRosa, John Crimmins and David Hackett. The next week the *Boston Globe* reported that Hackett was "known" to have been there. The *Boston Herald Traveler* also reported that Hackett attended the party.

Hackett was also named as being one of the individuals who gathered at the Kennedy compound at Hyannis Port immediately following the tragedy.[1]

Hackett's name is mentioned here at the outset because, amazingly enough, after all this early reportage, Mr. Hackett somehow disappeared from the official lists of those who publicly admitted attending the party, and who later testified at the Inquest into the death of Mary Jo. It is likely that these reports ultimately stemmed from the comments of Richard Drayne, Kennedy's press secretary, who had explained when the reporters first got onto the accident that it was a party for former Bobby Kennedy "boiler-room gals" and was in honor of David Hackett.[2] Normally one attends a party held in one's honor!

The importance of David Hackett's presence will be discussed completely in Chapter 13; the point here is to establish that widespread reportage indicated his presence; and how, from the very beginning, the story that the public received from Kennedy was at variance with the facts as they came to be established. *Human Events* Senior Book Editor, David Franke, also placed Hackett at the party in an article published 11-2-74. The *Vineyard Gazette*, the local Martha's Vineyard newspaper, stated on 7-22-69, that it was a "party for David Hackett." It had learned this from a "Kennedy staff member in Washington." We may assume that the reporter in both this later mention and the *New York Times* as above, was James "Scotty" Reston. Mr. Reston, former *NY Times* Executive Editor and retired op-ed columnist, owns with his family, the local *Vineyard Gazette*. Presumably the *Gazette* had been his busman's holiday and from local accounts, his Martha's Vineyard powerbase. To his eternal credit, Reston himself did not go easy on the young Kennedy in the aftermath of this tragedy, stating in his *New York Times* column that:

---

[1]   Jack Olsen, *The Bridge at Chappaquiddick*, Boston: Little, Brown & Co., 1970. p. 242. And, Richard L. & Thomas L. Tedrow, *Death at Chappaquiddick*, Ottawa, Illinois: Green Hill Publishers, Inc., 1976, Page 62.

[2]   *Boston Herald Traveler*, 7-20-69.

For the hard facts are that he ducked the main questions, evaded the press, pleaded guilty to the charge of not reporting the accident on time, which avoided cross-examination in the court. And in these circumstances — with all witnesses to the evening's proceedings gone from the Island and silenced, and all questions to the Senator barred in court — it is not clear why he and his counselors should raise the moral issue and appeal to the voters who have no means of questioning the cast of characters.

He has gone through a ghastly experience — not only on this Island [Reston was writing from Martha's Vineyard] recently, but ever since the murder of his two brothers. It may be that the pressures of the last year, when he became the proxy father to his brother Robert's children, the Democratic whip of the Senate and the leader and symbol of the Kennedy clan and its ambitions, were too much for him. But to end the Kennedy story on this tragic note, to ask for an impossible referendum on unknown facts by the people of Massachusetts is ridiculous.

The Kennedy strategy was to discard or add facts and information as suited their needs. It was necessary not simply to save the career of a senator and future presidential candidate. To repeat; Steve Smith; guardian of the Kennedy fortune, stated:

Our prime concern was whether or not the guy survived the thing, whether he rode out the still possible charge of manslaughter.

This brings us to the level of deepest need and necessity for the Kennedy family. From the very beginning, as the events began to unfold, Kennedy was surrounded by lawyers. These lawyers knew full well the laws of the state of Massachusetts; but more importantly, they knew that, even if Kennedy beat the charge of manslaughter, the very charge would wreck his political career. And as Smith stated there was a very real possibility that he might go to prison.

As will be proved in the following pages, in this case a conspiracy was formed, complete with illegal covert acts by three and possibly a fourth individual to obstruct justice with the specific intent of avoiding a charge of manslaughter. The irony as well as the horror, as will be shown, is that these very acts themselves, were, in the opinion of the author, the cause of the death of Mary Jo Kopechne.

In the state of Massachusetts, the statute describing manslaughter states that "willful and wanton conduct," must be an essential part of overt acts which result in death of another party. However, that does not mean and must not be interpreted to mean premeditation or the intent to kill. Also, by Massachusetts law, and pertaining directly to the point here, if an individual leaves the scene of an accident without reporting it, *if negligence is proved*, and that accident results in death, a manslaughter charge is *mandatory*. For example: driving under the influence of alcohol which results in death is cause for a manslaughter charge.

It would be most instructive to attempt to look into the mind of the local prosecutor, Walter Steele (now Judge Steele), to analyze his reactions and conclusions regarding the case as it was originally presented to him. We have his uncontested words as first reported in Jack Olsen's 1970 book[3] about the incidents at Chappaquiddick. Olsen, a former *Time* magazine senior editor,[4] rented an apartment and became a two month resident of Martha's Vineyard and consequently was known to the locals. He was thus able to move freely between the assembled press and the inside players. Consequently, we have good reason to put stock in Olsen's reconstructed dialogues. According to Olsen, Walter Steele was in conference with Police Chief Jim Arena the morning prior to their first meeting with Kennedy's attorneys. They were attempting to determine exactly what

---

[3] See Appendix A.

[4] Olsen wrote a moving eulogy in *Sports Illustrated* after JFK's assassination, and the Kennedy family was most appreciative. He explained to the author that when it was known that he intended to write on Chappaquiddick, he lost all access.

charges would or could be made. Steele's alleged remarks to the Chief were as follows:[5]

> But here's what we do have. One, we have his statement. Two, we can prove that he walked past at least two places that had night-lights on when he was leaving the scene, and his first report was made to you not less than nine hours after the accident. Third, there's no evidence of excessive speed or drunkenness. No evidence of speed or drunkenness. A lot of people are making a lot of wild-ass allegations, but I'm talking about evidence. Fourth, there's a medical examiner who says it's a classic case of death by drowning. And fifth, there's an unblemished body, and no trace of injury either by human hand or by banging against the car. In Massachusetts, there's no such thing as negligent manslaughter. I mean, you can't convict a man of manslaughter if he just screwed up and somebody dies as a result. The act has to be willful, wanton and reckless, which means something more than negligence and something less than murder. There's no way to stretch this case to manslaughter, and we'd be laughed out of court if we tried.
>
> The second that Kennedy walked past the first house on Dyke Road, he was guilty of leaving the scene.... it does mean that leaving the scene is the only criminal charge we can bring, no matter what some of the newspapers are saying.

Let's take a brief look at Judge Walter Steele for a moment. In 1962, Steele was a colleague of Senator Edward M. Kennedy. Kennedy's first job out of law school was as an Assistant District Attorney for Suffolk County; in a word, Boston. Steele was also an ADA on that staff and was known to be both hard-working and thorough. It has been reported that there was some grumbling on the staff regarding the fact that Kennedy wasn't pulling his load. The word was that Teddy was busy with his brother's campaign, and that he didn't have to worry about establishing his reputation at this level since his family's connections had made

---

[5]   Olsen, p. 209.

his career for him. The Burton Hersh biography disputes this, but the Hersh book appears to be a very friendly, even apologetic work which was written after Chappaquiddick.

In 1969, Steele maintained a private practice in Boston and acted as a part-time prosecutor for his beloved Martha's Vineyard, drawing a mere $5,000 in annual salary. Coincidentally, on another matter he had been at the Police Station when Kennedy and Paul Markham were there giving the statement, which will be presented in its entirety in the following chapter.

Mr. Steele knew Paul Markham as well. Markham was one of the individuals who had been at the party on Friday night. He accompanied Kennedy to the Police Station the following morning and, in fact, wrote out (and co-edited) the statement for Kennedy that was presented to the Police Chief as Kennedy's version of what had happened. Markham had recently given up the position of U.S. Attorney for Massachusetts. Paul Markham, a handsome Kennedy intimate, wore the highest Kennedy badge of honor: he had dislocated his shoulder in a touch football game at the compound some years before. Bobby Kennedy had convinced President Lyndon Johnson to appoint Markham as Assistant U.S. Attorney, and later prevailed on him to give Markham the top job as U.S. Attorney for Massachusetts.

Paul Markham got mixed reviews in his term as U.S. Attorney. He did send alleged Boston Mafia boss Raymond Patriarca to jail, but failed in his prosecution in the famous Plymouth robbery case.

In a zealous play for publicity as U.S. Attorney, Markham had personally led the police in a raid of suspected draft dodgers. Even though known as a liberal Kennedy man, no bleeding heart was he. He was an extremely hard-working family man with seven children, and was generally known to follow a moderate life style. As will be presented in Chapter 17, his movements for some months immediately following the tragedy lead to more than idle speculation regarding his actions during the fateful and telling nine hours following the accident.

Joe Gargan is Ted Kennedy's close cousin, and is two years older than the Senator. His mother was a sister of Rose Kennedy, and to some extent the two boys were raised like brothers. Gargan, trained as a lawyer, has been known as the Senator's "man" in Massachusetts. Some have deprecated Gargan, referring to his gofer status, but there can be no doubt that he served Teddy to the best of his abilities and that his loyalty remains unswerving. In fact his culpability as a participant after the fact, combined with the role of attorney which Kennedy thrust upon him, left him in an untenable position.

It was common knowledge that Joe Gargan was the individual who instigated the party, as well as its chief planner. He coordinated the social events of the Regatta weekend for the Kennedy entourage. When Markham and Kennedy went to the Police Station in the aftermath of the tragedy, Inquest testimony made it clear that Joe Gargan organized the sweeping-up of the debris of the party, and professionally and discretely escorted the ladies who had been at the party from the Island. Rumor once had it, most notably as published in Jack Anderson's *Washington Merry Go Round* column, that Joe Gargan had been set to take the rap as an alleged fall-guy, or driver of the vehicle which plunged into the water.[6] Whether Gargan was planning to do this or not is moot now. What is clear is that based on the evidence he was involved in executing a series of events to delay, if not avoid altogether, reporting the accident. Ultimately, it was the actions of the cover-up which, we will see, led to Mary Jo Kopechne's death. Joe Gargan has never been known to be a leader, and there is no reason to think that he was a leader in the planning after the accident. He remained faithful, and it my opinion that ultimately he continues to do so; contrary to the reportage by Leo Damore in his 1988 book, *Senatorial Privilege*.[7]

---

[6]   In Leo Damore's interviews with Gargan, Gargan allegedly told Damore that Kennedy suggested that Gargan and Markham take him back to the cottage, then he would go on to the Shiretown. Later Gargan could discover the car, and they could say that Mary Jo had been driving. Damore, op. cit. p. 81.

[7]   See, Appendix F, for comment on Damore's *Senatorial Privilege*, which is a well-written, scrupulously researched book. The issue here is to question whether Gargan was setting up Damore in order to keep the lid on an effective cover-up.

Damore undertook a massive investigation of the events and actions comprising the cover-up successfully staged by the Kennedy legal team. A close reading of Damore's book indicates that, at some point, if true, Joe Gargan was less than satisfied with his relationship with Senator Kennedy and, during this period, met with author Damore for several interviews. Gargan reportedly told Damore that, while Gargan and Markham unsuccessfully dove for Mary Jo, the Senator tried to convince them to say that Mary Jo had been driving the automobile. We have not seen Gargan challenge Damore's account of his remarks, and perhaps they are true. The very fact that Gargan broke his fourteen-year silence at that time (1983) was undoubtedly a major factor causing Random House to sign a book contract with Damore and advance him $150,000 to write the book which they ultimately rejected, and then sued him for return of the advance money. The rejection caused Damore to mount a herculean effort which ultimately saw his book published as a best seller through the last half of 1988, and became the No. 1 best selling paperback in July of 1969.

In order to complete the cast of major players in the events immediately following the discovery of Senator Kennedy's Oldsmobile in the waters of Poucha Pond, it is now necessary to look at Police Chief Dominik Arena.

The local chief, Dominik "Jim" Arena is a large man who stood 6'4" tall. He was serving in his third year as Chief of Police in Edgartown. Prior to that he served for thirteen years as a Sergeant with the Massachusetts State Police. Before that he had been a Staff Sergeant in the United States Marine Corps. Arena had known Senator Kennedy briefly in the past. As a state policeman assigned to governmental affairs, on several occasions he had officially chauffeured Senator Kennedy in Boston.

In fact several key players in the investigation had working relationships with the Massachusetts State Police. And it would not be overreaching to suggest that there may have been direct actions that could be seen as dereliction of duty if not obstruction of justice by two active State Patrolmen, Lieutenants George Killen and Bernie Flynn. Flynn admitted to author Damore that he surreptitiously met with Kennedy attorney Herbert Miller,[8] and a second time with Miller and Kennedy's brother-in-law Steve Smith, to assure them there would be no "surprises" from the D.A.'s office at the Inquest. This was clearly an obstruction of justice which Flynn now allegedly regrets.

Chief Arena wasn't looking for any challenges. In some ways he undoubtedly felt that his sinecure in Edgartown was a reward for a life devoted to service and honor. He was a good man. The minimal crime in Edgartown was certainly to his liking. He might investigate the rare burglary, stake out a location where seed-clam poachers were reported to be operating, quiet a local drunk, have a chat with a potential delinquent; but basically it was his presence rather than his actions that were required in Edgartown. Activity always heated-up in the summer, and there could be rowdiness on the streets, but the Police Department hired summer provisionals, which basically spread the increased work load. Arena was in charge, but hardly imposed upon.

At approximately 7:55 A.M., on Saturday, July 19, 1969, Chief Arena arrived at the Police Station in Edgartown, the largest and principal township of Martha's Vineyard. He retired to his small office to go over the log book, which contained a record of the previous night's activities. A stolen car had been found, a fight stopped, and a dozen cars had been ticketed for overnight parking. For a Friday night on Regatta weekend, it was a nothing; in fact, the calm before the storm. Heading to the street for his customary stroll, he noticed that Carmen Salvador, the day-shift desk policewoman, was on the phone, and he paused to let her to finish the call. She reported to him that a car had just been discovered in Poucha Pond. He decided to go out to Chappaquiddick to investigate himself.

As he occasionally liked to do in order to give the local old-timers who daily occupied the benches adjacent to the Court-

---

[8]   Mr. Miller went on to fame representing Richard Nixon in the Watergate scandal.

house a thrill, he ran out to his police car, and peeled-out. He drove to the ferry, crossed with the car and drove the 3.5 miles to Dyke Bridge. After observing the barely visible car, lying upside down in the water, he borrowed a bathing suit from the nearest neighbor, Mrs. Malm, who had reported the submerged car, and then called the Communications Center for backup. Almost as an afterthought, he told the Center to have the Fire Department's scuba diver come right over. Mrs. Malm had told him that around midnight she had heard a car "going faster than usual."[9]

He then made his way into the water. The tide was running swiftly, running out, and he was literally swept away each time he attempted to look into the car. Realizing that the trained scuba diver would soon arrive, he made his way to the rear end of the car that was now beginning to protrude from the water. He hoisted himself into a sitting position to await the diver.

A mere twenty-five minutes after receiving the summons on the telephone, John Farrar, who was Captain of the Scuba Search and Rescue Division of the Edgartown volunteer Fire Department, was on the scene strapping on his scuba gear. He had been reached by telephone at the Turf 'N Tackle Shop in Edgartown of which he was the manager. Farrar came from an old-money family and had matriculated at Milton Academy and Brown University. Milton Academy was also *alma mater* to Jack and Bobby Kennedy. (Bobby's roommate, David Hackett, entered the Kennedy circle as a result of this Milton connection.) Farrar, a Martha's Vineyard local, knew the Kennedys only in passing. Farrar had become a strongly conservative Republican. Yet, he had written to young Senator Ted thanking him for opposing Richard Nixon's nomination of Walter Hickel as Secretary of the Interior. This had led to an exchange of letters and Farrar had then surmised that maybe the young liberal Kennedy shouldn't be written off completely.

[9] Damore, op. cit. p. 5.

Because individuals had been known to survive for many hours in air pockets of submerged vehicles, Farrar realized from the outset that he might be involved in an actual rescue situation. He worked rapidly. Quickly donning his gear he slipped into the water. The tide hit him immediately and so he approached the car from the driver's side, which was nearly up against the bank. He dove down to peer into the upside-down driver's side window which was rolled down to within an inch of the bottom. Unable to see anything resembling a body in the murky darkness, he concluded that he could not enter the car from the drivers side window because of its proximity to the bank.[10]

Beyond purposes of idle or sensationalistic speculation it is important to question how, if in fact, Farrar could not enter the car, hard pressed by the bank, how could Kennedy, with a back brace and his corpulent bulk offsetting Farrar's diving tanks, have squirmed his way out through this window *without any recall* of having done so? Bear in mind, this is the only thing (how he got out of the car) that the Senator claimed that he cannot recall.

During this maneuvering for a vantage point, Farrar's mind hit upon the fact that only a high rate of speed could have caused the car to have shot so far over the bridge, flipping over in mid-air and coming to rest with its front end nearly facing the direction in which it had originally flown through the air. At a low speed, the car would have merely dribbled over the four-inch-high kick-railing and have been located close to the point where it had gone off the bridge. Kennedy claimed that he had used the brakes at the last moment, when he realized he was heading for the bridge.[11]

Moving to the back of the car along the driver's side, Farrar peered through the undamaged rear window and made out the shape of two feet in the back window area. Spurred to action, he quickly moved around the back of the car and approached

10 Author's interview, April, 1982.
11 His Inquest testimony.

the passenger's-side rear window which had been shattered, literally blown in by impact.[12] He put his head into the car and realized he was within eighteen inches of a young woman. From outside of the car he could easily reach her body, and, doing so, he instantly realized that she was several hours stiff. Her leg felt like metal in his hand.

What struck him as strange was her position, which was right side up to the water level, but upside down in relation to the overturned car. Her arms were grotesquely set at right angles to her body. Her hands were frozen in a clawed shape and were stiffly set in *rigor mortis,* still clutching the front of the rear seat. Her neck and head were extended, stretched, seeming to be reaching to the highest point in the overturned car, which was the footwell. (See illustration, Photo Section.)

He realized her position was not haphazard, and he reasoned that she must have strained with some energy in order to maintain this position. Her head was at the highest point in the automobile, the opposite position he expected to observe if the body had filled with water and sunk as in a normal drowning. She was completely covered by the water. Noting her clawed hands, set in *rigor mortis,* he immediately felt that something was wrong. The facts didn't add up. From outside he slowly and deliberately maneuvered her out of the car. As a safety precaution, in order not to lose the body to the current, he slipped the safety rope (the Chief held the other end topside) around her neck. He secured the rope with two half hitches, and remembers specifically not tightening the knot around her neck. He signalled the Chief, with two tugs on the rope, that he was coming up. With one hand on the rope (that was again, according to Farrar and the Chief, never pulled tight around her neck), and the other arm cross-chest around her, he propelled the body, which virtually floated in his arm, up, over his head and toward the surface.

---

[12] Damore, p. 8, claims that "shards of glass formed a ragged edge along the frame." This information has never been presented anywhere else and is not specifically cited by Damore. The photos of the car as it emerged from the water do not show any glass on the frame, let alone a "ragged edge.

2

INITIAL STATEMENT

One hour earlier that morning, at approximately 8:00 A.M., Paul Markham and Joe Gargan arrived at the Shiretown Inn in Edgartown and found Senator Kennedy with a group that was talking over morning coffee on the upstairs deck. This deck, just outside of Kennedy's room, had been the scene of a small gathering the evening before at the conclusion of the day's Regatta racing. In the morning, Markham and Gargan arrived "soaking wet" according to Ross Richards, the manager of the Narragansett Wire Company of Pawtucket, Rhode Island. The comment was made by Richards to investigating State Police Officer Lieutenant Dunn.[1] Richards later changed his testimony under oath at the Inquest, stating that they were "damp from the night's dew or fog or something."[2] However, Richards' testimony is suspect if not impeached by facts which emerged in the Damore book. It seems that Richards was so pleased that he had avoided mentioning the three rum-and-cokes that Kennedy had consumed on his boat directly after the race on Friday afternoon, that he had actually gone to Kennedy's house at Hyannis after testifying at the Inquest. He is reported to have been chagrined that Kennedy spoke to him for a few minutes on the porch, but pointedly did not invite him inside.[3]

When queried about early-morning (prior to 8:30 A.M.) travelers to or from Chappaquiddick, neither of the two ferry

---

[1] Damore, p. 255.
[2] Inquest testimony.
[3] Damore, p. 372.

crew members had any recollection of bringing either Markham or Gargan over to Edgartown. They certainly hadn't walked on the water. Why would they have swum, unless they were involved in covert acts of conspiracy to obstruct justice? Perhaps one of them had used a skiff part-way, while returning it to the *Victura,* Kennedy's yacht anchored in the harbor, and swam the rest of the way to Edgartown; this could explain Richards' "soaking wet" comment.

Ross Richards was a yachtsman who had won in his heat in the Friday afternoon running of the Regatta; after an impromptu congratulations party on Richards' boat, he and several members of his crew sat on the deck at the Shiretown Inn with Kennedy from 6:30 to around 7:00 P.M. Friday evening, discussing the race and drinking a beer. In his testimony Kennedy stated that he did not consume a full beer at this session[4] and he then headed over to Chappaquiddick to the cottage site. It was his intention to take a hot, soaking bath to relieve his aching back before the party began. Here we wonder whether Kennedy may have lied in order to establish that drinking was not a factor in his accident later that evening. It has been alleged that Stanley Moore knew that Kennedy had consumed three rum-and-cokes on Richard's yacht immediately following the race, and prior to the half beer that Kennedy himself stated that he had consumed.[5] Stanley Moore had picked Kennedy up from the *Victura* immediately after the race and brought him to the *Bettawin,* Ross Richards' yacht. Moore remembered that they had been out of beer and that he and Kennedy had both had three rum-and-cokes apiece. "I don't think it was anybody's business. Ted had three rum-and-cokes in about twenty minutes; but he wasn't laced or anything."[6]

On Saturday morning Richards had run into Kennedy at 7:30 A.M., five to seven hours after the accident,[7] and later testified

---

4   Maintaining the party line, Richards did substantiate this testimony.
5   Damore, p. 371.
6   Damore, p. 255, his interview with Stanley Moore, 8-23-83.
7   Inquest testimony.

that Kennedy was "not haggard or drawn." They had a quiet chat, discussing boating in general and the weather. They had met inadvertently on the street outside the Shiretown, and then gone up to the deck for another half-hour of idle chatting and coffee. When Markham and Gargan arrived, the atmosphere changed, with the three men withdrawing into Kennedy's room, leaving Richards and his wife behind on the deck.

Prior to meeting Richards at about 7:30 A.M., Kennedy had entered the office of the Shiretown, and inquired whether or not he could get the New York and Washington newspapers. The desk clerk had told him she would have them sent over for him and then loaned him a dime to make a call. He stepped outside, used the pay phone, and then returned the dime to her. Then he strolled out to the sidewalk in front of the hotel, and ran into Richards.

Shortly after Markham, Gargan and Kennedy retired into Kennedy's room, Charlie Tretter, who had been at the party on Chappaquiddick the previous night, came up on the deck and briefly entered the room where the three were huddled. According to those observing from the deck, as Tretter withdrew he looked thoroughly rebuked, as though he had stepped into a lion's den.[8] After remaining cloistered for approximately thirty minutes, Kennedy, Gargan and Markham left the Shiretown Inn. The three who were to receive so much press attention and criticism later on for their failure to report the accident still did not head for the police department.

At 8:30 A.M., Dick Hewitt, the morning ferry operator, and deck hand Steve Ewing, were just about to cast off to head the *On Time* over to the Chappaquiddick side, when Senator Kennedy, Gargan and Markham arrived. Kennedy gave an enthusiastic "Hi!" and the three clambered aboard for the six-minute crossing. Upon their arrival, they sequestered themselves in the

---

[8]   There was heavy business taking place inside the room. According to Gargan's interviews with Damore, the Senator had said, "I'm going to say that Mary Jo was driving." Markham had replied, "There's no way you can say that you can be placed at the scene." Then poor Tretter walked in and Gargan said, "Hey you! Get out of here!" Damore, p. 90.

little shack, 100 feet from the ferry landing on the Chappaquiddick side. They later claimed that they simply wanted to get to
a pay phone affording some privacy.[9] Any observer in Edgartown
will realize that this is a ridiculous claim. The small tourist town
is loaded with pay telephones and, at that time of the morning
(8:25 A.M.) on a Regatta weekend, few indeed are up and
about to disturb anyone's privacy.

At this point, the three were not aware that the car had
been found in the water. And Kennedy had not indicated either
verbally or by his attitude, according to both the desk clerk and
Ross Richards, that anything was amiss. If the local authorities,
Chief Arena and Prosecutor Walter Steele, had had any inclina-
tion to investigate this tragedy professionally, and if they had
been looking for a conspiracy to obstruct justice, this movement
by Kennedy and his associates could have easily been shown as
another covert act in their conspiracy.

Kennedy, Markham and Gargan hung out in the shack,
making telephone calls all over the country. As a result of the
automobile traffic (including a hearse) arriving on the Chappaquiddick side via the ferry, it became obvious to the ferry operators that something was up. Finally, they overheard conversations
from the professional people streaming to the accident site.

Hewitt and Ewing left the ferry and approached the group of
three men at 9:45. Hewitt said, "Senator Kennedy, are you aware
of the accident?" Kennedy furtively slipped around the cars
parked nearby, and Markham answered for him, "Yes, we just
heard about it."[10] This was a blatant lie on Markham's part; he
had heard about the accident ten hours earlier from Kennedy
himself.

After another few minutes of consultation, Gargan left for
the cottage, and Kennedy and Markham boarded the ferry to go
back to Edgartown. In contrast to the jovial mood he had had as
he crossed just an hour before, Kennedy sat with his head

---

[9]   Inquest testimony. Gargan has stated that he knew from experience that people
would be lined up two and three people deep at all the phones.
[10] Olsen, p. 132.

slumped. As they rode back across, Paul Markham spoke quietly to the Senator, occasionally making emphatic gestures to underscore points.[11]

Ironically, nearly the same time that the Senator's spirits seemed to diminish, as evidenced by his hang-dog appearance noted by the ferry operators, John Farrar was discovering Mary Jo Kopechne's distorted body in the back of the Senator's submerged automobile.

The public ordeal had begun.

Kennedy bounded off the ferry when it reached the other side, and headed up the street, with Markham struggling to keep up. Now that he was forced into public action, it may have seemed as if by walking fast he could somehow make up for the lost ten hours in which the accident was not reported.

When Kennedy arrived at the Police Station, he asked to use the phone and Officer Carmen Salvador, directly showed him into the chief's unoccupied office. As she returned to the main office, Paul Markham entered from the street. He seemed out of breath, and had obviously been left behind in Senator Kennedy's rapid movements to the station. Markham, too, asked to use a phone. She gave him her own phone, and, because the department had only two lines, thus cut herself and the Police Station off from the world. According to Officer Salvador, owing to his state of being, Markham was having difficulty with the phone and asked her to dial five numbers for him. The calls were placed, one each, to New York, Pennsylvania, Massachusetts and a couple to Washington, D.C. His conversations were short, and in a hushed voice. She was unable to make sense out of what she heard him say.

While the Kennedy team continued its outreach for political and legal counsel (calls to Ted Sorensen and Burke Marshall among others) and set up activities that will be proved to be part of a cover-up, they effectively cut-off the police department

[11] Ibid.

from the communications loop, because they tied up its two sole telephone lines.

Meanwhile the Senator, in the Chief's office, was talking out loud on his calls and Officer Salvador overheard snippets of the conversations. She heard him comment, "Well, we'll have to notify her parents." And some minutes later, on a different call, he said, "I have some sad news to tell you."

The fact is that the man finally summoned the courage to call Mary Jo's parents himself. Yet, a few minutes later he was again on the phone, "delivering explicit instructions on returning a body to the mainland...."[12]

In between these outgoing phone conversations, while the phone was briefly on the receiver, one call slipped into the police department. Kennedy himself answered the Police Station phone and received a call from Police Chief Arena who was calling in to report the discovery of the body, and to seek Kennedy's whereabouts. Jack Olsen's account of the dialogue between them has not been heretofore publicly denied by either of them, and clearly speaks for itself:[13]

> "Hello, Senator," Arena said. "Gee, I'm sorry, but I guess there's been another tragedy. Your car's been involved in an accident over here and there's a girl, you know — a girl died in the accident."
>
> "I know," Kennedy said.
>
> "Do you know whether there were any other passengers in the car?"
>
> "Yes, there were."
>
> Arena shuddered, "Well, do you think they might still be in the water?"
>
> "Well, no," Kennedy said. "Say, could I see you?"
>
> "Sure," Arena said. "Over here? Or would you like me to go over there?"
>
> "Over here if you don't mind," Kennedy said.
>
> "I'll be right there," the chief said, and hung up the phone.

---

12 Olsen, p. 140.
13 Olsen, p. 137, and 142-143.

By now it was a few minutes past ten, and the Chief rushed back to the Police Station. Upon his arrival he encountered Kennedy and Markham in his private office — Kennedy was sitting in the Chief's chair.

"I'm sorry about the accident," Arena said, still standing on the visitor's side of the desk.

"Yes, I know about it," Kennedy said. "I was the driver."

Arena tried to conceal his surprise. He blurted out, "Well, do you happen to know where Rosemary Keough comes from? I think we'd better notify her next of kin."

Kennedy began to move around from the chief's side of the desk, and as the two men hesitantly exchanged places, the Senator said, "Well, it wasn't Rosemary Keough. It was Mary Jo Kopechne. I've already notified her parents."

Arena took his place behind his desk and pulled out a pencil.

"Could you tell me how to spell that?" he said.

"I don't know," Kennedy said. "I only know how to pronounce it." He repeated the name and Arena jotted down

"Mary Jo Copachini [sic]." He asked if there had been any other passengers in the car, and Kennedy said there had not.

"Well, what do we do next?" Kennedy asked, and Arena was relieved to see that the reasonably calm young man seated across from him appeared to be interested only in helping out, instead of trying to throw his weight around. "We've got to do what's right," Kennedy was saying, "because if we don't, we'll both be criticized for it."

"Well," Arena said, "as far as I can see it's a motor vehicle accident. The first thing we're gonna have to do is I'd like to know what happened. Maybe you could give me a statement?"

Kennedy paused. "Is it okay if I write it out?" he said.

"Sure, it's all right by me. But why don't I let you in the back office, so we'll be out of your way? I saw a reporter hanging around outside and the rest of them'll be along any minute. This way you'll have privacy, and anyway I have to go back to the scene. They're still hunting for bodies over there, and I have to go back and clean up the turmoil."

As the two men walked down the hall toward the town accountant's office in the rear, Kennedy said that he hoped the wrecker would not have to tow the car through the center of Edgartown.

"The people will all **be staring** at it," he said. "They'll make a **big thing** out of it." [Emphàsis Added.]

They certainly should have! Kennedy knew that a close examination of the car at that time would reveal a great deal of evidence which he wished to conceal. He wanted the car to disappear. It wasn't merely the luck of the Irish that it did; after the Inquest, Kennedy's attorney, Edward Hanify, purchased the auto from the insurance company and had it crushed.

If the car had been closely inspected, or examined at the time the officials would have discovered that something was amiss. They would have learned that the story that Senator Kennedy told in the following official statement does not hang together. A close examination of the car at that point would have raised questions never raised heretofore in the official record, at the Inquest, or in any commercially published work. Questions that fairly and squarely point to a different interpretation of the facts.

Official Police Statement

On July 18, 1969 at approximately 11:15 pm on Chappaquiddick Island, Martha's Vineyard, I was driving my car on Main Street on my way to get the ferry back to Edgartown. I was unfamiliar with the road[14] and turned right onto Dyke Road instead of bearing left on Main Street. After proceeding for approximately a half mile on Dyke Road I descended a hill[15] and came upon a narrow bridge. The car went off the side of the bridge. There was one passenger in the car with me, Miss   , a former secretary of my brother Robert Kennedy. The car turned over and sank into the water and landed with

---

[14]   He had traveled that road only hours before.
[15]   There was no hill, only a slight incline.

the roof resting on the bottom. I attempted to open the door and window of the car but have no recollection of how I got out of the car.[16] I came to the surface and then repeatedly dove down to the car in an attempt to see if the passenger was still in the car. I was unsuccessful in the attempt. I was exhausted and in a state of shock. I recall walking back to where my friends were eating. There was a car parked in front of the cottage and I climbed into the back seat. I then asked for someone to bring me back to Edgartown.[17] I remember walking around for a period of time[18] and then going back to my hotel room. When I fully realized what happened this morning,[19] I immediately contacted the police.

The Chief claimed that Miss Kopechne's name was left out of the report because no one knew how to spell it at the time. The statement was written out in longhand by Paul Markham, Ted Kennedy's friend and the former U.S. Attorney for Massachusetts. Markham, a criminal prosecutor at the highest level, could be counted on to draft a statement that would cast Kennedy in a most favorable light, anticipating various legal defenses for the actions leading to Mary Jo Kopechne's death. But, more than that, Paul Markham was accountable for two roles that were at cross purposes. First, he could arguably be claimed by Kennedy as an attorney to Kennedy;[20] therefore duly bound by law to protect and defend the Senator and to legally hold in confidence any and all things that the Senator told him. Yet, as a participant in the activities the preceding night (the public only learns this later, and not from this police report drafted by Kennedy and Markham) Markham's role was much more than that of an attorney defending his client's rights. He was in fact

---

[16] Of the entire evening, "how I got out of the car," is the only thing that he does not recall exactly.

[17] His own testimony defeats this.

[18] He would have been observed because so many people filled the streets on the Regatta party night. At the inquest he contradicts this.

[19] He took the ferry to make phone calls. His own testimony later on bears this out.

[20] In fact Kennedy did surprise Markham when Edward Hanify, Kennedy's chief attorney told Markham that Kennedy felt that Markham was an attorney of record and could not speak of what had happened because of client privilege.

directly involved, as will be seen, as a co-conspirator to obstruct justice and thus a witting participant in a conspiracy to avoid a charge of manslaughter.

Markham wrote out the statement and then Chief Arena typed it up. Upon completion of his secretarial chore, Arena showed the statement to Kennedy, and he agreed to go with it; but amazingly, the Chief did not get Kennedy's signature on the statement of alleged facts.

The Chief didn't ask Kennedy any specific questions regarding the accident or the party when he was in the station. In fact, it was only after Kennedy had left the Island for Hyannis Port, that the Chief discovered that there had been a party the previous night. Soon after the business of the statement had been taken care of, the town prosecutor Walter Steele showed up. While Steele's home was on the mainland, he maintained a cabin near the township of Vineyard Haven, Martha's Vineyard, and had dropped by the station on other business.

He knew Edward Kennedy from years before when both had served as Assistant District Attorneys for Suffolk County. This had been the young Kennedy's first job out of law school. Steele was not a personal friend of the Senator's, and he, like many other Assistant D.A.'s, had felt that the young Teddy had not carried his fair share of the case work. But here and now things had changed. Even though he was in the station with Kennedy and Markham in his capacity as the local prosecutor, one could say that his conduct at this first meeting was, if not outright sociable, at least politic. It became clear enough that, in this particular case, Walter Steele had no appetite for the public role of local prosecutor.

By that time the press was beginning to accumulate outside the station. However, Steele did not suggest that Arena question Kennedy or Markham. He certainly didn't question them himself; in fact, his solicitous behavior indicated that he knew where the power resided. In that it clearly didn't reside with him, he behaved as if he wasn't about to upset any apple carts in his adopted favorite town.

When Markham decided to go back to the Shiretown to retrieve his "clothes,"[21] Steele went along. As they returned, according to author Jack Olsen, the following occurred:[22]

> Markham spoke in a slow stream of consciousness as the two companions left the inn and headed down the driveway to return to the Police Station, and by the time they had retraced their steps to the Edgartown town offices, the prosecutor had become aware that Ted Kennedy had driven off the Dyke Bridge in his car, that a young woman was dead, that Kennedy had almost drowned, and that nine hours had gone by before the accident had been reported. When it appeared that Markham was going to say nothing more, Steele said, "Jesus Christ, Paul, nine hours! This is gonna be a tough one. I feel sorry for the Senator, but Paul, nine hours is a long time." He was thinking that something was amiss, but based on Markham's skimpy narrative, he was not sure what it was.
>
> By the time the pair came abreast of the crowd in front of the building, Markham had settled down, and for a brief few seconds the two men stopped and faced each other. "Paul," Steele said gently, "your problem is not with me, and it's not with the chief. We have that district attorney in New Bedford to think about. You know who the D.A. is down here." Edmund Dinis, the flamboyant district attorney of the area, had a widespread reputation for unpredictability. "You know, they say he's kind of an intractable guy," Steele told Markham.
>
> "Oh, my God," Markham said. He pressed his hands together again, and then the two men stepped inside.

George "Red" Kennedy, no relation to the Kennedy family, was the local representative from the Motor Vehicle Registry called in to investigate the accident for the state. He spent a

---

[21] Steele observed Markham picking up his clothes that were scattered around the room. Had Markham been staying at the party cottage on Chappaquiddick as was reported in the Judge's final report on the inquest, Markham's clothes and personal effects wouldn't have been scattered around the room he was sharing with the Senator, they would have been out at the cottage.

[22] Olsen, pp. 157-158.

couple of hours at the Dyke Bridge and then returned to the Police Station. Upon his arrival at the station, and, in his role as the official state investigator, George Kennedy asked the Senator a question regarding the accident. He received a curt, "I have no comment."[23]

Thus intimidated, George Kennedy didn't push, he didn't pry. Apparently he couldn't summon the strength to pursue the issue and demand answers. He was merely an investigator for the State; whereas the Senator acted as if he possessed a God-given immunity to questions.

After spending approximately four hours at the station, and receiving the courtesy a U.S. Senator could expect at a banquet in his honor, Kennedy was privately ushered out the back door to avoid the press.

In order to let George Kennedy know just how important that *he* was, he was enlisted by the Chief to become Kennedy's driver, taking Kennedy and Markham to the airport. There, local Democratic Party activist, Edgartown alderman and staunch Kennedy loyalist, Robert Carroll flew them in his private plane to Hyannis and the relative safety of the Kennedy compound.

However, we find a small amount of light was shed during these proceedings. George Kennedy had been around Joe Gargan for some period of time at the station. Limited, perhaps chagrined by Senatorial imperative, and unable to get answers to his questions, George Kennedy had made careful observations of Gargan's physical condition. George Kennedy's later Inquest testimony regarding Gargan's good condition (no observable injuries), provided a key clue which we will see later.

The flight to Hyannis Port was merely ten minutes long in real time, but light-years away from the reality of a thorough interrogation into the facts of the events surrounding the accident. Such an interrogation would have led to conclusions and would have forced the issue at the outset, causing Arena and Steele to realize that there was much more to the incident than

---

[23] Damore, p. 27.

Kennedy and Markham had divulged in the brief and incomplete initial statement. Although the odds, stacked by favoritism and downright awe of political power were against any real exploration of the incident, it is entirely conceivable that Steele and even Chief Arena, had they determined any important facts through questioning, might have conducted themselves differently; and consequently they might have been drawn into conducting a legitimate inquiry that could have led to justice. It appears that human nature, combined with an altogether understandable sense of priorities, and, perhaps, real trust that a Senator would do the right thing, froze the process, allowing the guilty parties to walk away.

3

BY POUCHA POND

John Farrar had been submerged for some time. Chief Arena was meanwhile holding a safety rope for the scuba diver and could see that Farrar had worked his way around to the passenger side of the car, which faced the flowing channel. Arena was perched on the back of the vehicle, which was slowly surfacing as the tide raced out. He was shocked to see a blonde woman emerge from the water in Farrar's arms. He had been alerted by Farrar's pre-arranged signal, the tug on the rope. Arena had not pulled the rope taut, and now the woman surfaced with Farrar, who held her in a cross-chest carry. Arena cradled her stiff body in his arms as a skiff was brought out. She was brought to the shore and placed in the back of the police cruiser to shield her body from the eyes of spectators. As word had spread on the islands like an explosive sneeze, many people had arrived to observe.

Dr. Donald Randall Mills had been on duty that morning in his capacity as Associate Medical Examiner. (The Chief Medical Examiner for Martha's Vineyard, Dr. Robert Nevin, took weekends off.) Dr. Mills was 63 years old at the time and was known widely as a good and kindly man. His experience and record as a general practitioner were never in doubt. He was one of five physicians on Martha's Vineyard and he had been practicing medicine since 1935. While not born on the Island, he had spent his entire adult life there and had been gone only for a period of four years, while he served with the U.S. Army Medical Corps in the South Pacific during World War II. He was a widely admired figure and held many positions beyond his private practice: contract physician for the U.S. Public Health Service; Medical Examiner for the Federal Aviation Agency; additionally, he held several local advisory positions and board memberships. His role as Martha's Vineyard Associate Medical Examiner was his way of giving back to the community that had given so much to him.

When the call came that morning, he was worried about going to Chappaquiddick because he had a patient at the hospital about to go into labor.

Yet, it should be noted that Dr. Nevin, the Chief Medical Examiner, later described Mills as "a sweet, gentle, kind person who hooked rugs and plays the organ, and whose mother wanted him to be a musician. He won't take a stand unless pushed." When Mills heard of this remark he had retorted that Dr. Nevin was a "strange man, twice married, who doesn't make friends and has formed an impression in this case without knowing the facts."[1]

This example of interpersonal enmity was reported after the tragedy. The case was being tried in the press, during the delay for the Hearing for Exhumation and Autopsy that was to be held in the state of Pennsylvania, because Pennsylvania had jurisdiction and possession of Mary Jo's body. Perhaps Dr. Nevin was miffed because Dr. Mills had so forcibly been thrust into the spotlight, when in fact, Dr. Mills was only the Associate Medical Examiner. Though considerable attention has been paid herein to avoid idle speculation, it is important to try to assess the attitudes of the main players in order to determine not only the veracity of their statements, but also, their very ability and experience in order to professionally perform their appointed tasks under the glare of attention from the world press. Therefore, it is crucial to point out that in his entire 35 years of professional practice, Dr. Mills had previously handled only six drownings, none of which had any strange or unusual elements.

---

[1]   Sherrill, p. 81.

As before, we'll look at Olsen's reconstruction of events and dialogue when Dr. Mills arrived at the scene:[2]

"Hi, Doc," the young summertime officer said. "It's a girl. The body's in the cruiser. We'll take her out for you, Doc."

Donald Mills watches as a policeman and a fireman opened the back of the Edgartown police cruiser and lifted out a litter with a blue wool blanket on top of it. From all sides of him, he could hear murmured conversations: "I don't know, maybe about midnight. . . ." He heard someone ask, "Do you suppose there'll be more bodies?" And he heard old Tony Bettencourt answer, "There might be some more. That time of the night, the tide was running out like a bullet. The bodies could be miles from here by now, out Cape Poge Bay, or even in the Sound."

Now the litter was placed on the seaward side of the police cruiser, providing a measure of privacy from the Dyke Bridge and the other side. Scuba diver John Farrar came up as the doctor removed the blanket, and he said, "We took her out of the car in the water, Doc. We were too late."

"I see," Mills said softly. He looked down at the stiffened body of an attractive woman in her late twenties, fully clothed and neatly buttoned, dressed in black slacks, a white long-sleeved shirtwaist, and sandals. Her hair was upswept and slightly disheveled; there were three gold bracelets on her right wrist, and her color was a pale, chalky white.

"Golly!" he said to himself. "What a shame! This lovely young person. What an absolute shame!"

There was white foam about the woman's nose and mouth; Dr. Mills knew that the foam and the tiny web of blood at the corner of her nose were signs of death by drowning. The body lay on its back, and the arms were sticking almost straight upward; the doctor noticed that the hands were peculiarly cupped, almost in a claw-like position, as though they had been gripping something with a curved edge. He pulled the mouth open and saw a water level inside. He undid the buttons on the woman's blouse and laid it back, exposing a dressy blue brassiere, and percussed the chest lightly. With each tap

---

[2] Olsen, pp. 143-46.

of his fingers, water came from the mouth, and when Mills pressed hard on the rib cage the water spurted out both nose and mouth, washing away some of the foam. Whatever had happened in the car, he told himself, the girl had not been dead when she reached the bottom of Poucha Pond. She had stayed alive long enough to inhale water and die by drowning. She was *full* of water.

"Why, she's the most drowned person I've ever seen!" he said aloud.

He looked and probed around the body and could find no visible signs of injury, marks or obvious lesions. The neck was white and unblemished. There were no apparent bruises on the face or upper body. The major bones were unbroken. Under the nails, there was a small amount of foreign matter, but the nails themselves were unbroken and nicely manicured, and Dr. Mills could see no significance to the debris. He ran his hands across the scalp; it was smooth and regular. The woman had not bumped herself in going off the bridge. He pulled down the slacks and observed that the woman had been wearing nothing underneath. The abdomen was flat. He pushed against the abdominal wall and noted that the uterus was normal, unenlarged. It was not impossible that the victim had been in the early months of pregnancy, but looking at her small white belly and feeling the uterus, Dr. Mills doubted it. As he tipped the body to examine the back for signs of injury, more water gushed forth, and one of the undertakers, standing alongside, said, "That probably came from her stomach."

"No, it didn't," Mills said. "I'm pressing on her chest. There's definitely water in the lungs." The rigidly extended arms made it difficult for him to turn the body completely over, so he tipped it first to one side and then the other, saw nothing unusual on the back, and returned the body to its prone position. "Death by drowning," he said to a young patrolman standing nearby. "Not a question about it."

He saw old Tony Bettencourt, and to himself he said wryly, "They didn't need me on this one, Tony could have made the diagnosis!"

"What now?" Undertaker Eugene Frieh said.

"Well, I'm finished," Mills said, pulling the blue blanket over the body. "You can transfer her to the hearse."

The gray Buick was backed slowly across the bridge until it was within ten or twelve feet of the body, and the remains of the young woman were put inside in a large carrying bag. Mills turned to chat with the bystanders, many of whom he had treated in the past. "Say, who is this girl?" he said.

"Nobody knows for sure," one of the fireman said. "But she had something to do with Kennedy."

"Kennedy?"

"Senator Ted Kennedy. There's a search going on for him right now."

When Dr. Mills heard that there was a Kennedy connection in the case, he stiffened. He had never made a more routine or certain diagnosis, but now there were other considerations. Anything touching on the Kennedy family, pro or con, was potentially explosive, and one never knew whether the blast was going to come from the Kennedy backers or the Kennedy haters. For an instant he said to himself that a drowning death was a drowning death, and no political considerations could change that fact, but then he realized that certain decisions were not in his area of expertise. These included the matter of an autopsy for political purposes.

"Gee," he said to Gene Frieh, "if there's any Kennedy connection here at all, this is too big for me to handle alone. I'll call the D.A.'s office and ask about an autopsy." He started to add, "Hold the embalming for awhile, Gene," but he realized that such an instruction would be an insult to the undertaker's professional competence. Gene Frieh had been in the business for many years; he would know to hold the embalming.

Robert Sherrill (who wrote with the perspective of time, some five years later), adds an interesting note, he reported:[3]

But Eugene Frieh, the mortician who was standing by during this examination and closely observing Dr. Mills's actions, didn't see it that way. He says that when the doctor manipulated Miss Kopechne's chest "it produced some water flow, water and foam, mostly foam.' And on another occasion Frieh

---

[3] Sherrill, p. 82.

said, "Very little water was expelled from the lungs. I raised my eyebrows because I expected more water."

Later, Sherrill reports John Farrar, the scuba diver, approaching Dr. Mills, saying:[4]

"What do you think, Donald? It looks like we've got a drowning." Mills said, "Well, certainly from outward appearances she drowned. However, the autopsy will tell the complete story." Mills claims that when he released the body to undertaker Frieh, he said, "I'll notify the DA's office and ask for an autopsy. Hold the embalming."

The public ordeal now began for Dr. Mills. He returned to his office, checked on his patient at the hospital and then called the State Police Barracks at Oak Bluffs, on the mainland. He reached Trooper Richard P. DeRoche and detailed the ramifications of the case, explaining that the District Attorney, Edmund Dinis, who lived and maintained his office in Brookhaven should be informed, especially regarding the decision about whether to do an autopsy.

Shortly thereafter another State Trooper, Robert E. Lucas, called back and told him that they had been able to reach Lieutenant George Killen, the District Attorney's chief investigator; Lucas reported that Killen had said, that as long as Mills was satisfied that it was a drowning, there was no need for an autopsy. Killen also passed on word to take routine blood samples, which Mills in his nervousness had neglected to do by this point. District Attorney Edmund Dinis of Dukes County is known to have called Lieutenant Killen, "the best detective investigator in the country."[5]

The phone began ringing; reporters were calling from all over the country. Dr. Mills took several calls and tried in his

4   Ibid.
5   Olsen, p. 165.

good-natured way to give full disclosure of what he knew. On one call he inadvertently gave out some information that was not true (viz., that Mary Jo had been nude). He was able to call the reporter back to straighten it out, but he realized the strain was too much. Upset over these continued phone calls and the events of one of the longest days in his life, he was beside himself.

He later told a reporter from the *Medical World News:*[6]

The undertaker came back with a Kennedy representative and a death certificate for me to sign. "I've come up here to help things along," said the Kennedy man. For the first time I learned the girl's name. I was almost pushed to the point of irrationality and blackout as I did my best to answer the barrage of questions. By 5 P.M. I was desperate. I called Lieutenant Killen at Barnstable and asked him how to handle it and what to say. "Tell them the girl died of accidental drowning and that's all," he replied, "If they persist, slam down the receiver."

[6] Sherrill, p. 83.

4

BARGAINED VERDICT

Walter Steele, who was 43 years old at the time, had been delighted two months before to have been appointed "special prosecutor" for Martha's Vineyard. He had served as a Boston Assistant District Attorney for fourteen years before taking up a private criminal practice. He was widely respected in his field and, in addition to his private practice, he lectured on criminal prosecution at Boston University. The point is that Walter Steele was well connected with the Boston Criminal Bar. The $5,000-a-year post in Edgartown meant a minimum of real duties, and would provide him with a reason to be on the Island at least once a week, therefore enabling him to take part in his beloved surf fishing.

He had planned to stop by the Chief's office for just a few minutes before noon that Saturday morning. Surprised to see the crowd gathering outside the Police Station, he parked his car in the rear and entered through the back door. In the hallway he saw Thomas Teller, the clerk for the District Court, who told him that there had been an accidental death and that Kennedy was somehow involved. Steele didn't really believe that Kennedy was personally involved, and he was amazed at the brusque manner in which the Chief greeted him, nearly brushing him aside as Arena barreled down the hallway, still wearing only a bathing suit and T-shirt.

Steele moved into the main outer office and was greeted by a wave from Senator Kennedy, who was still on the telephone in the Chief's small office, just off the main office. Paul Markham, sitting on a bench in the main room, said good morning.

Joe Gargan soon arrived at the station. The Motor Vehicle Registry Inspector George Kennedy returned from the bridge, to be rebuffed by Kennedy; and, finally Robert Carroll was summoned to fly Kennedy and Markham back to Hyannis.

After they had gone, a series of strange, unusual, even downright weird occurrences began to occur. Steele and Arena were finally left alone to begin evaluating the case and its ramifications. It was they who would decide upon a course of legal action. When Kennedy and Markham left the Island, they told the Chief that they would call back that afternoon after reaching Burke Marshall, who Bobby Kennedy had considered to be the best attorney in the country. Marshall was a member of Bobby's Justice Department, and later distinguished himself as one of the best corporate (IBM) attorneys in the country. At Justice he headed the Civil Right Section, and was most effective in the tumultuous years of the Civil Rights movement in the South. He currently lectures at Yale Law School. In fact, Senator Kennedy summoned him in 1988 to testify against Robert Bork in Senate Congressional Hearings. Had the Republican staff done their homework (and raised the issue of Marshall's proximity to the Kennedy family), Marshall's testimony against his former colleague Robert Bork (they had both been on the Yale faculty together) could have been side-tracked by the fact that he was ultimately the senior attorney in the Chappaquiddick legal machinations.

So, by now Kennedy had left the Island and the press was clamoring for something, anything, some statement from the Chief. Near the front of the crowd of angry newsmen was James Reston of the *New York Times*. Reston was also the owner of the local *Vineyard Gazette*. His imperious presence was noted by the Chief. Arena felt pressured if not outright bullied by Reston, but he had promised Kennedy and Markham that he would not release the statement until they gave him the okay. For obvious reasons the appointed Chief of Police of a small town does not like the local newspaper owner upset with him.

Consequently the pressure from the press must have appeared to have career ramifications for the Chief. Finally, despite Steele's warning that by doing so he would be giving Kennedy a constitutional defense, on grounds he couldn't receive a fair trial, Arena read the statement that Markham had written, and which Kennedy had stated that he agreed with, to the gathered newsmen. After the Chief answered a few questions, Steele convinced him to withdraw from what turned into an impromptu press conference.

Steele sat with the Chief and began reviewing the statutes regarding automobile accidents and quickly came to the conclusion that they would have to immediately get out a complaint: for leaving the scene of an accident. Then the phone rang. The caller was Lieutenant George Killen of the State Police, who had been assigned as the chief investigator by District Attorney Edmund Dinis. As already stated, his boss, D.A. Dinis, publicly acknowledged regarding him as the top criminal investigator in the country. This detail is repeated to firmly plant the idea that there was expert help immediately in the vicinity, in fact Killen was on the phone.

Killen had been recently telephoned by Dr. Donald Mills, who had examined Mary Jo's body after it had been taken out of the water. Dr. Mills had called Killen to get an opinion from the District Attorney's office as to whether he should order an autopsy. Lieutenant Killen, according to Dr. Mills, was not particularly interested in an autopsy. According to author Olsen, the two of them had decided that an autopsy was not necessary is as much as Mills had determined that it was a case of death by drowning. As already noted, Dr. Mills had had little experience with drowning victims and, not being a wave-maker, it was predictable that he would go along with the opinion of this official law-enforcement figure. Killen was to later tell author Leo Damore, that failing to push for an autopsy was one of the biggest errors in his career.[1]

---

[1] Damore, p. xiii.

In the next chapter, we will examine the various efforts later made by the District Attorney in seeking disinterment and autopsy, but, it suffices to note that an autopsy was not high on anyone's list at this stage.

In his phone call, Killen made "common cause" with the Chief, commenting that this was a hot case, and wished Arena good luck, while making it clear that District Attorney Dinis would be leaving the matter to Arena and local prosecutor Steele. Ten minutes later, however, Dinis himself called and was quite excited. He literally yelled into the phone that, "We're taking over this case right away, Chief! We're in this case right now! He's all done; he's *gone*!"[2]

Incredibly, after only another five minutes, Lieutenant Killen called again, and in Arena's later reconstruction of the conversation it seemed that Killen was implying that there was no need for the district attorney's office to be involved after all. They had the following conversation:[3]

> "Look, Jim!" he said, "this is an automobile case, isn't it?"
> "Sure," Arena said. "That's exactly what it is."
> "Well, you've handled a lot of 'em. You don't need our help, do you?"
> "Not right now, anyway. Kennedy's given me an incriminating statement."
> "Okay. If you need help, let us know. I've talked to the D.A. and he says it's your case."

Steele was aghast when Arena repeated this latest conversation. He began to reexamine the medical examiner's statute. Armed with the facts, Steele then called Killen back himself, and indicated that he thought that there was every reason for an autopsy. Killen, curtly ended the conversation, stating, "Okay, Goodbye."

---

2   Damore, interview with Arena, 2-14-83, p. 31.
3   Olsen, p. 169.

What *was* afoot? One must have a greater familiarity with the individuals to gauge why this seemingly contradictory behavior was occurring. There is a connective thread. In a way, Killen's career had an element of similarity to that of Jack Crimmins, who was Senator Kennedy's chauffeur. Crimmins was regularly employed as an investigator for the Boston D.A.'s office, unless the Senator was in town. Similarly, Chief Jim Arena had been with the State Police, working out of Boston. All three of these men, Killen, Crimmins and Chief Arena, were intertwined as investigators, lawmen, enforcement officials, in a word: insiders, in the Boston criminal/political establishment. Not leaders, not politicians; they were the men in the background who got things done. They were professionals who had respect for their work, seriously undertook their responsibilities, and yet, at the bottom line, were still cronies who knew very well what their security depended upon. In exchange for their membership in this covey, their right to pensions down the line, they, as operatives for the government/establishment, understood the prime rule: you don't bite the hand that feeds you; especially if that hand is "city hall," or, in this case, a higher calling to the mysterious vapors and implicit power that surrounds a U.S. Senator, and in Massachusetts the ramification is magnified if a Kennedy is involved.

Naturally, Walter Steele, an experienced criminal prosecutor, had a very real sense of what was happening. He certainly knew enough to cover his back and to be quiet; to undertake the minimum role that was required of him until some external force exerted itself. Until some higher authorities started pushing the buttons. He and Arena were covered; they had alerted the District Attorney's office, they had suggested an autopsy; but, because the jurisdiction question was becoming obfuscated through enigmatic and contradictory opinions from the D.A. and his chief investigator, Steele wisely focused on what was at hand. And that was what, in fact, he could do or must do with the evidence right in front of him. There wasn't much.

There had been no real investigation. When all the players had left the Island, Steele had held hands with the Chief, attempting to keep Arena from becoming more upset while the media were jostling and crying for information from outside the Police Station. Neither Arena nor Steele had asked significant questions. They didn't even realize yet that there had been a party. So, there was virtually no evidence beyond the purely physical fact of a smashed-up automobile, Kennedy's statement and the body of Mary Jo Kopechne. With so little evidence there was no viable charge beyond leaving the scene of an accident. Arena and Steele were certainly not looking for negligence.

Leaving the scene of an accident which causes death, and in which negligence is found, calls for a mandatory manslaughter charge. They didn't want to know!

It was simply too big, there were too many power ramifications, and they were awe-struck, paralyzed into inaction. Meanwhile, over at the Kennedy compound, that very issue, the avoidance of a manslaughter charge, was the main issue, the deepest concern.

Senator Kennedy had left the scene of an accident without reporting it. That was a chargeable offense, and Steele urged Arena to make the formal charge. Kennedy had agreed to call them back after he got to Hyannis and reached his attorney. He didn't call. The fact that the Kennedy people were not reaching out to them, were letting them twist slowly in the wind, certainly caused no sympathy to run through Steele's mind as a trained prosecutor. Yet, he didn't want to hit hard; and at the same time he had become convinced that he didn't have anything significant to hit with.

Not long after the particular series of phone calls from Killen and Dinis, the Chief received another call that was even more perplexing than the others. Paul Markham called and the Chief winced: he fully expected Markham to be outraged that he had released the prepared statement to the press, without express permission from the Senator. After all, Arena had told Kennedy and Markham that he would hold the statement until he heard from them. But instead the following conversation ensued.[4]

> "Listen, Chief," Markham said, "we haven't been able to get hold of Burke Marshall. Could you hold onto the statement a little longer?"
> "Gee, I've already given it out."
> "Oh, you gave it out? Well, that's okay. Goodbye Chief."

This proved to be the last communication between Hyannis and Edgartown for several days, and it appears that the Chief was certainly not about to call them unless he was summoned. He knew his place in the scheme of things. Recall, it was only a few years before that, as a State Trooper, he had been assigned occasionally to be Senator Edward Kennedy's driver, his chauffeur, implicitly his servant.

But, the nasty business of officially getting out a complaint for leaving the scene had to be undertaken. Arena and Steele had mutually concluded that Kennedy was alert and clear-eyed in the morning when they had been with him.

So the charge was filed stating that one Edward M. Kennedy was guilty of, "leaving the scene of an accident *without negligence* involved." [Emphasis added.] More to the point, Steele, in his official report, inexplicably stated that Kennedy was driving "with extreme caution." It strains credibility past the breaking point to realize that this law enforcement officer and, in the case of Steele, Officer of the Court, could have reached these conclusions without the benefit of an investigation or close questioning of the Senator himself. Somehow they just "knew" that Kennedy, regardless of his infamous past driving record and known predilection for consuming alcohol, wouldn't strain any of the established rules and laws — even during a Regatta Week-

---

[4]   Olsen, p. 177.

end, known for its hi-jinks and partying — not on their watch, not in their jurisdiction.[5]

A few days later the internal maneuvering began. The call finally came from Hyannis in the personage of no less than the widely respected Honorable Judge Robert Clark of Massachusetts. Judge Clark was now back in private practice, and considered the top lawyer in the state regarding automobile accidents and personal-injury cases arising out of them. Private and, more to the point, secret meetings were set up between Judge Clark, Chief Arena and Prosecutor Steele to decide on a strategy and tactics, in pursuit of a plea bargain.

Here again we rely on author Olsen to bring us to the scene. In his book, he wrote about the meetings held on Martha's Vineyard at Walter Steele's secluded cabin. He quoted the principals as follows, starting with Judge Clark:[6]

> "I'm not one of those people that are invited over to the compound for cookouts and parties. I'm not a social friend of the Kennedys. When I go over to the compound on this case, I'm not a free agent. As you know, there's another attorney in charge.[7] At the compound, the ones who seem to have the most to say about the case are Stephen Smith and Ted Sorensen. We have conferences, but Smith and Sorensen seem to be calling the shots. The Senator walks in and out, but he really doesn't participate."
>
> "I understand all that," Steele said, "but I think they should rely on you, because you know this game a little better than they do."
>
> "Maybe you're right," Clark said rising to his feet, "but, I've got to clear everything first. Now suppose we start talking out loud about pleading guilty. What would you recommend to the Judge?"

---

5   Even though Arena had found no skid marks, and he assumed that Kennedy drove straight off the bridge as though he hadn't seen it, that didn't indicate negligence to him.

6   Olsen, pp. 212-13.

7   Burke Marshall or Edward Hanify.

"A suspended sentence," Steele said. "Anything else would be preposterous. I'd recommend a suspended sentence for **anyone** on a first offense leaving the scene."

"What about this Judge?" Clark said. "Do you think he'd go along?"

"I think so."

"Can you be sure?"

"You can't be sure of anything with Judge Boyle," Steele said, "but he's the Judge we've got. If he was a whore, it'd be different. If he was like some judges, we could get on the phone and say, 'Judge, they want to plead guilty and we'll recommend a suspended sentence, how do you feel?' and he'd say, 'Fine, okay.' But if I ever called Judge Boyle up, he'd throw me in jail. I'll tell you this; if you're ever gonna get a fair shot, you'll get it before this guy. He won't be influenced by the press, he won't be influenced by you or Kennedy, and he won't be influenced by me or Arena. He goes strictly by the facts."

Clark turned toward the massive Arena, standing in the shadows against the wall. "How do you feel about it Chief?" he asked.

"Well, gee, Judge," Arena said hesitantly, "I go along with Walter. I think the Judge'll suspend. I think the Judge should suspend."

"I'm glad to see you're not out to hang the senator," the elder Clark said, smiling.

"No," Steele said. "We're not. A suspended sentence in a case like this would be fair to everybody."

"Okay," Clark said, as he arose to shake hands with the two men. "As I told you, I'm not a free agent. I've got to go to the compound and see what they say about this. We'll fly back and talk tomorrow."

So, the plea bargain was setup, and the only wild card would be Judge James A. Boyle. The Kennedy defense attorneys were actually allowed to assist the Chief in editing and preparing the "statement of facts" that he would present to the Court. Therefore, the elimination of all untoward eventualities had proceeded as far as was possible. Apparently this was necessary, because Judge Boyle wasn't "a whore." Naturally the Kennedy team wanted to minimize any possibility of wild cards. That is precisely what a "good" lawyer does. Chief Arena was sympathetic and helpful. Unfortunately for the Chief in terms of the historic record, he was sympathetic *to a fault*.

After filing his charge, Arena had told the press that he had asked Lieutenant George Killen to investigate by speaking to the individuals who had allegedly attended the party. He made it clear that his request of Killen had simply been as a personal favor. Four days later Killen informed the press: "It is not true that I have been assigned to this case. I have no intention of interrogating any witnesses. All I know is that to all intents and purposes the investigation is over."[8] Poor Jim Arena was getting no help.

More to the point, the beleaguered Arena, who had turned to tranquilizers because of the stress, announced "that people in high places" had warned him that he was, "talking too much .... A state official has told me to keep my mouth shut."[9] Such an announcement by the distraught Arena indicated that strange things were beginning to happen at higher official levels.

Richard J. McCarran, age 39, one of Kennedy's attorneys, was in attendance at the strategy meetings held in Hyannis. He was a fine young man out of Boston, and Harvard-educated. In addition to his private practice, he was also town counsel for Edgartown. In other words he represented the very jurisdiction that was, in effect, prosecuting the Senator. He apparently reasoned that, because his position in Edgartown did not involve advice on police matters, there was no conflict of interest.

Cronyism mattered not one wit; and the word yuppie (in 1969 we only had Yippies) had not yet been invented. Mr. McCarran is not to be held up in public contempt at this late date; he is mentioned simply because he did represent and speak for Senator Kennedy at the disposition of the matter. But more to the point, the local political climate was such that he could

8   Rust, p. 50.
9   Sherrill, p. 75.

convince himself that it was fine to work both sides of the street as long as a Kennedy was involved. At the Hearing, it was McCarran who spoke for a suspended sentence for the Senator in as much as "the Senator's character is well-known in the United States and the world." Walter Steele, the prosecutor, joined in with the suggestion that the defendant be given a suspended sentence. A suspended sentence was the minimum allowed in such a case. And so it was: two months in detention, suspended for one year.

One week after the tragic death, on Friday, July 25, the Hearing was held. In answering the charge, Kennedy stood and said "Guilty," but in a voice so muted he was asked to repeat it, in order to be heard by the Court.

At the Hearing, Judge Boyle almost threw a kink into the carefully worked-out plan by asking, just before awarding a suspended sentence, "I would be most interested in determining from the defendant or the Commonwealth if there was a deliberate effort to conceal the identity of the defendant." Arena stated, "Identity of the defendant — not to my knowledge, your honor." Arena's performance as an arfing seal effectively diffused the concern. This comment from the Judge was thought to have arisen because rumors, which were mentioned in the press by the *NY Times* and later explored by Jack Anderson, had stated that Joe Gargan, Ted's cousin, was being set up to take the fall for Ted. And, according to this speculation, that was why they had not gone to the Police Station to report the accident the first thing in the morning, and instead had spent so much time on the telephone taking counsel from clearer, if not wiser heads.

McCarran then nearly threw it all away. He had been advised by Steele not to attempt to introduce any type of defense, but to accept the Judge's ruling silently, with all due respect to the Court. McCarran, perhaps acting on even higher authority, i.e., orders from Hyannis, did get on the record before being admonished by Judge Boyle. He claimed that a legal defense could have been erected by Kennedy, even though he was pleading guilty. Boyle, rightly offended at this arrogant legal tactic of gaining comment on the record, interrupted him vigorously, and Walter Steele wisely intervened.

Mr. Steele: May it please your Honor, the Commonwealth suggests for your Honor's consideration that this defendant be incarcerated in the house of correction for a period of two months and that the execution of this sentence be suspended.

Judge Boyle: There is no record, Mrs. Tyra?
Helen Tyra: None, your Honor.

Judge Boyle: Considering — the unblemished record of the defendant — and the Commonwealth represents that this is not a case where he was trying to conceal his identity....
Mr. Steele: No, sir.

Judge Boyle: Where it is my understanding, he has already been and will continue to be punished far beyond anything this court can impose — the ends of justice would be satisfied by the imposition of the minimum jail sentence and the suspension of that sentence, assuming the defendant accepts the suspension.

Mr. McCarran: The defendant will accept the suspension, your Honor.

Mrs. Helen Tyra was in charge of the local probation office. She either consciously overlooked the Senator's previous driving convictions in Virginia, or wasn't aware of them.[10] The Hearing

---

[10] March, 1957, convicted of speeding, Charlottesville, Virginia; March, 1958, convicted of reckless driving, Charlottesville, Virginia; April 1958, convicted of speeding, Charlottesville, Virginia; December 1958, convicted of running red light, Charlottesville, Virginia. These convictions had been printed in the newspapers that very morning. Helen Tyra apparently missed the papers.

had managed to only minimally task the Commonwealth, as the entire proceeding lasted only for some nine minutes.

Before the Hearing took place, it became known that local Deputy Sheriff Look, a lifetime Martha's Vineyard and Chappaquiddick Island resident, whom we will meet later, was speaking out regarding having seen the car on the Island after the time that Kennedy swore it entered the water. Steele said it was "unfortunate" that the Deputy Sheriff was talking, he thought Look was "seeking a little publicity in a big story."[11]

Following the Hearing, hard-working and brilliant Scripps-Howard reporter, Dan Thomasson, was thrown out of a press conference by Walter Steele. He wanted to know or, more appropriately, to see what existed in the public record to support Steele's statements to the Court that Kennedy had been driving "with extreme care." Not getting an answer, he then asked Steele if in fact, he wasn't a "friend and former co-worker with Kennedy in Suffolk County." Steele angrily retorted, "That's true! And if you're going to ask questions like that, you can leave. In fact, I'll have you shown out. Take him out."[12] He commanded the police officers, who were quick to obey. Ultimately, virtual Gestapo tactics were to be used by Steele to completely shut the matter away from the public eye.

Thomasson clearly had his day later on when he published material that made it perfectly clear that it was Steele who led, if not controlled, Chief Arena, and that it was Steele himself who "ruled out the more serious charge of negligence...."

Author Sherrill quoted Jack Olsen quoting Walter Steele:[13]

"What's keeping this case alive, besides politics, is the public wants to know what the hell is a United States Senator doing on the Island of Chappaquiddick having a few pops and ending up on a lonely road with a blonde. Now that's all very interesting, but it's not a criminal matter. The public's gonna keep on

---

[11] Sherrill, Ibid.
[12] Sherrill, p. 103.
[13] Ibid.

kidding itself for months and months, when in fact there's not a single goddamned reason to keep this case open."

This can be easily held to be the gratuitous comment of a true friend and Steele never denied, in fact confirmed this friendship. Aside from the clear violation of professional ethics and formal canons, the fact that Steele, a trained prosecutor, neither investigated the matter, nor removed himself as prosecutor from a case in which he had an admitted, even if somewhat removed, personal interest, is finally, repellent in the extreme. However, as we will see as the record unfolds, Steele's behavior is consistent with that of many officials we will encounter in the Commonwealth of Massachusetts. Ultimately, we must realize that at some points in history the issues, the personalities, the past — especially writ large as in the Kennedy history in Massachusetts — go to create an inexorable force. This last comment speaks to the issue of "Public Policy", a term little understood but which is, in fact, the determining vortex by which our laws are predicated and enforced. "It doesn't pay to fight City Hall" is a folk way of saying the same thing. In the final analysis, we could do far worse than to have Walter Steele sitting on the bench as a Judge in Massachusetts, as he now does. He is a learned scholar, and had been an active and effective prosecutor throughout his career before assuming his present post.

Consistent with the total mismanagement of the prosecution, and telling in retrospect is the fact that in January of 1976 the entire set of police records and papers was discovered missing from Edgartown. Chief Arena, then living in Maine, had the official documents. For what purpose? To write a book? We've never seen it.

More likely, this fiercely loyal Marine and ex-State Trooper was simply continuing to keep the case on ice. After all, he was and is a man of service, and, in order to keep those various pensions intact, he may have been practicing prudence, even though the prudence might be in direct conflict with the public's right to information that exists in the formal public record.

During the first week following the tragedy, reporters were tripping over each other asking both Chief Arena and Walter Steele about the newly surfacing rumors of heavy drinking at the party. Arena responded, "I did not ask that question of the Senator. I'm not pursuing that line at all. There is not a single iota of negligence in the accident."

No, because if one doesn't investigate, doesn't seek evidence at all, one doesn't find anything. As the Chief correctly stated, "There is no material evidence."

Steele's response to the heavy drinking question was clear and straightforward: "not a scintilla of evidence of erratic driving or anything that even suggests booze."[14]

They both should have looked at the car which Senator Kennedy had been so concerned about as it was towed through town, right past the Police Station. After we complete the establishment of the record we will look closely at the car.

Years later Steele said, "I really should have known better. If I had to do it over again, I would have held out for a probable cause Hearing for manslaughter and an autopsy." He felt the charge would not have held up, "but it would have wiped out a lot of doubts."[15]

[14] Sherrill, p. 75.
[15] *Cape Cod Standard Times*, 7-14-79.

5

PREPARED
PUBLIC REMARKS

On Friday evening, July 25, 1969, Ted Kennedy, having earlier that day pleaded guilty to leaving the scene of the accident which resulted in the death of Mary Jo Kopechne, appeared on *national* television to address the people of his *home* state. He did not have to face a charge of manslaughter, because no evidence had been presented that any wanton or willful conduct, negligence or alcohol was involved.

His speech, furthermore, had been prepared for him by a formidable crew: the Camelot Court had been hastily reconvened. The overall speech architect was Ted Sorensen, an attorney from New York City who had been considered by some to be President Jack Kennedy's alter ego. Sorensen is a brilliant strategist and tactician. In fact he wrote the platform for the 1988 Democrat Party Convention. If the Democrats ever return to the White House, Mr. Sorensen will be sure to have the ear of the President. Regarding the details and nuances of the Chappaquiddick tragedy, he rightfully kept himself beside the action; he had no need or desire to be one of the guys. Sorensen was reported to have been outspokenly outraged with Markham and Gargan for not reporting the incident and thus leaving the Senator vulnerable. He had much to learn about this incident, and from the reports that filtered out of the compound it seems likely that Mr. Sorensen was never really given the facts, never in fact informed of what actually happened on Chappaquiddick Island. By intelligence-community standards, he had no "need to know."

Reportedly, Robert McNamara left the compound in disgust, because it was apparent that these powerful and wise advisors were being dealt with strictly on this need-to-know basis. The recent record shows that Sorensen has moved away from support of the Senator. David Burke, the Senator's Washington-office administrative assistant, and Milton Gwirtzman, former Ted Kennedy staff member, speech writer and lawyer, were the other principal drafters of this infamous document. Burke Marshall, mentioned above, thought by Bobby Kennedy to be the most brilliant lawyer in America, was alleged to have been the executive editor of the speech.

David Burke, formerly Vice-President for ABC News and now President of CBS News, was the subject of articles in *Mother Jones* magazine in 1986 and 1987. At ABC he was ideally placed to argue against the showing of the ABC Marilyn Monroe documentary, which alleged that she had relationships with Jack and Bobby Kennedy. David Burke, who was not at Chappaquiddick, had no direct knowledge of the real events which took place. Naturally, he behaved as would any professional in protecting his boss. Burke has come far; he is in a position to determine to some extent exactly what the American people will see on television news, what they will know about. Obviously he proved his mettle with regard to Chappaquiddick, after the incident.

Earlier, even before Senator Kennedy returned to Hyannis Port, the clarion call had sounded, the word went out and the former Court of Camelot reconvened in order to preserve their options. The miraculous could happen again; might they not be summoned back to Washington, and power? And this time they would know how to do it right. Those present at Hyannis Port were a formidable group:

LeMoyne Billings	Jack Kennedy's college roommate, and closest friend; "uncle" to the Kennedy children.
David Burke	Ted Kennedy's Administrative Assistant, lawyer.
Robert Clark	Former District Court Judge in Massachusetts.
Robert Clark, III	Son of the above, lawyer.
John Culver	U.S. Congressman, Ted's friend.
John Driscoll	Lawyer.
Joe Gargan	Kennedy's close cousin, [alleged herein] co-conspirator, lawyer.
Milton Gwirtzman	Speech writer, lawyer.
Richard Goodwin	Special Assistant to President John Kennedy, his envoy to Castro, author, compassionate lawyer.
David Hackett	Bobby Kennedy's close friend and advisor, Kennedy family intelligence advisor.
Robert McNamara	Former Ford Motor Co. President; Secretary of Defense; World Bank President; currently, ambivalent statesman.
Richard McCarran	Edgartown town counsel.
Frank Mankiewicz	Formerly George McGovern's Press Secretary; Public Broadcasting System President; Public Relations/Lobbyist.
Paul Markham	Former U.S. Attorney for Massachusetts, [alleged herein] co-conspirator, lawyer.
Burke Marshall	Former Deputy U.S. Attorney General; IBM General Counsel; currently Yale Law School Professor.

Frank O'Conner	Ted Kennedy assistant
Sargent Shriver	Brother-in-law, former Director of the Peace Corps, Maria's Dad.
Steve Smith	Brother-in-law, Kennedy family financial counselor.
Theodore Sorensen	Special Assistant to President John Kennedy, speechwriter, author, lawyer.
John Tunney	U.S. Congressman, college friend, lawyer.

Not actually present but consulted by telephone were John Kenneth Galbraith, Harvard economist, "professional" liberal, *eminence grise* and Arthur Schlesinger, Jr., noted historian and Kennedy family archivist.

Members of this august body had been called together before by Jack and Bobby to give their well-considered advice to help resolve the Cuban Missile Crisis. What they were asked to do here was to make the incredible seem credible — to manufacture a *truth* out of fractured remains.

So the advisors advised and, to repeat what Judge Clark said, "At the compound, the ones who seem to have the most to say about the case are Stephen Smith and Ted Sorensen. We have conferences, but Smith and Sorensen seem to be calling the shots. The Senator walks in and out, but he really doesn't participate."

Ultimately the deal had been cut, and, Ted Kennedy pleaded guilty to a minor offense, but now the job, the real work, began in earnest. They had the politics to deal with. They had to go public. The Senator and his spokesmen had been telling the press that he couldn't speak about the incident until after disposition from the District Court. This had occurred, so now, to satisfy political imperatives, he needed to come forward to address the people of his state, the ones who would be needed to re-elect him if his career as Senator were to continue. And so, the networks gave *national television* time so he could speak to the people of Massachusetts.

The speech that Senator Kennedy delivered on television that Friday night is presented in its entirety, as follows:

My fellow citizens:

I have requested this opportunity to talk to the people of Massachusetts about the tragedy which happened last Friday evening. This morning I entered a plea of guilty to the charge of leaving the scene of an accident. Prior to my appearance in court it would have been improper for me to comment on these matters. But tonight I am free to tell you what happened and to say what it means to me.

On the weekend of July 18, I was on Martha's Vineyard Island participating with my nephew Joe Kennedy – as for thirty years my family has participated – in the annual Edgartown sailing regatta. Only reasons of health prevented my wife from accompanying me.[1]

On Chappaquiddick Island, off Martha's Vineyard, I attended on Friday evening, July 18, a cookout[2] I had encouraged and helped sponsor for a devoted group of Kennedy campaign secretaries. When I left the party, around 11:15 P.M., I was accompanied by one of these girls, Miss Mary Jo Kopechne. Mary Jo was one of the most devoted members of the staff of Senator Robert Kennedy. She worked for him for four years and was broken up over his death. For this reason, and because she was such a gentle, kind and idealistic person, all of us tried to help her feel that she still had a home with the Kennedy family.

[1]   Joan was four months pregnant at the time.
[2]   Not mentioned in the Police Statement.

There is no truth, no truth whatever, to the widely circulated suspicions of immoral conduct that have been leveled at my behavior and hers regarding that evening. There has never been a private relationship between us of any kind. I know of nothing in Mary Jo's conduct on that or any other occasion — the same is true of the other girls at that party — that would lend any substance to such ugly speculation about their character. Nor was I driving under the influence of liquor.[3]

Little over one mile away, the car that I was driving on an unlit road went off a narrow bridge which had no guard-rails and was built on a left angle to the road.[4] The car overturned in a deep pond and immediately filled with water. I remember thinking as the cold water rushed in around my head that I was for certain drowning. Then water entered my lungs and I actually felt the sensation of drowning. But somehow I struggled to the surface alive.[5] I made immediate and repeated efforts to save Mary Jo by diving into the strong and murky current but succeeded only in increasing my state of utter exhaustion and alarm.[6]

My conduct and conversations during the next several hours to the extent that I can remember them make no sense to me at all. Although my doctors informed me that I suffered a cerebral concussion as well as shock, I do not

---

3   We only have his word for it. Had he reported the accident immediately after its occurrence, we might know for sure. It is believed by many that his ingestion of alcohol was the precise reason why the accident was not reported.

4   By now he had dropped the reference to a "hill" which was mentioned in the Police Statement.

5   In Chapter 8, his Inquest testimony will reiterate a complete recall of entering the water, trying the door and window, flapping about, being "kicked and punched" by Mary Jo, but amazingly a total amnesia about how he got out of the car.

6   According to his timetable he left the cottage at 11:15 P.M., in fact the tide was slack until after 1:00 A.M.

seek to escape responsibility for my actions by placing the blame either on the physical, emotional trauma brought on by the accident or on anyone else. I regard as indefensible the fact that I did not report the accident to the police immediately.

Instead of looking directly for a telephone after lying exhausted in the grass for an undetermined time, I walked back to the cottage[7] where the party was being held and requested the help of two friends, my cousin Joseph Gargan and Paul Markham,[8] and directed them to return immediately to the scene with me — this was some time after midnight — in order to undertake a new effort to dive down and locate Miss Kopechne. Their strenuous efforts, undertaken at some risks to their own lives, also proved futile.

All kinds of scrambled thoughts — all of them confused, some of them irrational, many of them which I cannot recall and some of which I would not have seriously entertained under normal circumstances — went through my mind during this period. They were reflected in the various inexplicable, inconsistent and inconclusive things I said and did, including such questions as whether the girl might still be alive somewhere out of that immediate area, whether some awful curse did actually hang over all the Kennedys, whether there was some justifiable reason for me to doubt what had happened and to delay my report, whether somehow the awful weight of this incredible incident might in some way pass from my shoulders. I was overcome, I'm frank to say, by a jumble

---

[7] He passed two homes with night lights, and the Fire Department with a red light glowing.

[8] Neither gentleman was mentioned in the Police Statement.

of emotions — grief, fear, doubt, exhaustion, panic, confusion and shock.[9]

Instructing Gargan and Markham not to alarm Mary Jo's friends that night I returned to the ferry crossing. The ferry having shut down for the night, I suddenly jumped into the water and impulsively swam across, nearly drowning[10] once again in the effort and returned to my hotel about 2 A.M. and collapsed in my room. I remember going out at one point and saying something to the room clerk.[11]

In the morning, with my mind somewhat more lucid, I made an effort to call a family legal adviser, Burke Marshall, from a public telephone on the Chappaquiddick side of the ferry and belatedly reported the accident to the Martha's Vineyard police.

Today, as I mentioned, I felt morally obligated to plead to the charge of leaving the scene of an accident. No words on my part can possibly express the terrible pain and suffering I feel over this tragic incident. This last week has been an agonizing one for me and the members of my family, and the grief we feel over the loss of a wonderful friend will remain with us the rest of our lives.

These events, the publicity, innuendo and whispers which have surrounded them and my admission of guilt this morning raise the question in my mind of whether my standing among the people of my state has been so

---

[9]   Here he sets up the conditions for a plea of temporary insanity if he needs it later.

[10] It is common knowledge that the ferry can be summoned at any hour of the night; that night the operator stayed on duty until 1:20 A.M., in part because *he knew* that the Senator was on the Island.

[11] That "something" was "What time is it, I misplaced my watch?" Therefore he established a time.

impaired that I should resign my seat in the United States Senate. If at any time the citizens of Massachusetts should lack confidence in their senator's character or his ability, with or without justification, he could not in my opinion adequately perform his duty and should not continue in office.

The people of this state, the state which sent John Quincy Adams and Daniel Webster and Charles Sumner and Henry Cabot Lodge and John Kennedy to the United States Senate, are entitled to representation in that body by men who inspire their utmost confidence. For this reason, I would understand full well why some might think it right for me to resign. For me this will be a difficult decision to make.

It has been seven years since my first election to the Senate. You and I share many memories — some of them have been glorious, some have been very sad. The opportunity to work with you and serve Massachusetts has made my life worthwhile.

And so I ask you tonight, people of Massachusetts, to think this through with me. In facing this decision, I seek your advice and opinion. In making it, I seek your prayers. For this is a decision that I will have finally to make on my own.

It has been written a man does what he must in spite of personal consequences, in spite of obstacles and dangers and pressures, and that is the basis of all human morality. Whatever may be the sacrifices he faces, if he follows his conscience — the loss of his friends, his fortune, his contentment, even the esteem of his fellow man — each man must decide for himself the course he will follow. The stories of past courage cannot supply courage itself. For this, each man must look into his own soul.

I pray that I can have the courage to make the right decision. Whatever is decided and whatever the future holds for me, I hope that I shall be able to put this most recent tragedy behind me and make some further contribution to our state and mankind, whether it be in public or private life.

Thank you and good night.

The reader is referred to the Police Statement, above, which contains the remarks that the Senator caused to be written out the morning after the tragedy. The contrast between the two statements is obvious with only a cursory reading. Notably, Markham and Gargan are represented as heros in the TV version, when in fact they aren't so much as mentioned in the original statement. It has been argued, that as attorneys for Senator Kennedy, they had a legal obligation not to speak out, and Paul Markham never has except to say that his testimony told all.[12] But their very deliberate silence immediately following the tragedy, their not reporting the accident, and their leaving the Island as soon as possible also makes them guilty of withholding information, obstructing justice and being accessories after the fact. As will be shown later, they were co-conspirators in an effort to obstruct justice that ultimately caused the death of Mary Jo Kopechne.

Following the TV speech, the press moved as rapidly as the Kennedy supporters, who had spread the word for an inpouring of positive messages to be sent to the Senator.

Columnists Robert S. Allen and John A. Goldsmith wrote:

The word was being spread by telephone and other means to Kennedy's liegemen and devotees throughout the country to make every effort to ensure a deluge of favorable responses. A

[12] *LA Times*, 12/24/79.

boiler-room team was set up to solicit supporting messages from all parts of the country.

Ted Lewis, *NY Daily News*:

Loyal precinct workers in Rockwell, Lexington, Concord and Chicopee Falls were responsible for getting out the favorable masses. The Wisconsin Labor Journal said that labor leaders in Massachusetts were requested to get their members to respond favorably.

Harper's, David Halberstam wrote:

The statement itself was of such cheapness and bathos as to be a rejection of everything the Kennedys had stood for in candor and style. It was as if these men had forgotten everything which made the Kennedys distinctive in American politics and simply told the youngest brother that he could get away with whatever he wanted because he was a Kennedy in Massachusetts.

Finally, an anonymous Edgartown newspaperman reported privately:

Edgartown got sick to its stomach watching him on TV. People here know this area and they know the Dyke Bridge, and they can't be conned. They sat in front of their screens and listened to Ted Kennedy tell stories that made him sound like Superman, and they laughed and said, "Come on Teddy, you've got to be kidding!" Phones were ringing all over town as soon as he went off the air. Everybody agreed he must be lying, that he must be covering up for something much worse. Now they're wondering what that *something* is.

But the last word, should be given to pundit Mike Royko, who said it for us all. He wrote scathingly right after the TV speech in the *Chicago Daily News*:

It's unfortunate Sen. Edward Kennedy isn't answering questions about his accident.

A few points still need clearing up.

However, he did go on TV and make a long statement after spending the day with the Kennedy team's top speech writers, brain-trusters and tacticians.

So maybe in his eloquent and heart-twanging statement, the answers can be found:

Q. Senator, people are still wondering why you turned down that dangerous dirt road, instead of following the paved road to the ferry landing?

A. It has been written a man does what he must in spite of personal consequences, in spite of obstacles, dangers and pressures, and that is the basis of all human morality.

Q. Gee, Senator; Ted Sorensen couldn't have said it better. But about that wrong turn: The white line went left; the reflectorized arrow points left; you had driven that road many times before. So how come you went the other way, and kept going?

A. Whatever the sacrifice he faces if he follows his conscience, the loss of his friends, his contentments, even the esteem of his fellow men, each must decide for himself the course he will follow.

Q. Gosh, Senator; Arthur Schlesinger couldn't have said it better. But about that turn. A deputy sheriff said he saw your car was stopped near the intersection before you made the wrong turn. Could you explain that?

A. And so I ask you tonight, the people of Massachusetts, to think this through with me in facing this decision. I seek your advice and opinion in making it. I seek your prayers. For this is a decision I will have finally to make on my own.

Q. Touchingly put, Senator; Richard Goodwin couldn't have said it better. But about the weekend: You originally told the police that you were in shock, and that after the accident you returned to the cottage and crawled into the back seat of a car, right?

A. It has been seven years since my first election to the Senate. You and I share many memories, some of them glorious, some have been very sad. The opportunity to work with you and serve Massachusetts has made my life worthwhile.

Q. That's very nice, but now you have changed the story so that you returned to the cottage summoned two companions, Gargan and Markham, and all of you went diving for the girl. Would you explain this change?

A. The stories of past courage cannot supply courage itself. For this each man must look into his own soul.

Q. I see. Well, then, after the dives failed, you say you were too shook up to report the accident. But why didn't Gargan and Markham, both lawyers, report it? Were they in shock, too?

A. The people of this state, the state which sent John Quincy Adams, Daniel Webster, Charles Sumner, Henry Cabot Lodge and John Kennedy to the United States Senate, are entitled to representation in that body by men who inspire their utmost confidence.

Q. Great guys, Senator. But about Gargan and Markham: when you impulsively jumped into the ocean to swim back to Edgartown through treacherous tides, almost drowning once, what did your companions do?

A. I pray that I can have the courage to make the right decision. Whatever is decided, whatever the future holds for me, I hope that I shall be able to put this most recent tragedy behind me and make some future contribution to our state and mankind, whether it be in public life or in private life.

Q. Poignantly put, Senator; Sorensen, Schlesinger and Goodwin couldn't have written a better phrase. But about your companions: When you went swimming into the inky night, didn't they do anything? Didn't they even yell, "Hey, come back," or get a rowboat and accompany you? Weren't they even mildly curious whether you eventually made it across?

A. And so I ask you tonight, the people of Massachusetts, to think this through with me in facing this decision.

Q. Senator, do you plan on ever answering some of these questions?

A. Thank you and good night.

6

OPEN COURT BRIEFLY

What follows is presented for the record, and hopefully
will aid anyone who is not an attorney to comprehend the legal
elements of the case. The complete written decision from Judge
Bernard C. Brominski of Wilkes-Barre, Pennsylvania, regarding
the unsuccessful attempt by District Attorney Edmund Dinis to
have Mary Jo Kopechne's body disinterred and autopsied, is
reprinted because it formally states many of the facts of the case.
The Hearing was held in October, but this decision was released
only on December 8, 1969, just after Judge Brominski was re-
elected to the bench. The implication is that Brominski did not
want the findings he made to get in the way of his re-election.

In this chapter, the reader should pay particular attention to
three basic facts. First, on Sunday morning, twenty-four hours
after the death of Mary Jo, the District Attorney, Mr. Dinis, was
reported to have made efforts to have an autopsy performed
before the body left the Island. Second, as will be shown, there
is an unresolved, if not suspicious, element concerning whether
the District Attorney actually made the request, or whether he
was misinformed by his own investigator, Lieutenant George
Killen, regarding the actual removal of the body. Third, we have
the fact that Mr. Dunn Gifford, Legislative Assistant to Edward
Kennedy, came to the Island for the purpose of managing the
removal of the body to Pennsylvania, out of the jurisdictional
reach of the local authorities to be able to demand an autopsy.

In fact, Kennedy himself had been overheard by Police
Officer Carmen Salvador on the telephone, making arrangements
for her speedy removal. In all fairness, this may have been at the

request of Mary Jo's family, but it also fit Kennedy's own personal necessity. Remember his remarks about the car being
towed through town: "The people will all be staring at it," he
said. "They'll make a big thing out of it." [Emphasis Added.]

It is here, in Judge Brominski's court, that the issue of blood
on Mary Jo's blouse is raised for the first time. Pay particular
attention here and later in Chapter 10 to the ramifications of
the blood on her blouse, and pause to consider why the Kopechne family attorney was so professionally prepared, such an
authority, on the issue of blood. This attorney, actually hired by
Kennedy to represent the Kopechne family, did everything he
could to fight exhumation and autopsy. A principal premise of
this book is that an autopsy could have changed the ultimate
disposition in this matter. The fact that the Kennedy/Kopechne
legal and lay resources fought so strongly (and ultimately, successfully) to avoid autopsy indicates the extreme need Kennedy
felt to keep the ultimate truth buried in the ground with Mary
Jo Kopechne.

Autopsy Hearing
Wilkes-Barre, Pennsylvania
October 20, 1969

- - - - - - - - - - - - - -

IN RE: KOPECHNE   IN THE COURT OF
                                   COMMON PLEAS OF
                                   LUZERNE COUNTY --
                                   CRIMINAL

PETITION FOR
EXHUMATION
AND AUTOPSY
                                   NO. 1114 of 1969.

- - - - - - - - - - - - - -

DECISION

This matter comes before the court upon petition and the amended petition for exhumation and autopsy of the body of Mary Jo Kopechne. The petitioners are Edmund Dinis, District Attorney for the Southern District of Massachusetts, and Robert W. Nevin, M.D., Medical Examiner for Dukes County, Massachusetts. The amended petition sets forth the following allegations of fact:

1. The death of Mary Jo Kopechne on July 18 or 19, 1969.

2. Her burial in Larksville, Luzerne County, Pennsylvania.

3. A search on July 19, 1969 which resulted in the recovery of the body of Mary Jo Kopechne from a submerged car off Dykes Bridge, Edgartown, Dukes County, Massachusetts.

4. A determination by Dr. Mills that the death of Mary Jo Kopechne was caused by asphyxiation from immersion (i.e., drowning); that the cause of death was determined without benefit of autopsy; that Dr. Mills did not perform an autopsy because he found no external signs of violence or foul play; that the body of the deceased had been submerged eight hours before his observation; that it was assumed Mary Jo Kopechne was not only the driver of the car, but was its sole occupant; and that death occurred five to eight hours prior to 9:30 A.M.

5. That the operator of the motor vehicle in which the deceased's body was found did not report the accident to the police until approximately ten hours after he said it occurred; that said operator reported that the accident happened at 11:15 P.M. on July 18, 1969; that there is a witness who claims to have seen the car at 12:40 A.M. on July 19, 1969, with two or possibly three persons in it.

6. That said operator pleaded guilty to a motor vehicle law infraction.

7. That the report of the accident made to the Chief of Police of Edgartown, Massachusetts by the operator on July 19, 1969, differed from a report of the accident broadcast by the operator on July 25, 1969.

8. That the broadcast and police reports are silent on many important details.

9. That persons who were not directly involved in the accident but who were cognizant of it, did not call the authorities.

10. That there appear on the white shirt worn by the deceased "washed out" stains that give a positive benzidine reaction, an indication of the presence of the residual traces of blood.

11. That there was present a certain amount of blood in both the deceased's mouth and nose which may or may not be inconsistent with death by drowning.

12. That the information in paragraphs 10 and 11 (5-I and 5-J) was not available to the petitioners until after interment.

13. That the public interest and proper administration of justice requires confirmation of Dr. Mills' original determination of the cause of death which can be accomplished only by an autopsy.

14. The passage of time from the date of death on July 18 or 19, 1969, has not diminished to any significant degree the findings which could be made from an autopsy conducted at the present time.

15. There is now pending in Dukes County, Massachusetts, an Inquest into the death of Mary Jo Kopechne.

16. That the purpose of the Inquest is to determine whether or not there is any reason sufficient to believe that the sudden death of Mary Jo Kopechne may have resulted from the act or negligence of a person or persons other than the deceased.

17. That in order that the circumstances of death be clearly established and the doubt and suspicion surrounding the death be resolved, an exhumation and autopsy will be required.

18. That once Dr. Mills' determination of the cause of death is confirmed by an autopsy, the Inquest can proceed with certainty that Mary Jo Kopechne's death was caused by drowning. However, if the autopsy should disclose that her death resulted from some cause other than drowning, the Inquest may then proceed in the direction appropriate in light of the information thus revealed.

19. That in either event, an autopsy would further serve the public interest and promote the proper administration of justice in that it will disclose either the presence or absence of other conditions beside the cause of death having a critical bearing on the events and circumstances culminating in the death of Mary Jo Kopechne.

20. That the public interest in general and the proper administration of justice in particular require that all facts relative to the Inquest be established with the utmost attainable degree of certainty.

Courts have never hesitated to have a body exhumed where the application under the particular circumstances appeared reasonable and was for the purpose of eliciting the truth in the promotion of justice.

On the other hand, an application for disinterment for the purpose of performing an autopsy should not be granted where there is no basis or justification for an order. Disinterment for the purpose of examination or autopsy should not be ordered unless it is clearly established that good cause and urgent necessity for such action exist. An order should not be made except on a strong showing that the facts sought will be established by an examination or autopsy. In the search for the truth, the problems of religion, the wishes of decedent, the sensitivities of loved ones and friends, or even the elements of public health and welfare, should not be disregarded. The law will not reach into the grave in search of the facts except in the rarest of cases, and not even then unless it is clearly necessary and there is reasonable probability that such a violation of the sepulchre will establish that which is sought.

The positive criteria in law are then that the application for exhumation and autopsy:

1. Must be reasonable under the circumstances.

2. Its purpose is to elicit the truth in the promotion of justice.

3. It must be clearly established that:

    (a) good cause and
    (b) urgent necessity for such action exist.

4. There must be a strong showing that the facts sought will be established by an exhumation and autopsy.

5. That the law will reach into the grave in:

    (a) Only the rarest of cases, and
    (b) not even then, unless clearly necessary, and
    (c) where there is a reasonable probability that such a violation of the sepulchre will establish that which is sought.

Let us now turn to the facts established at the Hearing on the petition for exhumation and autopsy.

Essentially, they must be examined in two categories. First, from the purely legal point of view as they obtain to the eliciting of the truth in the promotion of justice and the good cause and urgent necessity that must exist to warrant an exhumation and autopsy; and, second, from the medical-legal aspect that there must be a strong showing that the facts sought will be established by an autopsy and the reasonable probability that the violation of the sepulchre will establish that which is sought.

As to the former, we are obviously referring to such facts as would cause one in authority to conclude that the death of Mary Jo Kopechne resulted from a cause other than by drowning.

A review of the record of testimony, in light of the allegations of the petition from Edmund Dinis, reveals that there is some question as to whether the vehicle in question departed the Dyke Bridge at about 11:15 P.M., July 18, 1969, or about 12:40 A.M. July 19, 1969. That the driver of the vehicle failed to report the incident until some ten hours after it happened. That the report given by the driver to the Edgartown police varied from his broadcast on July 25, 1969, and that the police report and broadcast are silent on many important details of the accident. That persons not directly involved in the accident who were cognizant of it, did not call the authorities. That there were washed-out stains on the back of the blouse of the deceased which, when exposed to a benzidine test, indicated the presence of blood and that there was present a certain amount of blood in both the deceased's mouth and nose which may or many not be inconsistent with death by drowning.

That a witness saw the car in question July 19, 1969 at about 12:40 A.M. in which there appeared to be a man and a woman in the front seat and a person or a sweater or pocketbook or something on the back seat and that this car stopped and, upon approach by the witness, left hurriedly and that this was the same car that was found in Poucha Pond off the Dyke Bridge the following morning. That the witness also saw two other unidentified girls and a man that night near the scene. That there is an Inquest now pending in Edgartown, Massachusetts, and that an autopsy is necessary to resolve the circumstances surrounding the death of Mary Jo Kopechne.

Starting with the premise that the purpose of this autopsy is to establish the cause of death of Mary Jo Kopechne, are there any credible facts of record here that could objectively cause one to conclude that a reasonable probability exists that the cause of death was other than death by drowning?

Let us first consider the fact that the driver failed to report the accident until ten hours after it occurred. Disposition of same need not be considered here since the Massachusetts authorities have accepted the driver's plea of guilty to leaving the scene of an accident. Furthermore, the fact that the vehicle

operated by the driver may have entered the water at 12:40
A.M., July 19, 1969, rather than at 11:15 P.M., July 18, 1969
does not suggest a cause of death other than death by drowning.

Reference is then made to the difference between the driver's
broadcast and the police report. Essentially, there are but two
basic differences between the two. First, in the broadcast the
driver made reference to seeking aid from Joseph Gargan and
Paul Markham. In the police report, no reference was made to
them. Second, in the police statement, he said he went back to
the party[1] and had someone (unidentified) drive him back to
Edgartown, while in his broadcast he refers to the aforesaid
Gargan and Markham assisting him. These discrepancies do
not alter the determination of cause of death.

The next reference is that the police report and the broadcast
are silent on many important details of the accident. While this
is possibly so, proper subpoenaing of witnesses may or may not
have substantiated this, but at the moment this court is not at
liberty to speculate as to what those details might be.

Again, reference is made to witnesses who had knowledge of
the accident and did not call the authorities. The court is
unable to determine from the record who these witnesses were,
to what they would testify, or why they were not subpoenaed.

One of the more substantial references in the petition was
concerning the evidence of blood on the back of the deceased's
blouse, as well as in her mouth and nose. Yet, the only positive testimony as to these was that this evidence was wholly
consistent with death by drowning.

Equally significant was the testimony of Christopher Look, Jr.[2]
who testified as to the presence of the car of the driver near
the bridge at about 12:40 A.M. on July 19, 1969 with a man

---

1   The Judge errs here, the Police Report made no mention of a party, but merely to
     where "my friends were eating."

2   Judge Brominski's failure to cite the fact that Look was a Deputy Sheriff, off-duty,
     but in uniform, can be seen as an indication of his prejudice.

and a woman in the front and a person or a sweater in the back, which left the scene hurriedly when his presence was evident and that this was the same car found in Poucha Pond that same day; also that he saw two unidentified girls and a man nearby. Again, this course of conduct by the driver does not suggest a cause of death other than as has been found.

With this in mind, let us examine the testimony in the petitioners' case that refutes their own contentions. In Chief Dominick Arena's police report, he states: "It was felt that because of the evidence at the scene, condition of the roadway and accident scene that there was no negligence on the part of the operator in the accident."[3] The testimony of John N. Farrar, the scuba diver, is that at the scene there was nothing outstanding about the body other than that she was attractively dressed and fully clothed.[4] That the submerged car had its ignition on, the car was in drive, the brake off, the light switch on, and it was full of gas. Also that the window on the driver's side was down and the door was locked. Dr. Donald Mills' testimony, reference to which will be made at length in the legal-medical portion of this opinion was that he found no signs of foul play or any criminal conduct. Finally, Eugene Frieh, the mortician, testified that in cleansing the body of Mary Jo Kopechne, he found no bruises, contusions or abrasion, except on a knuckle of her left hand.

In view of the above, it is difficult for this court to conclude that exhumation and autopsy are warranted. If there is testimony available to the petitioners that might establish the relief they seek, it has not been presented here.

Let us now address ourselves to the medical-legal aspect of this matter. As stated before, the petitioners must establish by a

---

3   Ironically, this statement had been controlled by Kennedy's own attorneys before the original Hearing where Kennedy pleaded guilty.

4   He fails to mention Farrar's significant remarks regarding the position of her body (straining her head up to an air pocket) and the significant fact that her arms were bent at right angles with her hands clawed from clutching the back seat. Both Judge Brominski and Judge Boyle completely ignored air pockets, because they would imply that she lived, and therefore failure to report the accident would constitute negligence.

strong showing that the facts sought will be established by an exhumation and autopsy, and there must be reasonable probability that a violation of the sepulchre will establish those facts.

In cases of death resulting from unnatural causes, autopsies before burial are performed as a matter of course. After interment, the legal test recited on pages four and five of this decision controls. As stated in this court's decision of October 9, 1969, "... It must not be overlooked that the Massachusetts authorities had the statutory right and opportunity to perform an autopsy prior to interment of the body of Mary Jo Kopechne, but once burial is complete, the aforementioned legal principles as to exhumation and autopsy must be considered."

Let us first review the medical testimony offered by the pathologists for the petitioners, that of Doctors Joseph W. Spellman, George G. Katsas, and Cyril H. Wecht. They all testified that if the body of Mary Jo Kopechne were exhumed and an autopsy performed, an interpretation of results would be more difficult, but it would be entirely possible to make observations and draw valid conclusions. In the instance of Dr. Spellman, he testified he has performed autopsies on bodies interred for a period of five years. They also testified autopsies have frequently revealed causes of death not revealed by external examination, such as fractured skulls, hemorrhages within the brain, broken necks, broken ribs, ruptured internal organs and natural disease processes. In the case of Dr. Spellman, he testified that he attaches little significance to froth about the mouth or nose of a victim since it is found in other kinds of deaths such as heart failure, overdose of drugs, and death from respiratory depression. Dr. Katsas referred specifically to tests that might confirm death by drowning such as the presence of foreign material deep in the tracheae or bronchi, hemorrhage in the middle ear and presence of diatoms and algae in the bones and remote areas of the body.

However, on cross-examination, he testified that if all three tests proved negative, he would conclude that the cause of death was by drowning if he didn't find any other evidence of disease or injury in the remainder of the body. The only reference to reasonable medical certainty developed in the testimony of Dr. Wecht, who after reciting many general areas of causes of death, stated: "There would be an excellent opportunity to arrive at a quite substantial valid medical opinion that could be rendered by any competent pathologists with more than a reasonable degree of certainty." But of what?

Even if we assume that an autopsy would reveal a broken neck or any other bone in the body, a fractured skull, the rupture of an internal organ, none of these would be incompatible with the manner in which the accident occurred. To consider any other cause of death at this time would give loose rein to speculation unsupported by any medical facts of record.

When we weigh this evidence with that of Dr. Donald Mills, who was also called on behalf of the petitioners, we immediately find an inconsistency within the petitioners' cause. Dr. Mills, after examination of the body of Mary Jo Kopechne, concluded and issued the death certificate with the cause of death as: "Asphyxiation by immersion — (Overturned submerged automobile)"[5] i.e. death by drowning. His examination included a view of the body, finding a dead girl, well nourished, fully clothed, in total *rigor mortis*. He opened her blouse, put a stethoscope to her heart, percussed her chest with slight pressure and water came out of her nose and mouth.

There was a fine white froth about her nose and mouth which was present before percussion. There were little cobwebs of blood on the foam which went directly to a little capillary area just on the left hand edge of her nostril. She obviously had much water in her respiratory tract since he applied pressure a number of times in varying degrees and each time water would well up and out. This pressure was on the chest, not the stomach. He saw no evidence of trauma of any kind after feeling her legs, arms, skull and back. That although he did not disrobe her, he did open her blouse and pulled her slacks down over her abdomen. To him, it was an "obvious case of drowning" since the foam about the nose and mouth, the

---

[5] This death certificate was brought to Dr. Mills (already filled out) for his signature by the assistant undertaker who was accompanied by Dun Gifford, a Kennedy administrative assistant.

cobwebs of blood from her nostril, the splashing sound of water in her chest and the emission of water from deep down are all common concomitants of drowning. It was his opinion that for all practical purposes his external examination excluded other causes of death. He also added that there was no evidence of foul play or any criminal conduct. To this we add the report of the blood test of the blood of the deceased which was negative as to barbiturates and evidence of the consumption of only a small amount of alcoholic beverages.[6]

While this may actually belong to the first category of consideration, the eliciting of truth in the promotion of justice, the fact is that after his examination Dr. Mills released the body to Mr. Frieh, the mortician, with a caveat that there should be no embalming until he cleared with the District Attorney's Office and the State Police. Only after it had been determined that there was no necessity for an autopsy did Dr. Mills then direct Mr. Frieh to embalm the body. This testimony of the delay in embalming was corroborated by Mr. Frieh, also a witness for petitioners.[7]

Turning to the testimony of Dr. Werner Spitz, the pathologist testifying for the respondents, while his colleagues in his field did not attach particular significance to pinkish foam about the nose and mouth in drowning cases, he explained that when water enters the lungs under pressure, particularly salt water, there is a rupture of very small vessels and the blood from the rupture gives the foam a pinkish appearance. That when resuscitation stops, foam develops and being lighter than water, comes up. While there may be differences of opinion among pathologists, it would be illogical for this court not to accept that which is a logical explanation in view of all the attending circumstances. In addition, Dr. Spitz gave the only explanations

[6] 0.9% alcohol is not legally drunk, based on weight it can indicate 2 cocktails or 3 ounces of liquor consumed in an hour, let alone what had left her bloodstream in the approximately twelve hours between the party and the taking of the blood sample. That the Judge failed to take this into consideration would seem to point to prejudice, and to at least a willful limiting of the record.

[7] Of major import is that he ignores Mr. Frieh's testimony that he was surprised that she had so little water in her body. This goes directly to the question of drowning vs. asphyxiation by being deprived of air.

as to the presence of blood on the back of the blouse of the deceased. He stated that when this pinkish foam begins to form, it runs down the face along the neck and makes a puddle behind the head and hence the blood on the back of the blouse.[8] He said he couldn't imagine a drowning victim looking any different. He concedes that he would have liked to have had an autopsy when the body was first removed from the water, but that an exhumation and autopsy would be but of academic importance and added that, in his opinion, within medical certainty, Mary Jo Kopechne died from drowning.[9]

The testimony of Dr. Henry C. Freimuth, a toxicologist, lends verity to the testimony of Drs. Mills and Spitz in that the stains on the blouse of the decedent were characteristic of the stains produced by pinkish foam from drowning victims.

In evaluating this medical testimony as it relates to the law of the Commonwealth of Pennsylvania, it must be concluded that the petitioners have failed to meet their burden of proof by a "strong showing that the facts sought will be established by an exhumation and autopsy" and that there is a "reasonable probability" that that which is sought warrants a violation of the sepulchre. A *fortiori*, from the testimony before this court, every reasonable probability leads to a conclusion that supports the original finding of the cause of death of Mary Jo Kopechne, asphyxiation by immersion, i.e., death by drowning.

In view of the testimony and law considered herein, and bearing in mind that courts are not reluctant to grant autopsies in given cases, we must be mindful that Joseph A. Kopechne and Gwen L. Kopechne, the parents of Mary Jo Kopechne, have indicated that they are unalterably opposed to exhumation and autopsy. Thus, it is incumbent that this court give weight to their objections. While their disapproval is not an absolute

---

[8] How could it make a puddle when she was upright (see illustration, Photo Section) especially when the car was filled with water? The blood would have flowed away and certainly not have set on her blouse unless it set before the car went in the water.

[9] Dr. Spitz also said in his testimony, "Well, my reservations are that she may have injuries which I cannot determine upon external examination of the body." Therefore Dr. Mills cursory examination had been incomplete.

bar to an exhumation and autopsy, in view of the facts presented to this court, their objections are well taken.

It is the conclusion of this court that the facts presented herein are insufficient to support a finding of the cause of death of Mary Jo Kopechne other than asphyxiation by immersion.

Therefore, we enter the following:

ORDER

Now this 8th day of December, 1969, at 11:55 A.M., EST, it is hereby ordered and decreed that the objections of Joseph A. Kopechne and Gwen L. Kopechne, parents of Mary Jo Kopechne, are hereby sustained and the petitioner's request for exhumation and autopsy of the body of Mary Jo Kopechne is hereby denied.

BY THE COURT

_____

P.J.

*   *   *   *

Signed, sealed and delivered. While this Court Decision was not to be the end of the matter, many have said that this action effectively took the fire out of the belly of D.A. Dinis. He seemed to give his best effort in this maneuver, but saw failure all about him. His own co-petitioner, Dr. Robert Nevin, the Martha's Vineyard Chief Medical Examiner, had inexplicably withdrawn his support for the petition without telling Dinis, after Brominski had ordered them to submit a second petition, deeming the original to be inadequate for ordering disinterment and autopsy.

Amazingly, in the Decision above, Judge Brominski failed to seriously consider the sheer volume of blood stains that were found on Mary Jo's blouse. And, also significant, the Judge stating that Dinis "voluntarily" let the body go without autopsy, ignoring Dinis' own testimony to the contrary.

Below, we present key testimonies from this Hearing:

Direct Examination by Assistant D.A. Fernandes:

Q. Are you the duly elected District Attorney for the Southern District of Massachusetts?

Edmund Dinis, called in behalf of Petitioners and duly sworn:

A. I am.

Q. And will you please tell the Court what this district and area embraces?
A. This District is a District established by statute and it encompasses four counties in Massachusetts, the Counties of Bristol, Barnstable, Dukes and Nantucket.

Q. And does Dukes County embrace Edgartown and Chappaquiddick?
A. Dukes County includes the Elizabeth Island, Martha's Vineyard Island and Chappaquiddick Island which is part of the Township of Edgartown.

. . . . . .

Q. With reference to the death of Mary Jo Kopechne, if anything, what investigations, if any, has your office conducted?
A. The . . . .

Flanagan: Objection, your Honor.[10]

The Court: Overruled.

A. The District Attorney's office has endeavored to speak to the parties who were present prior to and after the estimated time

---

[10] Attorney for the Kopechne family, opposed to autopsy.

of death of Mary Jo Kopechne and has been unable to do so, none of these witnesses are available.

Flanagan: Your Honor, I ask that that answer be stricken.

The Court: It may be stricken from the record.

Q. Is it your opinion as the chief law enforcement officer for Dukes County or for the Southern District that your request for an Inquest for autopsy in this particular case would promote the interests of justice?

Flanagan: Objection, calling for a conclusion.

The Court: Sustained.

. . . . . .

Q. As chief law enforcement officer for the Southern District of Massachusetts are you satisfied with the cause of death as determined today?
A. I am not satisfied.

Flanagan: Objection.

. . . . . .

Q. Was this information available to you soon after the death in this case?
A. What information?

Q. The information that Dr. Mills testified to yesterday with reference to his observations and his conclusions, his medical opinion as to the cause of death?
A. Not within the first twenty-four hours and not before the body left the Island.

Q. Well, after that information was made available to you, what, if anything, did you do?
A. I ordered an autopsy.

Flanagan: Objection, your Honor.

The Court: Overruled.

Q. And could you tell this court when you ordered an autopsy?
A. Ten A.M. on July the 20th.

Q. Would this be a Sunday, the day after the body was discovered?
A. That's correct.

Q. To whom did you make this request?
A. I made this request to Lieutenant George E. Killen of the State Police.

Q. And what if any information was given to you with reference to the possibility of an autopsy at that time?
A. I was informed by Lieutenant Killen that the body had already been flown off the Island by the Kennedy people.

Flanagan: Objection, your Honor.

The Court: Make your objections timely, would you please, before the answer is given.

Flanagan: We ask that the answer be stricken as hearsay.

The Court: Too late now.

. . . . . .

Cross Examination By Mr. Flanagan:

Q. Is it not a fact, sir, that there was a conversation with Dr. Mills where you concurred in his opinion that no autopsy was necessary?

Mr. Dinis: This is not true.

Q. Did you hear Dr. Mills testify to that here yesterday.
A. I did.

. . . . . .

The Court: Gentlemen, you are both members of the Bar
and you recognize the problems of the Court
Reporter. You are both talking at the same
time, now, please, one at a time, if you will.

. . . . . .

Q. How did you receive the information, Mr. Dinis, to the effect
that the body was flown out at ten A.M. on Sunday morning?
A. Lieutenant Killen, at my — when I called Lieutenant Killen at
ten A.M. or thereabouts on July the 20th, he informed me that
he had been in touch with Mr. Frieh, I believe it was, and he
informed me that the body had been flown out at nine-thirty,
that arrangements were made the day before to take the body
out at that particular time.

Q. Did he tell you that the body had actually been flown out or
that arrangements were made to fly the body out?
A. Well, the impression that I had at the time, my best memory
tells me he told me the body had left at nine-thirty.

Q. So you did nothing further after that to try to stop either the
body that had not been flown out or contact officials here in
Luzerne County?
A. No, I did not.

Q. Did you yourself call the undertaker to find out whether the
body had in fact left.
A. No, I did not.

. . . . . .

Q. In that conversation [with Dr. Mills] did you discuss an autopsy with him?
A. My memory tells me that I questioned him concerning his
certainty with regards to all of the facts that we had at that

time when he made the determination not to have an autopsy, as to whether he was certain of his position.

Q. Well, isn't it a fact, Mr. Dinis, that you asked him whether he was satisfied that there was no foul play?
A. That is not true. Medical Examiners are not charged with that responsibility.

Q. Will you answer the question that was asked? I ask that the last remark be stricken.

The Court: All right, it is of no consequence. Go ahead.

Flanagan: No further questions your Honor.

Fernandes: No further questions.

The Court: You may step down, Mr. Dinis.

. . . . . .

Direct Examination by Mr. Flanagan:

KILVERT DUNN GIFFORD called in behalf of Respondents (Kopechne family) and duly sworn.

A. I'm presently employed as Legislative Assistant to Senator Edward Kennedy.

Q. Did you know Mary Jo Kopechne?
A. Yes, I did.

. . . . . .

Q. Mr. Gifford, when did you first learn of the death of Mary Jo Kopechne?
A. In the middle of the morning on July 19th, Saturday morning.

Q. Where were you at that time?
A. I was in Nantucket, Massachusetts .... shortly after learning of her death I went to Martha's Vineyard Island .... to assist Mr.

and Mrs. Kopechne in any way in making arrangements for getting the body of their daughter to Wilkes-Barre where it was to be buried. .... I had previously spoken by telephone with Mr. Frieh. .... I told him I was available to help him as I was to the Kopechne family in any way that made sense to him. ..... when I got to Martha's Vineyard at the County Airport I engaged a taxi and had it take me to the funeral home in Vineyard Haven.

Q. Was the body of Mary Jo Kopechne there before you arrived?
A. Yes, it was.

Q. Were you asked to identify the body?
A. I was.

Q. And did you identify the body?
A. I did.

Q. Did you take any further steps to assist Mr. Frieh and Mr. Gay?
A. Yes, I did, there was understandably considerable paper work involved in matters of this sort, there were questions about such things as her Social Security Number, the — her employer of record as of that date, matters of this sort — relating to filling out the forms and certificates and various other forms.

Q. Did you have any contact Saturday with Chief Arena?
A. Yes, I did.

Q. What time and where?
A. After spending some time with Mr. Frieh and Mr. Gay at the funeral home and getting as much of the paper work as we could there, there was a need for various signatures on the forms, so I drove in a car with Mr. Gay to the Town and County Building in which the office of Chief Arena is, I introduced myself to him, told him I was there on the Island to help in any way I could with any information or anything else he needed, if he needed any in terms of helping the Kopechne family and the funeral directors in getting the body of Miss Kopechne to Wilkes-Barre.

Q. Did you ask either Chief Arena or the undertakers or anyone else whether there were any other requirements that had to be met before the body could be transported back to Wilkes-Barre for burial?

A. Yes, I did, in the funeral home in Vineyard Haven while going over the various forms and trying to get the information such as Social Security Numbers etc., on the form was a notation, the death certificate, I believe, that death was due to asphyxiation by immersion. I asked what that meant and I was told that that meant drowning. I said, "How do we know?" and Dr. Mills made that finding. I asked if there were need for more tests.

Mr. Dinis: I object, your Honor.

The Court: He can say what he asked, go ahead, over-ruled for the moment. Proceed.

A. I asked, as I was saying, what was meant, I asked how that determination had been made on that form, I asked if there were steps such as an autopsy which had to be taken. I asked very similar questions of Chief Arena when I was with him in the Town and Country Building.

Q. Was there any request for an autopsy, do you know?

A. To my knowledge, at that particular time in the proceeding, there had been none .... I was with Mr. Gay [undertaker's assistant] as we were endeavoring to complete the variety of forms, we stopped by to see Dr. Mills, his signature was necessary on one of the forms, I asked him many of the same questions I asked of the other gentlemen I spoke to earlier. He answered similarly, I then, at some time around seven-thirty or eight P.M. called Mr. Gay who had returned to the funeral home by then and said was there anything else I could help on and he said, no, everything was fine as far as he knew and so I then left the Island of Martha's Vineyard and flew back to the Island of Nantucket where my family were and spent the night there. .... I left Nantucket about eight A.M. Sunday morning and flew to Martha's Vineyard. .... I waited there in the airport for the arrival of the gentlemen from the funeral home, we had previously, as they have testified previously that the plans were to leave the Island about nine-thirty in the

morning, in a chartered aircraft, there was some difficulty with
the weather, with the type of aircraft, and one of the aircraft
previously engaged had mechanical difficulty of one sort, there
was a question of where there was a Hold on the body because
of a possible autopsy, it was, just .... [11]

Q. What happened as you waited there?
A. Well, we waited with no word, no airplane and no word back
about the Hold or anything like that.

Q. Did you take steps to find out what was going on?
A. ... I did, however, at about ten o'clock..... leave the airport and
go downtown, downtown to Edgartown to see Chief Arena and
say that we were very much slowed up in what had previously
been arranged for various reasons, among them being the
weather and the business about a Hold for an Autopsy, and
was there anything I needed to do as far as he was concerned
before we left. .... he said "No," he got all the forms filled out,
they're not my forms anyway but "Goodbye," he said "Goodbye." I left the Police Station and went back to the airport. ....
waited some more, and we waited until about, oh, I should say,
sometime around noon when the plane was there waiting, we
were waiting and I asked about whether there was, what about
the Hold for an autopsy, can we go now, what's — you know,
is it all right and there was some more waiting and in a
subsequent conversation they said OK to go.[12]

Q. What did you do?
A. We left, sir.

Q. Did you accompany Mr. Kielty and his assistant to the funeral
home. .... located in Plymouth, Pennsylvania. .... did you stay
there for a period of time?

---

[11] Nowhere does the record disclose just exactly what comprised a "Hold".

[12] Again, who said: "OK to go." The State Police? Did they talk to Killen who had
told Dinis the body had left at 9:30? According to Chief Arena he had nothing to
do with a "Hold." Ultimately Gifford's concern was allayed by undertaker Eugene
Frieh, who assured him there was no such hold. As to where this "Hold" business
began, we have only Mr. Gifford to ask.

A. I did, I would say that when we arrived there about, I'd say three or three-fifteen, there was to be a viewing of the body that evening by members of the Kopechne family.

Q. Were, you present while Mr. Kielty was preparing the body?
A. Yes, I was.

Q. What did you observe while you were present?
A. That there were no visible marks on the body of any sort.

Q. Now, Mr. Gifford, the matters that you have testified to that you did, did you do those because of your friendship with Miss Kopechne?
A. Yes, I did them in part because of that, and part because the Kopechne's didn't have, there was nobody more or less that knew, I never had met them before but I did know Mary Jo and I just wanted to help in any way, this was a — I felt very pleased to be able to help them in any way.

That's all, you may cross-examine.

Mr. Dinis: No questions.

The Court: You may step down, sir.

By failing to ask Gifford if he was personally in touch with the State Police Barracks, and if not, who was, who in fact said "OK to go", Dinis failed to elicit a very important point.

One wonders if in fact Dinis' own testimony was designed to protect himself, relative to his own upcoming re-election, where he would appear on the Democratic Party ticket with Edward Kennedy. But Dunn Gifford did claim later "to be specific, that until noon he had kept in touch with the state police through the Edgartown undertaker and that the state police had told him no autopsy was requested."[13]

[13] Sherrill, p. 84.

At 10:00 A.M., on Sunday morning, 24 hours after Mary Jo's body was discoverd, Dinis got the medical report and immediately ordered an autopsy through his investigator, State Police Detective Lieutenant Killen. Killen told Dinis that the body had left. The body didn't actually leave until 12:30, and that was not only owing to the weather but because of some "Hold for Autopsy" that Gifford testified to above. Who issued such a "Hold"? But, more to the point, who lifted it? If this is in fact the way it happened, Lieutenant Killen could be accused of extreme negligence, if not complicity. On the other hand, Killen's conduct may have been misreported.

It wasn't until one week after the tragedy when Dinis saw the TV speech, that he had any knowledge of the inconsistencies in the Police Report. It was then that he swung into high gear for an autopsy that he was ultimately unable to effect. Was the D.A. conned, merely lackadaisical, or was he realistically appraising the fact that his own political fortunes were tied to the Senator's, in that they were both up for re-election the following year.

Regarding the blood on Mary Jo's blouse, the very fact of the extremely diligent efforts by Attorney Flanagan on behalf of Mary Jo's parents hints at the truth, but there was even more pressure placed on the Kopechne's than we read about in the papers.

In their book, *Death at Chappaquiddick*, 1976, from Green Hill Publishers, authors Richard and Thomas Tedrow, father and son, state on pages 81-82:

> On behalf of the Senator, there appeared on the scene in Wilkes-Barre, Pennsylvania, no less a personage than His Eminence (the late) Richard Cardinal Cushing, one of the foremost Churchmen in the United States and a longtime intimate friend of the Kennedys. He called on the Kopechnes and advised them it was their Christian duty to oppose the efforts to exhume the body and perform an autopsy. He said they must do all in their power to prevent such a desecration of their daughter's body.

So the Kopechnes retained Joseph Flanagan of Wilkes-Barre to appear before Judge Brominski on their behalf. Mr. Kopechne took the stand and testified they were against any autopsy, they saw no value in one and it would be like another funeral.

It is not known by what arguments the Kennedy forces persuaded Cardinal Cushing to go to the Kopechnes, but Teddy had benefited by the Cardinal before. In his 1962 campaign for the Democratic Senatorial Nomination, one of Teddy's publicity props was a picture of the Cardinal and himself; his opponent Eddie McCormack yelled foul.

The Tedrows quote a source for this material, but the quoted source actually refers to a photo opportunity, and it is not clear how they came by the information regarding the Cardinal's visit to the Kopechnes. No one has denied that the visit took place.

There are many citations from expert medical authorities who have stated that it is ridiculous to claim that there was no need for an autopsy for the body of a woman who had been in an auto underwater nine hours, and has been examined for eight to ten minutes at the accident site by a general practitioner who had no experience or training as a forensic pathologist. The fact that Dr. Mills examination was cursory at best strengthens the contention that an autopsy ought to have been performed.

Judge Brominski also ignored the testimony on the blood "froth," and how it would be extremely unlikely, if not impossible, that any such froth could have set on a blouse that was wet the entire time. We shall examine this aspect in complete detail in Chapter 11.

In dubious cases, an autopsy, will not only determine the medical cause of death, but often points to the legal cause of death as well. That Judge Brominski ruled that this autopsy would, "give rein to speculations unsupported by medical facts...," is an aberration when, in fact, an autopsy should by its very nature *halt* conjecture as a result of its objective disclosure.

Finally, from Judge Brominski: "even if the autopsy showed injuries, that could have been caused in the accident, that would not necessarily change the origins of death by drowning." Massachusetts law maintained that only an autopsy could change the determination of the *medical* cause of death. However, further actions and investigations could have led to discovering a different *legal* cause of death.

However, by the very competency with which Dunn Gifford served his employer, and perhaps with a little help from the State Police in the personage of Lieutenant Killen, an autopsy was never performed.[14]

Frustrated, but informed by reading Judge Brominski's Decision, we shall now turn to a further manipulation, of the Massachusetts Supreme Court, by Senator Kennedy's attorneys; another extraordinary example of the influence which powerful individuals can exert in our constitutional government by law.

---

[14] While Dinis had always claimed he had asked for this autopsy, his long-suffering investigator, Lt. George Killen, had a different take on the matter which he divulged shortly before his death. According to an interview with Leo Damore on 8-15-79, he stated, "If he'd asked for an autopsy, he'd have gotten one." Killen also told Damore, on 7-26-79: "Kennedy killed that girl the same as if he put a gun to her head and pulled the trigger."

7

WELL MANAGED (IN)JUSTICE

By early September, the press was reporting that a horse-race was developing between District Attorney Dinis' attempts *vis-a-vis* the Autopsy Hearing and his intention to hold a routine Inquest into the matter. Each legal procedure was delayed and delayed by the Kennedy forces, who used time to their legal advantage. Rather than a full-fledged horse-race, it turned out to be more like a dog-and-pony show; jurisdiction questions and procedures, motions, hearings, delayed rulings; in other words, the usual slowdown in proceeding to justice in our litigious society; which sometimes protects the rights of injured parties, more often serving the wealthier party, and always keeping the attorneys rolling in hay. It is quite clear that if the Kennedy legal team had nothing to hide, they would have had no need to litigate in the fashion they chose. However, if the actual facts had been closely scrutinized while timely legal action was possible, serious trouble would have been in the offing for the Senator. So, naturally they did everything in their power to make sure that the facts were obscured.

Leslie Leland, the local Vineyard Haven, Martha's Vineyard, druggist and foreman of the local Grand Jury began making waves by inquiring as to whether or not he could call the Grand Jury into session to consider the issues in this case. He was wrongly informed that he could not. Later on, he found out that it would have been legally correct for him as foreman, to call the Grand Jury into session himself. With Leland beginning to make noise, Dinis realized he must act if he was to maintain control over the case. He had to face the reality that he was up for election the next year. Dinis came up with the idea of an Inquest, to bring the ball back into his hands.

Because Dinis went over the head of Judge Boyle (who had given Kennedy a suspended sentence) in making his Inquest request, Dinis became subject to the Judge's wrath. This will be clearly shown later in the way Judge Boyle frustrated Dinis and the Assistant District Attorney Fernandes when they attempt to examine Kennedy and the other witnesses under oath. Judge Boyle set the Inquest for September 3, 1969, and laid out extremely abnormal ground rules for the Inquest:

> Only one witness at a time could appear in the court room; he could have counsel who would come and go with him and advise him of his constitutional rights;
>
> Any sequestering of witnesses would be decided by the judge;
>
> No listening devices or cameras would be allowed, but counsel could arrange for stenographic transcripts;
>
> Courtroom seats were to be reserved exclusively for the press;
>
> The presence of Senator Kennedy would be required.

Kennedy's attorneys proceeded to have a field day with these rules, and moved initially for a Hearing to try to have the Inquest conducted along the lines of a criminal proceeding. Traditionally, beginning literally hundreds of years ago in England, the coroner's Inquest was held in the outlying areas, so as to establish the facts while they were fresh, before the King's magistrate could arrive to hold trial. This procedure had been adopted in the United States and had stood the test of time.

In Massachusetts, the Inquest procedure was invoked in 1877 in order to protect individuals against the rapacious Robber Barons acting as railroad magnates. The procedure was implemented to allow an average citizen protection under the law, and allowed for discovery proceedings under the watchful and wide eye of the public forum. The Kennedy attorneys had four basic requests:

(1) that all witnesses and their attorneys should have the right to examine and cross-examine witnesses;
(2) they should have the right to call their own witnesses;
(3) they wanted the right to refuse to testify; and
(4) they wanted the press banned.

Judge Boyle refused their motions all the way around. So, the scene was set for September 3, to begin the proceeding. Kennedy's attorneys waited until September 2, when the Massachusetts Supreme Court was not in formal session and when the august Justice Paul Reardon of the Court would be sitting by himself in a special branch to hear special or unusual writs and petitions.

Justice Reardon had the ultimate in legal establishment credentials. He was Past President of the Harvard Alumni Association, and chairman of the executive committee of the Harvard Overseers. His schooling was at Phillips Andover Academy; he was Phi Beta Kappa at Harvard, and a graduate of Harvard Law School. Under the auspices of the American Bar Association, he was the author of the infamous Reardon Report; which gave teeth to magistrates in barring reporters from courtrooms, in fining newspapers for printing their own research in current cases, and notably in preventing public officials from commenting on cases that were due to come up or were currently on trial.

Reardon, a staunch Republican, may not have been in love with the career of the young, pragmatic and learning-to-be-a-liberal Edward Kennedy, but he knew his law, and immediately stayed Judge Boyle's Order until the full Massachusetts Supreme Court could rule on the matter when it reconvened in late October.

The Kennedy attorneys were brilliantly led by Edward B. Hanify, a Boston Brahmin if ever there was one. A significant point, which will be elaborated on later, was that Hanify was also a director of the New England Telephone Company. Hanify headed the venerable Boston law firm of Ropes & Gray, and he himself led the oral arguments before the Massachusetts Supreme Court. He argued for an "infusion of constitutionality" to protect the right of due process for his client and to further safeguard the rights of all Massachusetts citizens for all time. The Court agreed and set precedent, actually making new law, which is normally and appropriately left to the legislatures of our states and nation, which represent the voters, and therefore, ideally, the will of the people.

This Court ruled in its Order that:

1. Upon completion of the Inquest, Judge Boyle's report and **the transcript of the proceedings shall remain impounded.**

2. Access both to the Judge's report and to the transcript shall be afforded only to the attorney general, the appropriate district attorney, and counsel to any person reported to be actually or possibly responsible for Mary Jo Kopechne's death. **Any witness at the Inquest shall be permitted to check the accuracy of the transcript of his own testimony.**

3. The transcript of the Inquest and Judge Boyle's report shall be made available to the public only upon order of a judge of the Superior Court and only if one of the following conditions is met:

    a. The district attorney has filed with the Superior Court a written certificate that there **will be no prosecution.**

b. An indictment shall have been sought and **not returned**.
c. The trial against the person named in the record as responsible shall have been completed.
d. A judge of the Superior Court shall determine that no criminal trial is likely. [Emphasis Added Above].

And most insolently, considering the fact that they were making new law, they also ordered that these new rules would apply for any and all future Inquests in the state of Massachusetts. This policy fairly flew in the face of the intent and origin of Inquest law. Prior to this ruling, literally hundreds of Inquests had been held that were open to the public. The lack of secrecy, the very openness itself, was designed to eliminate subterfuge and to reinforce democratic ideals.

Even more amazing as we evaluate the extreme lengths the Massachusetts Supreme Court went to to safeguard the Senator is the fact that, by Massachusetts law, they were bound *not* to hear Kennedy's attorneys very application for a ruling on a writ of certiorari (which is a petition to appeal a lower court ruling) until the case was tried and finished in the lower courts. By hearing the case and ruling prior to Inquest, a trial, or whatever else may have occurred at the lower level, the Supreme Court in fact was making *new* law. Therefore, to repeat, they took the initiative away from existing legislation, which had arguably been the voice of the people through its duly elected representatives, and then proceeded to make a ruling that they were bound by law not to make until the Inquest had reached a conclusion.

Even more outrageous, the Massachusetts Supreme Court in fact denied that they had actually ruled on the Kennedy case and maintained that they had simply benefited old antiquated laws with what Kennedy's attorney Edward Hanify called, an "infusion of constitutionality." They knew better!

But in recognition of brilliance (even though he was simply dealing for the most part with Boston buddies on the Supreme Court bench, and in fact the ruling that he inspired was ultimately reversed by the U.S. Supreme Court) we must hand it to Mr. Hanify, Senator Kennedy's lawyer; he stands as a pillar amongst his sisters and brothers in the legal theater. He had gone past and literally transcended the "practicing" of law and had actually, on the strength of his compelling arguments as a working attorney, "made" or "written" law. In this case his "new law" only held up long enough to protect his client from a public viewing of the procedures and testimony. That was enough.

There was some notice taken of this highly unusual State Supreme Court Order. Notably, Sigma Delta Chi, the national fraternity of Journalism said through its president:

We find it extremely ironic that the Court cites "great public interest" as a reason for closing the Hearing to the public . . . There is further irony in the Court's own statement that it will not make "any special rule for a particular case."

Several years later, as was reported in the *New York Times,* January 25, 1982, the United States Supreme Court reversed the "Kennedy Decision" with its ruling on a Massachusetts sex trial. The United States Supreme Court said in part that a lower court: "... cannot exclude public or the press..." that the "... law was too broad in that it's mandatory..."; and "... an individual judge can exclude the press with good reason."

However, Judge Boyle had not sought the opinion of the United States Supreme Court and had meekly followed the orders of his own state's highest judicial body. But then, why not? He had spent most of his life as a court clerk before being appointed a judge. In the words of author Robert Sherrill, "... as a legal scholar, Judge Boyle was a good golfer."

The Massachusetts Supreme Court made its ruling on October 28, 1969. The autopsy Hearing had already occurred and therefore won Kennedy the race; but the final decision would not come in, as noted above, until December 8, 1969.

The next act of what was becoming a grotesque comedy was to begin on January 5, 1970, when the Inquest would finally be held in Edgartown, on Martha's Vineyard Island in the proud Commonwealth of Massachusetts.

8

FRIENDLY
"KANGAROO" COURT

It is clear from the preceding chapter that the Senator's legal team was more than formidable; in fact it seems to have contained the Massachusetts Supreme Court itself. The wagons had circled. Power is not easily usurped, challenged or denied; it can only be taken. Judge Boyle got the message. He was not about to make an appeal to the U.S. Supreme Court; very frankly he had invested his entire career at the Massachusetts Bar; he had his future security at stake, which included the desire to retire into serenity.

The Massachusetts Supreme Court, as we have seen, assumed jurisdiction where it had none; changed the law to protect a single Senator and denied it was doing so; and arrogantly sealed the Inquest proceeding from the prying eyes of the public and press until the information *could not* be used to prosecute.

By withholding, even from his advisors and legal defense team, knowledge of what had really happened, Kennedy successfully managed matters. Whether the support groups would or could have acted so strongly in his interest had they known what was really involved is a question that will never be answered. Adhering to the business aspect of legal practice, attorneys have learned to think of themselves as inculpable hired guns. The point is arguable. Advocacy is essential in a democracy governed by a Constitution and various laws. The point here is that more than mere advocacy was involved in this case.

We have seen over and over how the Senator was protected from the very beginning in this sordid affair. Now we will see what he himself had to say, under oath. Bear in mind that the complete transcript which follows was scrutinized by the Kennedy legal team before being publicly released. Incredibly, they were given the right to secretly and privately alter the text if it didn't conform to their *recollection* of the actual testimony. Of course they may not have touched it, fearing that it might leak that they had, in fact, edited it. But *we don't know* whether they changed any of the Senator's answers, nor is it likely that we will ever know whether this is exactly what the Senator said that day. We do know that they decided to let us see this much, to come this close to Senator Kennedy's words on the subject: his *only* specific words on the facts.

TESTIMONY OF
EDWARD M. KENNEDY

Before: Hon. James A. Boyle, Justice of Edgartown District Court

Present: Edmund Dinis, District Attorney for the Southern District of Massachusetts, Armand Fernandes, Assistant District Attorney, Peter Gay, Assistant District Attorney.

            Edward B. Hanify, Esq. and Robert G. Clark, Jr., Esq., in behalf of Edward M. Kennedy.

            Thomas Teller, Clerk of Courts
            Helen S. Tyra, Temporary Court Officer
            Harold T. McNeil, and
            Sidney R. Lipman, Official Court Stenographer,

Edgartown, Massachusetts
Monday, January 5, 1970

The Court: Senator, would you take the witness stand?

Kennedy: Yes.

Edward M. Kennedy, Sworn

Examination By Mr. Dinis:

Q. Please give your name to the Court.
A. Edward Moore Kennedy.

Q. And where is your legal residence, Mr. Kennedy?
A. 3 Charles River Square, Boston.

Q. Directing your attention to July 18, 1969, were there plans
   made by you to have a gathering on Martha's Vineyard Island?
A. There were.

Q. And what were these plans, Mr. Kennedy?
A. There were plans to participate in an annual sailing regatta in
   Edgartown on the dates of Friday, July 18th and Saturday, July
   19th, and with my cousin Joe Gargan, Mr. Markham, Mr.
   LaRosa and a number of other people, a number of other
   individuals.

Q. When were these plans made?
A. Well, I had planned to participate in the regatta for some
   period of weeks.[1]

Q. And were there any particular arrangements made for this
   gathering that we have just discussed?
A. Well, I had entered my boat in the regatta and had listed my
   crew. I had made those arrangements through my cousin, Joe
   Gargan.

[1]   His family had participated for the past 30 years.

Q. Were there any particular arrangements made to rent a house on Chappaquiddick?
A. I had made no such arrangements myself.

Q. Do you know who did?
A. Yes, I do.

Q. May we have that name?
A. Mr. Gargan.

Q. Mr. Gargan. When did you arrive on the Island in conjunction with this gathering?
A. On July 18th about 1 o'clock.

Q. 1:00 P.M.?
A. That is correct.

Q. Was there anyone with you?
A. No, I arrived by myself.

Q. And where did you stay, Senator?
A. Well, at the Shiretown Inn.

Q. Could you tell the Court what your activities were during that afternoon from the time of your arrival?
A. Well, I arrived shortly after 1 o'clock on July 18th, was met by Mr. John B. Crimmins, driven through town, made a brief stop to pick up some fried clams, traveled by ferry to Chappaquiddick Island to a small cottage there where I changed into a bathing suit, later visited the beach[2] on I imagine the east side of that Island for a brief swim, returned to the cottage and changed into another bathing suit, returned to the ferry slip and waded out to my boat, the *Victura*, later participated in a race which ended approximately at 6 o'clock.

Q. When did you check into the Shiretown Inn that day?
A. Sometime after 6:30 before 7 o'clock.

---

[2] He was driven down Dyke Road, and over the bridge at this time.

Q. Was anyone else in your party staying at the Shiretown Inn?
A. My cousin Joe Gargan.

Q. Did your nephew Joseph Kennedy, stay there?
A. Not to my knowledge.

Q. Now, following your checking in at the Shiretown Inn, what were your activities after that?
A. I returned to my room, visited with a few friends just prior to returning to that room on the porch which is outside the room of the Shiretown — outside my room at the Shiretown Inn, washed up briefly and returned to Chappaquiddick Island.

Q. What time did you return to Chappaquiddick Island at that time?
A. It was sometime shortly after 7:00 o'clock.

Q. And these friends that you had some conversation with at the Shiretown, do you have their names?
A. I do.

Q. May we have them?
A. Well, they are Mr. Ross Richards; I believe Mr. Stanley Moore was there that evening, and perhaps one or two of their crew, maybe Mrs. Richards. I am not familiar with the names. I know the other members of his crew, but I would say a group of approximately five or six.

Q. Do you recall the number of the room in which you were staying?
A. I believe it was 9:00, 7:00 or 9:00.

Q. Now, you say you returned to Chappaquiddick around 7:30 P.M.?
A. About 7:30.

Q. About that time. Now, were you familiar with the Island of Chappaquiddick? Had you been there before?

A. *Never been on Chappaquiddick Island before that day.*[3]

Q. I believe you did state in one of your prepared statements that you had been visiting this Island for about thirty years?
A. Martha's Vineyard Island.

Q. But you had never been to Chappaquiddick?
A. *Never been to Chappaquiddick before 1:30 on the day of July 18th.*[4]

Q. Now, when you left the Shiretown Inn and returned to Chappaquiddick around 7:30 P.M., was there anyone with you?
A. Mr. Crimmins.

The Court: Might I just impose a moment and ask this question? You said you took a swim on Chappaquiddick Island Friday afternoon?
Kennedy: That is correct.

The Court: Did you travel over the Dyke Bridge to go to the beach on that swim?
Kennedy: Yes, I did.
If your Honor would permit me, at the time of the afternoon upon arrival on Chappaquiddick Island as at the time that I was met at Martha's Vineyard Airport I was driven by Mr. Crimmins to the cottage and to the beach, returned to the cottage subsequent to the point of rendezvous with the *Victura*.

Q. What automobile was being used at that time?
A. A four-door Oldsmobile 88.

The Court: Might I ask you just a question? Who drove you to the beach?
Kennedy: Mr. Crimmins.

---

[3] In the following testimony, bold and italicized text are the author's attempts to add emphasis to various comments.

[4] On 1-20-80, the *New York Post*, presented evidence given by five different individuals who had seen Ted Kennedy on Chappaquiddick "several times" and "at least half-a-dozen times."

The Court: Was the car operated over the Dyke Bridge or was
it left on the side?

Kennedy: No, it was operated over the Dyke Bridge.

Q. Was there anyone at the cottage when you arrived there at
7:30 P.M.?
A. No, I don't believe so.

Q. Had there been anyone there, when you changed your swimming suits early in the afternoon?
A. Not when I first arrived there. Subsequently, a group returned
to the cottage after the swim.

Q. When you returned?
A. They were either outside the cottage or in its immediate
vicinity. I wasn't aware whether they were inside the cottage or
outside at the time that I changed.

Q. Do you have the names of these persons who were there?
A. I can only give them in a general way because I am not
absolutely sure which people were there at that particular time
and which were in town making arrangements.

Q. Were they a part of the group there later that evening?
A. Yes, they were.

Q. Were there any persons other than the crew that participated
in the cookout there?
A. No.

Q. Were there any other automobiles at that house on Chappaquiddick that afternoon?
A. Yes, there were.

Q. Do you know how many?
A. Just two to my best knowledge. One other vehicle, so there
were two in total to my best knowledge.

Q. Did you have any plans at that time to stay on Chappaquiddick
Island?

A. No, I did not.

Q. Did you plan on staying overnight?
A. No, I did not.

Q. And how long did you actually stay on Chappaquiddick Island that evening?
A. Well, to my best knowledge, I would say 1:30 in the morning on July 19th.

The Court: When you left?

Kennedy: When I left.

Q. What transpired after you arrived at the cottage after your arrival at 7:30 P.M.?
A. Well, after my arrival I took a bath in the tub that was available at the cottage, which was not available at the Shiretown Inn, and soaked my back; I later was joined by Mr. Markham who arrived some time about 8 o'clock, engaged in conversation with Mr. Markham until about 8:30, and the rest of the group arrived at 8:30 or shortly thereafter. During this period of time Mr. Crimmins made me a drink of rum and Coca-Cola.

Q. Now, did you have dinner at the cottage?
A. Well, at 8:30 the rest of the group arrived and were made to feel relaxed and at home, enjoyed some hors d'oeuvres, were served a drink, those who wanted them, and steaks were cooked on an outdoor burner by Mr. Gargan at about approximately quarter of 10:00, I would think.

Q. Do you recall who did the cooking? Was there any cooking at that time?
A. Yes, there was.

Q. And do you recall who performed the job?
A. Well, principally Mr. Gargan. I think the young ladies did some of the cooking of the hors d'oeuvres and some of the gentlemen helped in starting the charcoal fire, and also the cooking of the steaks, the making of the salad, and so forth.

Q. Were there any drinks served, cocktails served?
A. There were.

Q. Did anyone in particular tend bar or have charge of this particular responsibility?
A. Well, I tried initially to respond to any of the requests of the guests, when they arrived and then I think most of the individuals made their drinks after that that they wanted.

Q. And I believe you said earlier that Mr. Gargan was in charge of the arrangements of renting the cottage and making the preparation for the cookout, as far as you know?
A. That is correct, I would say the other gentlemen did some of the purchasing of the food and others got the stuff for the cookout. Others — some brought the steaks, others brought the other ingredients for the cookout.

Q. Did you have occasion to leave the cottage at any time during that evening?
A. That is correct.

Q. Did you leave more than once?
A. That is correct.

Q. Well, will you please give us the sequence of events with regard to your activities after 8:30 P.M.?
A. Well, during the course of the evening, as I mentioned, I engaged in conversation and recollections with those that were attending this group which were old friends of myself and our families. Some alcoholic beverages were served.

The Court: Excuse me. Read the question back to me. [Question read.]

Q. How many times did you leave the cottage that evening, Senator?
A. Two different occasions.

Q. Would you please tell us about the first time?
A. The first I left at *approximately 11:15* the evening of July 18th and I left a second time, sometime after midnight, by my best

judgment it would be **approximately 12:15 for the second time.**
On the second occasion I never left the cottage itself, I left the
immediate vicinity of the cottage which was probably fifteen or
twenty feet outside the front door.

Q. And when you left the second time, did you then return to
Edgartown?
A. Sometime after I left the second time, I returned to Edgar-
town. I did not return immediately to Edgartown.

Q. Now, when you left on the first occasion, were you alone?
A. I was not alone.

Q. And who was with you?
A. Miss Mary Jo Kopechne was with me.

Q. Anyone else?
A. No.

Q. And did you use the 88 Oldsmobile that was later taken from
the river?
A. I used — yes, I did.

Q. What time did Miss Kopechne arrive at the cottage that
evening?
A. My best knowledge approximately 8:30.

Q. At 8:30 P.M.?
A. That is correct.

Q. Do you know how she arrived?
A. To my best knowledge she arrived in a white Valiant that
brought some of the people to that party.

Q. Do you know who owned that car?
A. I believe it was a rented car.

Q. Do you know who rented it?
A. No. One of the group that was there, I would say. I'm not
sure.

Q. When you left at 11:15 with Miss Kopechne, had you had any prior conversations with her?

A. Yes, I had.

Q. Will you please give that conversation to the Court?

A. At 11:15 I was talking with Miss Kopechne perhaps for some minutes before that period of time. I noticed the time, *desired to leave and return to the Shiretown Inn* and indicated to her that I was leaving and returning to town. She indicated to me that she was desirous of leaving, if I would be kind enough to drop her back at her hotel.[5] I said, well, I'm leaving immediately; spoke with Mr. Crimmins, requested the keys for the car and left at that time.

Q. Does Mr. Crimmins usually drive your car or drive you?

A. On practically every occasion.

Q. On practically every occasion?

A. Yes.

Q. Was there anything in particular that changed those circumstances at this particular time?

A. Only to the extent that Mr. Crimmins, as well as some of the other fellows that were attending the cookout, were concluding their meal, enjoying the fellowship, and it didn't appear to me to be necessary to require him to bring me back to Edgartown.

Q. Do you know whether or not Miss Kopechne had her pocketbook with her at the time you left?

A. I do not.

Q. Mr. Kennedy, how were you dressed at the time you left the first time at 11:15?

A. In a pair of light slacks, and a dark jersey and I believe shoes, moccasins, and a back brace.

Q. Do you know how Miss Kopechne was dressed, do you recall that?

[5] She did not take her pocketbook, which contained her motel room key, airline tickets, etc.

A. Only from what I have read in the — I understand, slacks and a blouse, sandals, perhaps a sweater; I'm not completely —

Q. And when you left the house at Chappaquiddick at 11:15, you were driving?
A. That is correct.

Q. And where was Miss Kopechne seated?
A. In the front seat.

Q. Was there any other person — was there any other person in the car at that time?
A. No.

Q. Was there any other item, thing, or object in the car at that time of any size?
A. Well, not to my knowledge at that particular time. I have read subsequently in newspapers that there was another person in that car, but that is only what I have read about and to my knowledge at that time there wasn't any other object that I was aware of.

Q. Well, Senator, was there any other person in the car?
A. No, there was not.

Q. And on leaving the cottage, Senator Mr. Kennedy, where did you go?
A. Well, I travelled down, I believe it is Main Street, *took a right on Dyke Road and drove off the bridge at Dyke Bridge.*

Q. Did you at any time drive into Cemetery Road?
A. *At no time did I drive into Cemetery Road.*

Q. Did you back that car up at any time?
A. *At no time did I back that car up.*

Q. Did you see anyone on the road between the cottage and the bridge that night?
A. I saw no one on the road between the cottage and the bridge.

The Court: Did you stop the car at any time?

Kennedy: I did not stop the car at any time.

Q. Did you pass any other vehicle at that time?
A. I passed no other vehicle at that time. I passed no other
vehicle and I saw no other person and I did not stop the car
at any time between the time I left the cottage and went off
the bridge.

Q. Now, would you describe your automobile to the Court?
A. Well, it is a four-door black sedan Oldsmobile.

Q. Do you recall the registration plate?
A. I do not recall the registration plate.

Q. Senator, I show you a photograph and ask you whether or not
you can identify that?
A. I believe that to be my car.

Q. Your automobile?
A. Yes.

Dinis: This is the automobile that the Senator identifies
as his.

The Court: I think we ought to have a little more. This location is —

Kennedy: I have no —

The Court: Mr. Kennedy says this is his automobile after the
accident and he doesn't know the location of where
the automobile is or when this picture was taken.
Mark that Exhibit 1.

Q. I show you two photographs. Are you able to identify the
automobile in the photographs?
A. In my best judgment that is my automobile that went off the
bridge.

Q. In examining the registration plate, would that help you at all?

A. I would believe that is my vehicle.

Dinis: Your Honor please, these are photographs that
                have been taken of the car which has been remov-
                ed from the water.

The Court: Well, are you going to have any witness testify
                when these were taken?

Dinis: Yes, your Honor, we can have that?

The Court: And where they were taken.

Dinis: Yes, your Honor.

The Court: You identify the car as being your car?

Kennedy: I do, your Honor, it is my best judgment that is my
                car. I don't think there is really much question.

The Court: I would prefer that you wait until you put on the
                witness that is going to say —[6]

Dinis: May it be allowed *de bene*, your Honor? The
                sequence in presenting this evidence is for the
                purpose of — we — couldn't, all I want to establish
                is that the Senator says they look like his car and
                then we will later have testimony as to where they
                were taken.

The Court: Well, I would rather not get into the trial tech-
                nique.

Dinis: I appreciate that.

---

[6] Here Judge Boyle begins his interventions — whether out of pique with Mr. Dinis,
or in support of Kennedy we cannot say. The point is that he effectively diffused
and confounded the D.A.'s efforts.

The Court: *De bene*, I prefer you wait until you have the witness to identify it. I want to avoid as much as possible, Mr Dinis, any trial technique.[7]

Kennedy: I would just say to the best knowledge that those are pictures of my car that were shown to me.

Q. In your conversation with Miss Kopechne prior to your leaving at 11:15, did she indicate to you any necessity for returning to Martha's Vineyard or to Edgartown?
A. Prior to that conversation, no.

Q. Well, when she left with you, where was she going?
A. Back to her hotel.

Q. Now, when you left at 11:15 do you know how many persons remained at the house on Chappaquiddick?
A. To my best judgement most of them were in the cottage when I left. I didn't make a count of who was there, but I think most of them were there.

The Court: Well, do you know of anyone having left before?
Kennedy: No, I don't, except on one occasion where —

The Court: No, I mean having left permanently.
Kennedy: No, no.

Q. Did anyone else have access to your automobile that afternoon or evening?
A. Oh, yes. Well, Mr. Crimmins certainly had access that afternoon and I believe Mr. Tretter borrowed the car to return to Edgartown briefly. I couldn't say of my own knowledge that he used that car rather than the Valiant, but he may very well have, and I would say during the course of the afternoon it was generally available to any of the group to use for transportation.

7 Ask your favorite lawyer if it is possible to have an inquest without asking questions; the Judge clearly shows his prejudice by calling Dinis' questioning "trial technique." On the first day of the Inquest, Judge Boyle had certainly raised Dinis' hackles by stating that Dinis shouldn't act as a "prosecutor, but as an aide to the court." Sherrill, p. 152.

Q. Do you recall how fast you were driving when you made the right on Dyke Road?
A. No, I would say approximately seven or eight miles an hour.

Q. And what were the lighting conditions and weather conditions that evening?
A. Well, as you know, there are no lights on that road. The road was dry. There was a reasonable amount of humidity. The night was clear, extremely dark.

Q. Were the windows opened or closed of the automobile?
A. Some of the windows were open and some were closed.

Q. Do you have an air conditioner in that car?
A. No, I don't.

The Court: Could we know which were opened and which were closed?
Kennedy: I read, your Honor —

The Court: No, no, of your own knowledge.
Kennedy: Of my own knowledge?

The Court: What about the window on your side?
Kennedy: I would expect it was open.

The Court: You don't remember that?
Kennedy: I don't remember that.

The Court: How about the window in the passenger's side?
Kennedy: I really don't remember.

The Court: Was it a warm night?
Kennedy: I would think it was cool at that hour, but I really have no personal knowledge as to which windows were open or closed. I have read subsequently which ones were open or blown open, but at that time I really don't recall.

Q. Well, Mr. Kennedy, was the window on the driver's side, the driver's door open?

A. Yes, it was.

Q. Do you recall whether or not the window in the rear seat behind the driver was open?

A. I don't recall.

Q. And you have no recollection as to the windows on the passenger's side of the vehicle?

A. No, I really don't.

Q. How fast were you driving on Dyke Road?

A. Approximately twenty miles as hour.

Q. Were the brakes of your Oldsmobile in order at that time?

A. I believe so. There is no reason to assume otherwise. **Mr. Crimmins takes very good care of the car.**[8]

Q. Well, were you aware at the time that you were driving on a dirt road when you hit, when you turned onto Dyke Road?

A. Well, sometime during the drive down Dyke Road I was aware that I was on an unpaved road, yes.

Q. At what point, Mr. Kennedy, did you realize that you were driving on a dirt road?

A. Just sometime when I was I don't remember any specific time when I knew I was driving on an unpaved road. I was generally aware sometime going down that road that it was an unpaved, like many of the other roads here in Martha's Vineyard and Nantucket and Cape Cod.[9]

Q. When you left the house at 11:15, what was your destination?

A. The Katama Shores, the ferry slip, the Katama Shores, Shiretown.

[8] Later we will refer to this point as it has crucial bearing on the ultimate condition of the car.

[9] In order to turn right onto Dyke Road (a dirt road) one must ignore the large reflector arrow pointing to the left, and make a turn against the banking macadam paving, which is so banked to ease the natural turn to the left, to the ferry.

Q. Now, had you been over that road from the ferry slip to the cottage more than once that day?

A. Yes, I had.

Q. Did you recall at the time that you noticed you were driving on a dirt road, that the road from the ferry slip to the house had been paved?

A. **Well, Mr. Dinis, I would say that I, having lived on Cape Cod and having visited these Islands, I am aware some roads are paved.**[10]

The Court: I am sorry, that is not quite responsive. The question is whether or not you realized the road from the ferry slip to the cottage was paved.

Dinis: That is correct.

Kennedy: Yes.

The Court: That is, did you become aware of it during your trips?

Kennedy: Well, I would just say it was not of particular notice to me whether it was paved or unpaved.

The Court: Were you driving the car either one of those times?

Kennedy: I was not.

Q. Well, while you were driving down Dyke Road and after you noticed it was a dirt road and you were driving at 20 miles an hour, what happened, Mr. Kennedy?

A. Well, I became —

---

[10] The Senator's need to be sarcastic indicates the intensity of the emotions he must have felt. He was being asked to certify that he didn't know what he was doing, and he responded with some anger.

The Court: I'm going to ask one question. At any time after you got on the unpaved road, the so-called Dyke Road, did you have a realization that you were on the wrong road?

Kennedy: No.

The Court: Do you remember the question?

Kennedy: After I realized it was an unpaved road, what did I become aware of?

Q. Well, after you realized it was an unpaved road, and that you were driving at 20 miles an hour, what happened then?
A. I went off Dyke Bridge or I went off a bridge.

Q. You went off a bridge into the water?
A. That is correct.

Q. Did you apply the brakes of that automobile prior to going off into the water?
A. Perhaps a fraction of a second before.

Q. What prompted you to do that?
A. Well, I was about to go off a bridge and I applied the brakes.

Q. Were there any lights in that area?
A. *Absolutely no lights in that area I noticed* other than the lights on my vehicle.[11]

Q. Did you realize at that moment that you were not heading for the ferry?
A. At the moment I went off the bridge, I certainly did.

Q. Do you recall whether or not the strike that question well, what happened after that, Senator?

---

[11] One of the two homes (Malm House) in the area by the bridge had lights on until past midnight, the other home had a light on all night. Those lights would have stood out as beacons on the "dark" night.

A. Well, I remembered the vehicle itself just beginning to go off the Dyke Bridge and the next thing I recall is the movement of Mary Jo next to me, the struggling, *perhaps hitting or kicking me* and I, at this time, opened my eyes and realized I was upside down, that water was crashing in on me, that it was pitch black. I knew that and I was able to get a half a gulp, I would say, of air before I became completely immersed in the water. I realized that Mary Jo and I had to get out of the car.

I can remember reaching down to try to get the doorknob of the car and *lifting the door handle*[12] and pressing against the door and it was not moving. I can remember reaching what I thought was down, which was really up, to where I thought the window was and feeling along the side to see if the window was open *and the window was closed,*[13] and I can remember the last sensation of being completely out of air and inhaling a lung full of water and assuming that I was going to drown and the full realization that no one was going to be looking for us that night until the next morning and that I wasn't going to get out of that car alive and then somehow I can't remember coming up to the last energy of just pushing, pressing, and coming up to the surface.

Q. Senator, how did you realize that you were upside down in the car?

A. Because that was a feeling that I had as soon as I became aware that the water rushing in and the blackness, I knew that I was upside down. I really wasn't sure of anything, but I thought that I was upside down.

Q. Were you aware that there was any water rushing in on the passenger's side?

A. There was complete blackness. Water seemed to rush in from every point, from the windshield, from underneath me, above me. It almost seemed like you couldn't hold the water back even with your hands. What I was conscious of was the rushing

---

12 Had he done this, it would have pushed the knob up, unlocking the door -- the door was found with the knob down.

13 At this time — the only closed window was the passenger side, back seat window.

of the water, the blackness, the fact that it was impossible to even hold it back.

Q. And you say at that time you had a thought to the effect that you may not be found until morning?
A. I was sure that I was going to drown.

Q. Did you make any observations of the condition of Miss Kopechne at that time?
A. At what time?

Q. At that particular moment when you were thrashing around in the car?
A. Well, at the moment I was thrashing around I was trying to find a way that we both could get out of the car, and at some time after I tried the door and the windows I became convinced I was never going to get out.

Q. Was the window closed at that time?
A. The window was open.[14]

Q. On the driver's side?
A. That's correct.

Q. And did you go through the window to get out of the car?
A. **I have no idea in the world how I got out of that car.**[15]

Q. Do you have any recollection as to how the automobile left the bridge and went over into the water?
A. How it left the bridge?

Q. Yes. What particular path did it take.
A. No.

Q. Did it turn over.
A. I have no idea.

---

[14] He had just said it was closed.
[15] Pinpoint amnesia — he remembers everything else but the key fact.

The Court: I would like to inquire, Mr. Dinis, something about the operation of the car, if you are finished.

Dinis: Go right ahead, your Honor.

The Court: You are driving along the sandy dike road and you are approaching the Dyke Bridge. Now, you can describe to me what you saw, what you did, what happened from the point when you first saw the bridge.

Kennedy: I would estimate the time to be a fraction of a second from the time that I first saw the bridge and was on the bridge.

The Court: Did you have on your high beams, do you remember?

Kennedy: I can't remember.

The Court: Is it your custom to use high beams when you are driving?

Kennedy: I rarely drive.[16] I really couldn't tell you. I may have.

The Court: It is recommended.

Kennedy: It is recommended, but sometimes if there is a mist you see better with low beams.

The Court: Did you see the bridge before you actually reached it?

Kennedy: *The split second before I was on it.*[17]

The Court: Did you see that it was at an angle to the road?

Kennedy: The bridge was at an angle to the road?

The Court: Yes.

Kennedy: Just before going on it I saw that.

---

[16] Perhaps, yet the record of his convictions shows that when he does drive, he drives fast.

[17] Then he was preoccupied; the bridge is visible some *320* feet before, even at night.

The Court: Did you make any attempt to turn your wheels to
follow that angle?

Kennedy: I believe I did, your Honor. I would assume that I
did try to go on the bridge. It appeared to me at
that time that the road went straight.

The Court: Were you looking ahead at the time you were
driving the car, at that time?

Kennedy: Yes, I was.

The Court: Your attention was not diverted by anything else?

Kennedy: No, it wasn't.

The Court: I don't want to foreclose you, Mr. Dinis, I want to
go into the question of alcoholic beverages. Perhaps you had that in mind later?[18]

Dinis: Yes, your Honor.

The Court: All right.

Q. Going back to the cottage earlier in the day, you stated, you
volunteered the information that you had a rum and Coca-
Cola?

A. That is right.

Q. Did you have more than one.

A. Yes, I did.

Q. How many did you have?

A. I had two.

The Court: I would like to go back before that. I think you
said you visited some friends at the Shiretown Inn?

Kennedy: That is right.

The Court: Did you do some drinking then?

Kennedy: I had about a third of a beer at that time.

---

[18] The Judge jumps in to suggest a change in the D.A.'s line after he had already
taken over Dinis' line of questions regarding the Senator's recollections of being
underwater. Dinis was getting the point, and so he changed to liquor.

The Court: And you had nothing further until this?
Kennedy: *No, I had nothing further.*[19]

Q. And when did you have the second rum-and-coke?
A. The second, some time later on in the evening. I think before dinner, sometime about 9:15. It would be difficult for me to say.

Q. Now, during the afternoon of the 18th did you have occasion to spend some time with your nephew Joseph Kennedy?
A. I might have greeted him in a brief greeting, but otherwise, no. I knew he was concerned about where he was going to stay; that he had some reservations and that somehow they had gotten cancelled, but I would say other than a casual passing and a greeting. I would say no.

Q. He was at this time on Chappaquiddick Island?
A. Not to my knowledge. I never saw him at Chappaquiddick.

Q. Did you see him at the Shiretown Inn.
A. I might have seen him in inquiring whether he could stay at the Shiretown Inn.

Q. Did he stay with you in your room?
A. No, he did not.

The Court: I would like to ask some questions. You said you had a portion of beer late in the afternoon at the Shiretown Inn?
Kennedy: That is correct.

The Court: Then you had two rums and coke at this cottage at Chappaquiddick sometime after you arrived at about 8:30?
Kennedy: That is right.

---

[19] He had three rum-and-cokes on Richards' boat directly before the "third of a beer" up on the deck.

The Court: Who poured those drinks?
Kennedy: Mr. Crimmins poured the first one. I poured the
           second one.

The Court: What amount of rum did you put in?
Kennedy: It would be difficult, your Honor, to estimate.

The Court: Well, by ounces?
Kennedy: By ounces? I suppose two ounces.

The Court: I mean, some people pour heavy drinks. Some pour
           light drinks.
Kennedy: Yes.

The Court: When did you take the last one?
Kennedy: I would think about 9:00 o'clock. The only way I
           could judge that, your Honor, would be that I ate
           about 10:00 and it was sometime before I ate.

The Court: You had nothing alcoholic to drink after eating?
Kennedy: No, I didn't.

The Court: How much liquor was at this cottage?
Kennedy: There were several bottles so that I wouldn't be
           able to tell specifically.

The Court: Not a large supply?
Kennedy: I wouldn't be able to tell how much. There was an
           adequate supply.

The Court: Was there a sustained amount of drinking by the
           group?
Kennedy: No, there wasn't.

The Court: By any particular person?
Kennedy: Not that I noticed. There wasn't prior to the time
           I left.

The Court: Mr. Hanify, you have advised your client of his
           constitutional rights.
Hanify: Yes, I have, your Honor.

The Court: Were you at any time that evening under the influence of alcohol?

Kennedy: Absolutely not.

The Court: Did you imbibe in any narcotic drugs that evening?

Kennedy: Absolutely not.

The Court: Did anyone at the party to your knowledge?

Kennedy: No, absolutely not.[20]

The Court: In your opinion were you sober at the time that you operated the motor vehicle to the Dyke Bridge?

Kennedy: Absolutely sober.

Q. Senator Kennedy, what did you do immediately following your release from the automobile?

A. I was swept away by the tide that was flowing at an extraordinary rate through that narrow cut there and was swept

---

[20] The specter of drugs received some play in the course of events following the tragedy. Miss Esther Newberg, a party participant, got the ball rolling by stating in an interview three days after the accident to the *Baltimore Sun* that she didn't know when they left the party "because her Mickey Mouse watch — which had been a topic of joking conversation — was not working properly." Those who remember that watch know that the Mickey Mouse watch was small and had a brightly colored rainbow on the dial, and was a hip statement.

More to the point, Louise Hutchinson and William Jones reported in the *Chicago Tribune* that she had told them: "Miss Newberg said she was very vague about time during the evening partly because her watch was a *psychedelic one* that 'you couldn't read' and because no one was sitting around watching the clock... 'At no time were we aware of time' she explained." [Emphasis Added].

The *New York Times*, 7-25-69, in reporting by Warren Weaver, Jr. stated, "Miss Newberg described it as an informal group, with no one keeping particular track of who was there or who wasn't there at any given time. Thus, she said, no one specifically missed either the Senator or Miss Kopechne or noticed what time they left."

Yet, at the inquest under oath Miss Newberg was asked about the time they left the party, she said, "11:30 ... I have a rather large watch that I wear all the time and I looked at it."

In 1979, *High Times* magazine printed a story by a pseudonymous author that stated clearly that LSD had been brought to the party. We would have more on that, but the *High Times* cabal, after initially co-operating and going so far as to say that the story "was true...." labeled this author as CIA, and refused further comment. Imagine!

along by the tide and called Mary Jo's name until I was able to make my way to what would be the east side of that cut, waded up to about my waist and started back to the car, at this time I was gasping and belching and coughing, I went back just in front of the car.

Now the headlights of that car were still on and I was able to get to what I thought was the front of the car, although it was difficult — and I was able to identify the front of the car from the rear of the car by the lights themselves. Otherwise I don't think I would be able to tell.

Q. How far were you swept along by the current?
A. Approximately 30 to 40 feet.

Q. Did you pass under the bridge?
A. The vehicle went over the bridge on the south side and rested on the south side, and that was the direction the water was flowing, and I was swept I would think to the south or probably east, which would be the eastern shore.

Q. Some 30 feet?
A. I would think 30 to 40 feet.

Q. Now, in order to get back to the car was it necessary for you to swim?
A. I couldn't swim at that time because of the current. I waded into — to where I could wade and waded along the shore up to where I could go to the front of the car and start diving in an attempt to rescue Mary Jo.

Q. Was the front of the car facing a westerly direction?
A. I would think it was facing in a northerly direction.

Q. Well, in regard to the bridge could you describe the location of the automobile with relation to the bridge?
A. Well, your Honor, in the direction of north and south. I will do the best I can.

The Court: We don't have any map, do we?

Teller: The bridge runs north and south, fairly close to
            north and south.

The Court: That is coming towards Edgartown would be north
            and towards the ocean would be south?
Teller: Yes, sir.

Mr. Dinis: May we use the chalk, your Honor?
The Court: Yes, if it is helpful.

Q. Would that be helpful Mr. Kennedy?
A. It may be.

Q. I believe there is a board behind you. Assuming the bridge is
   north and south.
A. Yes. (Witness draws sketch on the blackboard.)
   I would bet that the bridge runs more east-west than north-
   south.

Teller: Not directly north, but southeast-north.

Q. Will you indicate, Mr. Kennedy, Edgartown?
A. I would rather have counsel draw and respond. I will be
   delighted to do whatever the court desires.

The Court: It is only for purposes of illustration.
Kennedy: I suppose the road runs something like this.

The Court: You are trying to get the relation of the car to the
            bridge?
Dinis: Yes, your Honor.

Q. As you went off the bridge?
A. I think it was like this.

The Court: All right, Mr. Dinis.

Q. Mr. Kennedy, after you emerged from the automobile you say
   you were swept some 30 feet away from the car, is that correct?
A. In this direction. (Indicating.)

Q. And how much time did it take you after you left the automobile to be swept down to about 30 feet, down the river?

A. By the time I came up I was, the best estimate would be
somewhat over here, which would be probably 8-10 feet, it is
difficult for me to estimate specifically, and I think by the time
I was able to regain my strength, I would say it is about 30
feet after which time I swam in this direction until I was able
to wade, and wade back up here to this point here, and went
over to the front of the car, where the front of the car was,
and crawled over to here, dove here, and the tide would sweep
out this way there, and then I dove repeatedly from this side
until, I would say, the end, and then I was swept away the first
couple of times, again back over to this side, I would come
back again and again to this point here, or try perhaps the
third or fourth time to gain entrance to some area here until
at the very end when I couldn't hold my breath any longer. I
was breathing so heavily it was down to just a matter of
seconds. I would hold my breath and I could barely get underneath the water. I was just able to hold on to the metal
undercarriage here, and the water itself came right out to
where I was breathing, and I could hold on, I knew that I just
could not get under water any more.

Q. And you were fully aware at that time of what was transpiring?

A. Well, I was fully aware that *I was trying to get the girl out of
that car and I was fully aware that I was doing everything I
possibly could to get her out of the car* and I was fully aware at
that time that my head was throbbing and my neck was aching
and I was breathless, and at that time, the last time, hopelessly
exhausted.

Q. You were not confused at that time?

A. Well, I knew that there was a girl in that car and *I had to get
her out.* I knew that.

Q. And you took steps to get her out?

A. I tried the best I thought I possibly could to get her out.

Q. But there was no confusion in your mind about the fact that there was a person in the car and that you were doing the best you could to get that person out?

A. *I was doing the very best I could to get her out.*

The Court: May I ask you some questions about the depth of the water?

Kennedy: Yes.[21]

The Court: You were not able to stand up at any point around any portion of that car?

Kennedy: No, it was not possible to stand. The highest level of the car to the surface were the wheels and the undercarriage itself. When I held on to the undercarriage and the tide would take me down, it was up to this point. (Indicating.)

Q. Mr. Kennedy, how many times if you recall did you make an effort to submerge and get into the car?

A. I would say seven or eight times. At the last point, the seventh or eighth attempts were barely more than five or eight second submersions below the surface. I just couldn't hold my breath any longer. I didn't have the strength even to come down even close to the windows or the door.

Q. And do you know how much time was used in these efforts?

A. It would be difficult for me to estimate, but I would think probably 15-20 minutes.

Q. And did you then remove yourself from the water?

A. I did.

Q. And how did you do that?

A. Well, in the last dive, I lost contact with the vehicle again and I started to come down this way here and I let myself float and came over to this shore and I came onto this shore here, and

---

[21] Clearly the Judge is foreclosing the prosecutor, by asking Kennedy if he can ask him a question, he proves his sympathy.

I sort of crawled and staggered up some place in here and was very exhausted and spent on the grass.

Q. On the west bank of the river?
A. Yes.

Q. As indicated by that chart?
A. Yes, that's correct.

Q. And how long did you spend resting?
A. Well, I would estimate probably 15-20 minutes trying to get my, I was coughing up the water and I was exhausted and I suppose the best estimate would be 15 or 20 minutes.

Q. Now, did you say earlier you spent 15-20 minutes trying to recover Miss Kopechne?
A. That is correct.

Q. And you spent another 15 or 20 minutes recovering on the west side of the river?
A. That is correct.

Q. Now, following your rest period, Senator, what did you do after that?
A. Well, I —

Q. You may remain seated.
A. All right, after I was able to regain my breath, I went back to the road and I started down the road and it was extremely dark and I could make out no forms or shapes or figures, and the only way that I could even see the path of the road was looking down the silhouettes of the trees on the two sides and I could watch the silhouette of the trees on the two sides and I started going down that road, walking, trotting, jogging, stumbling as fast as I possibly could.

Q. Did you pass any houses with lights on?

A. Not to my knowledge; *never saw a cottage with a light on.*[22]

Q. And did you then return to the cottage where your friends had been gathered?
A. That is correct.

Q. And how long did that take you to make that walk, do you recall?
A. I would say approximately 15 minutes.

Q. And then you arrived at the cottage, as you did, is that true?
A. That is true.

Q. Did you speak to anyone there?
A. Yes, I did.

Q. And with whom did you speak?
A. Mr. Ray LaRosa.

Q. And what did you tell him?
A. I said, get me Joe Gargan.

Q. And was Joe Gargan there?
A. He was there.

Q. He was at the party?
A. Yes.

The Court: Excuse me a moment. Did you go inside the cottage?
Kennedy: No, I didn't go inside.

Q. What did you do? Did you sit in the automobile at that time?
A. Well, I came up to the cottage, there was a car parked there, a white vehicle, and as I came up to the back of the vehicle, I saw Ray LaRosa at the door and I said Ray get me Joe, and

---

[22] According to his timetable here, he would have passed the Malm cottage when it was still fairly ablaze with light. They turned out their lights at midnight. Just across the road was another cottage with an outside light on all night.

he mentioned something like right away, and as he was going in to get Joe, I got in the back of the car.

Q. In this white car?
A. Yes.

Q. And now, did Joe come to you?
A. Yes, he did.

Q. And did you have conversation with him?
A. Yes I did.

Q. Would you tell us what the conversation was?
A. I said, you had better get Paul, too.

Q. Did you tell him what happened?
A. At that time I said, better get Paul, too.

Q. What happened after that?
A. Well, Paul came out, got in the car. I said, there has been a terrible accident, we have got to go, and we took off down the road, the main road there.

Q. How long had you known Mr. LaRosa prior to this evening?
A. Eight years, ten years, eight or ten years.

Q. Were you familiar with the fact or — strike that — did you have any knowledge that Mr. LaRosa had some experience in skindiving?
A. *No, I never did.*

Q. Now, before you drove down the road, did you make any further explanations to Mr. Gargan or Mr. Markham?
A. Before driving? No, sir. I said, there has been a terrible accident, let's go, and we took off —

Q. And they went —
A. Driving.

Q. And they drove hurriedly down?
A. That is right.

Q. And where did you stop the white automobile that you were riding in?
A. Mr. Gargan drove the vehicle across the bridge to some location here (indicating) and turned it so that its headlights shone over the water and over the submerged vehicle. (Indicating on blackboard.)

Q. What happened after the three of you arrived there?
A. *Mr. Gargan and Mr. Markham took off all their clothes, dove into the water*, and proceeded to dive repeatedly to try and save Mary Jo.

Q. Now, do you recall what particular time this is now when the three of you were at the —
A. *I think it was 12:20, Mr. Dinis. I believe that I looked at the Valiant's clock and believe that it was 12:20.*[23]

Q. Now, Mr. LaRosa remained at the cottage?
A. Yes, he did.

Q. Was Mr. LaRosa aware of the accident?
A. No, he hadn't heard — no, I don't believe so.

Q. No one else at the cottage was told of the accident?
A. No.

Q. How many times did you go back to Dyke Bridge that night?
A. Well, that was the only —

Q. After the accident, that was the only occasion?
A. The only time, the only occasion.

Q. Now, how long did Mr. Markham and Mr. Gargan remain there with you on that particular occasion?
A. I would think about 45 minutes.

---

[23] The rented Valiant had no factory-installed clock. Upon checking, it was determined that no drill holes were found, which indicated that the car *never* had a clock.

Q. And they were unsuccessful in entering the car?
A. *Well, Mr. Gargan got halfway in the car. When he came out he was scraped all the way from his elbow, underneath his arm was all bruised and bloodied, and this is the one time that he was able to gain entrance I believe into the car itself.*[24]

Q. And did he talk to you about his experience in trying to get into the car?
A. Well, I was unable to, being exhausted, to get into the water, but I could see exactly what was happening and made some suggestions.

Q. So that you participated in the rescue efforts?
A. Well, to that extent.

Q. You were fully aware of what was transpiring at that time?
A. Well, I was fully aware that Joe Gargan and Paul Markham were trying to get in that car and *rescue that girl*, I certainly would say that.

Q. Did you know at that time or did you have any idea how long Mary Jo had been in the water?
A. Well, I knew that some time had passed.

Q. Well, you testified earlier that you spent some 15 or 20 minutes of —
A. **Well, Mr. District Attorney,** I didn't add up the time that I was attempting to rescue her and time on the beach, the shore, and the time to get back and the time it took back and calculate it.[25]

---

[24] Here Kennedy introduced free-flowing blood directly into the car. This is very significant, crucial to the hypothesis which will follow. Also significant are Gargan's own recollections of being in the water: "Because in turning to feel around [he had gotten into the car after working himself down from the front of the car], I'd gotten jammed in. Instead of turning again calmly, I kind of pushed myself out fiercely." Interview with Damore, 2-15-83. He went on to tell Damore that "He felt something sharp rake his arms and chest as he passed out of the car." Yet, fifteen years before he — *testified* — that his back had also been scraped.

[25] Kennedy's sarcasm may indicate emotional agitation in that he has told a vast lie regarding Gargan's alleged bleeding; and now the D.A. is bearing in on the veracity of the time sequence.

Q. Was it fair to say that she was in the water about an hour?
A. Yes, it is.

Q. Was there any effort made to call for assistance?
A. *No, other than the assistance of Mr. Gargan and Mr. Markham.*

Q. I know, but they failed in their effort to recover —
A. That is right.

Q. Miss Kopechne?
A. That is correct.

(Discussion off the record.)[26]

Q. I believe, your Honor, before the witness left the courtroom the question was whether or not any assistance had been asked for?

The Court: I think the answer had been no.

Q. And now may I ask you, Mr. Kennedy, was there any reason why no additional assistance was asked for?
A. Was there any reason?

Q. Yes, was there any particular reason why you did not call either the police or the fire department?
A. *Well, I intended to report it to the police.*

The Court: That is not quite responsive to the question.

Q. Was there any reason why it did not happen at that time?

The Court: Call for assistance.
Kennedy: I intended to call for assistance and to report the accident to the police within a few short moments after going back into the car.

---

[26] Here Kennedy was led out of the courtroom by his counsel, undoubtedly to cool off after this highly emotional exchange.

The cottage where the party was held.

Edgartown waterfront,
Chappaquiddick Island on the right.

C The ferry *On Time* approaching Chappaquiddick.

EE Dyke Bridge, one year later.

Q. I see, and did something transpire to prevent this?
A. Yes.

Q. What was that?
A. With the Court's indulgence, to prevent this, if the Court would permit me I would like to be able to relate to the Court the immediate period following the time that Mr. Gargan, Markham and I got back in the car.

The Court: I have no objection.
Dinis: I have no objection.
Kennedy: Responding to the question of the District Attorney...

Dinis: Yes.
Kennedy: At some time, I believe it was about 45 minutes after Gargan and Markham dove they likewise became exhausted and no further efforts appeared to be of any avail and they so indicated to me and I agreed. So they came out of the water and came back into the car and said to me, Mr. Markham and Mr. Gargan at different times as we drove down the road towards the ferry that it was necessary to report this accident. A lot of different thoughts came into my mind at that time about how I was going to really be able to call Mrs. Kopechne at some time in the middle of the night to tell her that her daughter was drowned, to be able to call my own mother and my own father, relate to them, my wife, and I even — even though I knew that Mary Jo Kopechne was dead and believed firmly that she was in the back of the car, I willed that she remained alive.

As we drove down that road I was almost looking out the front window and windows trying to see her walking down the road. I related this to Gargan and Markham and they said they understood this feeling, but it was necessary to report it. And about this time we came to the ferry crossing and I got out of the car and we talked there just a few minutes.

I just wondered how all of this could possibly have happened. I also had sort of a thought and the wish and desire and the hope that suddenly this whole accident would disappear, and they reiterated that this has to be reported and I understood at the time I left that ferry boat, left the slip where the ferry was, that it had to be reported and *I had full intention of reporting it,* and I mentioned Gargan and Markham something like, "You take care of the girls, I will take care of the accident" that is what I said and I **dove into the water.**

Now, I started to swim out into the tide and the tide suddenly became, felt an extraordinary shove and almost pulling me down again, the water pulling me down and suddenly I realized at that time even as I failed to realize before I dove into the water that I was in a weakened condition, although as I had looked over that distance between the ferry slip and the other side, it seemed to me an inconsequential swim; but the water got colder, *the tide began to draw me out and for the second time that evening,* I knew I was going to drown and the strength continued to leave me. By this time I was probably 50 yards off the shore and I remembered *being swept down toward the direction of the Edgartown Light and well out into darkness,* and I continued to attempt to swim, tried to swim at a slower pace to be able to regain whatever kind of strength that was left in me.

And some time after, I think it was about the middle of the channel, a little further than that, the tide was much calmer, gentler, and I began to get my — make some progress, and finally was able to reach the other shore and all the nightmares before me again. And when I was able to gain this shore,

this Edgartown side, I pulled myself on the beach
and then attempted to gain some strength.

After that I walked up one of the streets in the
direction of the Shiretown Inn. By walking up one
of the streets I walked into a parking lot that was
adjacent to the Inn and I can remember almost
having no further strength to continue, and leaning
against a tree for a length of time, walking through
the parking lot, trying to really gather some kind
of idea as to what happened and feeling that I just
had to go to my room at that time, which I did by
walking through the parking lot, trying to really
gather some kind of ideas as to what happened and
feeling that I just had to go to my room at that
time, which I did by walking through the front
entrance of the Shiretown Inn up the stairs.[27]

Q. Do you have any idea what time you arrived at the Shiretown
Inn?

A. I would say some time before 2:00.

Q. Can you tell us now how great a distance you swam when you
left the ferry slip?

A. I left just adjacent to the ferry slip, I would say on the north
side of it and I was swept down for a number of yards and
then across. I don't think I can estimate the terms of the
yardage.

Q. When you arrived at the Shiretown Inn, did you talk to anyone
at that time?

A. I went to my room and I was shaking with chill. I took off all
my clothes and collapsed on the bed, and at this time, I was
very conscious of a throbbing headache, of pains in my neck,
of strain on my back, but what I was even more conscious of
is the tragedy and loss of a very devoted friend.

---

[27] Continuing the theme from his TV spiel, he gets on the record with this rambling
business about "having to go to his room" and sets up temporary insanity as a
possible defense if charged with the crime of manslaughter.

Q. Now, did you change your clothes?

A. I was unable really to determine, detect the amount of lapse of time and I could hear noise that was taking place. *It seemed around me, on top of me, almost in the room, and after a period of time, I wasn't sure whether it was morning or afternoon or nighttime,*[28] and I put on — and I wanted to find out and I put on some dry clothes that were there, a pants and shirt, and I opened the door and I saw what I believed to be a tourist, someone standing under the light off the balcony and asked what time it was. He mentioned to me it was, I think, 2:30, and I went back into the room.[29]

Q. Had you known Miss Kopechne prior to July 18th?

A. Well, I have known her — my family has known her for a number of years. She has visited my house, my wife. She has visited Mrs. Robert Kennedy's house. She worked in the Robert Kennedy Presidential campaign, and I would say that we have known her for a number of years.

Q. Now, directing your —

A. If the question is, have I have ever been out with Mary Jo...

Q. No, that is not the question. The question was whether you knew her socially prior to this event.

A. Well, could I give you a fuller explanation of my knowledge of Mary Jo, your Honor?

Dinis: I have no objection.

The Court: Go ahead.

Kennedy: I have never in my life, as I have stated on tele-
            vision, had any personal relationship with Mary Jo
            Kopechne. I never in my life have been either out

---

28 Ironic in the context of the previous reference to drugs, this type of speech sounds like drug babble, especially the feeling of being out of time.

29 Russell Peachey then came forward and told reporters that he had indeed had that conversation with Kennedy. A week before he had told the police that he hadn't seen Kennedy after he had checked in Friday night. Then later, as he reconsidered what he'd seen, he told *Newsweek,* 9-8-69: "He didn't look to me like a man who had come downstairs to complain about noise. He was just standing there. He was fully dressed. I think he was wearing a jacket and slacks. Usually, a man who just wants to complain about noise doesn't get up and get fully dressed to do it. Especially at 2:25 in the morning."

with Mary Jo Kopechne nor have I ever been with her prior to that occasion where we were not in a general assemblage of friends, associates, or members of our family.

Q. Directing your attention to the 19th at around 7:30 A.M., did you have any conversation with anyone at that time?
A. Could I hear the question, please?

Q. The 19th, which was that morning at around 7:00 A.M., 7:30 A.M.
A. Yes.

Q. Did you meet anyone at your room?
A. Not at 7:30 A.M., I did not.

Q. Did you meet anyone at any time that morning at your room?
A. Yes, I did.

Q. And whom did you meet there?
A. If your Honor would permit I would like to be specifically responsive, and I can. I think. It might be misleading to the Court if I just gave a specific response to it. Whatever the Court wants.

Q. Well, the point is, what time did you get up that morning?
A. *I never really went to bed that night.*[30]

Q. I see. After that noise at 2:30 in the morning, when did you first meet anyone, what time?
A. It was sometime after 8:00.

Q. And whom did you meet?
A. Sometime after 8:00 I met the woman that was behind the counter at the Shiretown Inn and I met Mr. Richards and Mr. Moore, very briefly Mrs. Richards, and Mr. Gargan and Mr. Markham, and I saw Mr. Tretter, but to be specifically respon-

---

[30] As we will see later, this is probably true.

sive as to who I met in my room, which I believe was the earlier question, was Mr. Markham and Mr. Gargan.

Q. What time was this, sometime around 8 o'clock?
A. I think it was close to 8:30.

Q. Did you have any conversation with Mr. Moore or Mrs. Moore or Mr. Richards or Mrs. Richards?
A. It is my impression that they did the talking.

Q. Well, what was the conversation, do you recall?
A. Mr. Moore was relating about how I believe some members of his crew were having difficulty with their housing arrangements?

Q. Now, what time did Mr. Markham and Mr. Gargan arrive?
A. About a few I — would think about 8:30, just a few minutes after I met Mr. Moore probably.

Q. And do you recall how they were dressed?
A. To the best of my knowledge, a shirt and slacks.

Q. Do you recall at this time the condition of their dress?
A. Well, they had an unkempt look about them.

Q. Nothing further, nothing more than that?
A. Well, I mean it was not pressed; it was messy looking. It was unkempt looking.

Q. Did you have any conversation with Mr. Markham or Mr. Gargan or both at that time?
A. Yes, I did.

Q. Can you give the Court, what the conversation was?
A. *Well, they asked, had I reported the accident, and why I hadn't reported the accident;* and I told them about my own thoughts and feelings as I swam across that channel and how I always willed that Mary Jo still lived: how I was hopeful even as that night went on and as I almost tossed and turned, paced that room and walked around that room that night that somehow when they arrived in the morning that they were going to say

that Mary Jo was still alive. I told them how I somehow believed that when the sun came up and it was a new morning that what had happened the night before would not have happened and did not happen, and how I just *couldn't gain the strength within me, the moral strength to call Mrs. Kopechne at 2:00 o'clock in the morning and tell her that her daughter was dead.*[31]

Q. Now, at some time did you actually call Mrs. Kopechne?
A. Yes, I did.

Q. And prior to calling Mrs. Kopechne, did you cross over on the Chappaquiddick Ferry to Chappaquiddick Island?
A. Yes, I did.

Q. And, was Mr. Markham and Mr. Gargan with you?
A. Yes, they were.

Q. Now, did you then return to Edgartown after some period of time?
A. Yes, I did.

Q. Did anything prompt or cause you to return to Edgartown once you were on Chappaquiddick Island that morning?
A. Anything prompt me to? Well, what do you mean by prompt?

Q. Well, did anything cause you to return? You crossed over to Chappaquiddick.
A. *Other than the intention of reporting the accident, the intention of which had been made earlier that morning.*[32]

Q. But you didn't go directly from your room to the police department?
A. No, I did not.

Q. Did you have a particular reason for going to Chappaquiddick first?

---

[31] Of course he ultimately did call her, after he had set his defense into action. Here he also got Markham and Gargan off the hook.

[32] The Police Station was, of course, in the opposite direction from which he travelled.

A. Yes, I did.

Q. What was that reason?
A. It was to make a private phone call to one of the dearest and oldest friends that I have and that was to Mr. Burke Marshall. *I didn't feel that I could use the phone that was available outside of the dining room at the Shiretown Inn,* and it was my thought that once I went to the Police Station, that I would be involved in a myriad of details and I wanted to talk to this friend before I undertook that responsibility.

Q. You mean that —

The Court: Excuse me, Mr. Dinis, we are now at 1 o'clock.
Dinis: The recess.

The Court: I think we will take the noon luncheon recess.[33]

AFTERNOON SESSION

The Court: All right, Mr. Dinis.

Q. Mr. Kennedy, you said that you made a phone call to a friend, Mr. Burke Marshall?
A. I made a phone call with the intention of reaching Mr. Burke Marshall.

Q. You did not reach him?
A. No, I did not.

Q. And then I believe the evidence is that you left Chappaquiddick Island, crossed over on the ferry and went over to the local police department?
A. That is correct.

---

[33] Saved by the judge's hunger for food, just as Dinis began to bear down about not reporting the accident.

Q. There you made a report to Chief Arena?
A. That is right.

Q. And you arrived at the Police Station at approximately 10 A.M.?
A. I think it was sometime before 10:00.

Q. And you made a statement in writing, is that correct?
A. That is correct.

Q. Did the chief reduce this to a typewritten statement, do you know?
A. No, he did not.[34]

Q. Now, I have in my hand what purports to be the statement that you made to Chief Arena at that time, and I would like to give you a copy of that, and in this statement you saw — well, would you read it first, Senator?
A. Yes, that is correct.

Q. Now, Senator, prior to the phone call you made, the effort you made to contact Burke Marshall by phone, did you make any other phone calls?
A. Yes, I did.

Q. Where did you make these phone calls?
A. I made one call after 8 o'clock in the morning from the public phone outside of the restaurant at the Shiretown Inn.

Q. One call?
A. *That is all. This was made sometime after 8:00.*

Q. And to whom did you make this call?
A. I was attempting to reach Mr. Stephen Smith, the party that I felt would know the number.

Q. Were you alone in the Police Station?

[34] Untrue.

A. No. At certain times I was, but if the thrust of the question is did I arrive at the Police Station with someone with me, I did.

Q. And who was that?
A. Mr. Markham.

Q. Mr. Markham?
A. Yes.

Q. With regard to the statement that you made at the Police Station, Senator, you wind up saying, "When I fully realized what had happened this morning, I immediately contacted the police." Now is that in fact what you did?

The Court: Mr. Dinis, are you going to ask the statement be put in the record?
Dinis: Yes, your Honor.

The Court: Mr. Kennedy already said this was a copy of the statement he made. **He already testified as to all his movements. Now, won't you let the record speak for itself?**[35]
Dinis: All right, your Honor.

The Court: This will be Exhibit
Teller: 2.
The Court: 2.

(Statement given to Chief Arena by Senator Kennedy marked Exhibit 2.)

Q. Senator, you testified earlier that when you arrived at the cottage you asked Mr. LaRosa to tell Mr. Markham you were outdoors, outside of the house, when you arrived back at the house?
A. No, that is not correct.

---

[35] Here come 'de judge. A prime technique of an interrogation in a court room situation is to ask witnesses the same question from different angles in order to test the witnesses' truthfulness. The Judge wasn't interested.

Q. Did you ask someone to call Mr. Markham?

A. I asked Joe Gargan when he entered the vehicle to call for Mr. Markham.

Q. Well, did you at that time ask anyone to take you back to Edgartown at that time when you arrived back at the house after the accident?

A. No. I asked Mr. Gargan to go to the scene of the accident.

Q. But you didn't ask anyone to take you directly back to Edgartown?

A. I asked them to take me to Edgartown after their diving.

Q. After the diving?

A. After their diving.

Q. I show you, Mr. Kennedy, what purports to be a copy of the televised broadcast which you made approximately a week after the accident. Would you read the statement and tell me whether or not this is an exact copy of what you said?

A. Yes. After a quick reading of it, I would say that this is accurate.

Dinis: Your Honor, may I introduce this statement made by Senator Kennedy in a televised broadcast?

The Court: You may, Exhibit No. 3. (Statement made by Senator Kennedy in televised broadcast marked Exhibit 3.)

Q. Now, Senator in that televised broadcast you said and I quote, "I instructed Gargan and Markham not to alarm Mary Jo's friends that night," is that correct?

A. That is correct. I would like to —

Q. Look at it?

A. — look at it. I believe that is correct.

Q. It would be on page 3.

(Witness examined the document.)

A. That is correct.

Q. Can you tell the Court what prompted you to give this instruction to Markham and Gargan?
A. Yes, I can.

Q. Will you do that please?
A. I felt strongly that if those girls were notified that an accident had taken place and that Mary Jo had in fact drowned, which I became convinced of by the time that Markham and Gargan and I left the scene of the accident, that it would only be a **matter of seconds** before all of those girls who were long and dear friends of Mary Jo's to go to the scene of the accident and dive themselves and enter the water with, I felt, a good chance that some serious mishap might have occurred to any one of them. It was for that reason that I restrained — asked Mr. Gargan and Mr. Markham not to alarm the girls.[36]

Q. I have no further questions of Mr. Kennedy.

The Court: And I have no further questions. Would you be available in the event we needed you back for anything?

Kennedy: I will make myself available, your Honor.

The Court: Well, were you planning to stay in Hyannis Port or some place near?

Kennedy: Well, I will. I will be glad to be available.

The Court: Otherwise you would go back to Boston?

Kennedy: No, I would return to Cape Cod tonight and I would hope to be able to return to Washington

---

[36] Of course one of the girls might have taken it on herself to report the accident, to summon professional help in "... a matter of seconds...."

sometime this week, but I would be glad to remain available to the Court if the Court so desired.

The Court: Well it is difficult for me to say right now.

Kennedy: Well, then, I will remain available as long —

The Court: We will try to give you as much notice as possible if we felt it essential to have you back.

Dinis: Your Honor, I think we could make it an overnight notice, so if the Senator had to be in Washington, we would arrange for his arrival the next day, if necessary, which may not be.

The Court: All right, subject to that, you are excused.

Kennedy: Your Honor, could I talk to my counsel before being released, just on one point that I might like to address the bench on?

The Court: Go ahead.

(Off the record discussion between Mr. Kennedy and lawyers.)

The Court: And I think we can put in the record this question. Why did you not seek further assistance after Mr. Markham and Mr. Gargan had exhausted their efforts in attempting to reach Mary Jo? Now, you give the answer.

Kennedy: It is because I was completely convinced at that time that no further help and assistance would do Mary Jo any more good. I realized that she must be drowned and still in the car at this time, and it appeared the question in my mind at that time, was, what should be done about the accident.

The Court: Anything further? Off the record.

(Discussion off the record.)

The Court: All right, take this.

Kennedy: Since the alcoholic intake is relevant; there is one
             further question, your Honor, and although I
             haven't been asked it, I feel that in all frankness
             and fairness and for a complete record that it
             should be included as a part of the complete pro-
             ceedings, and *that is that during the course of the
             race that afternoon that there were two other mem-
             bers of my crew and I shared what would be two
             beers* between us at different points in the race,
             and one other occasion in which there was some
             modest intake of alcohol would be after the race
             at the slip in which Ross Richards' boat was at-
             tached, moored, that *I shared a beer with Mr. John
             Driscoll. The sum and substance of that beer would
             be,* I think, less than a quarter of one, but I felt
             that for the complete record that at least the Court
             should at least be aware of these instances as
             well.[37]

The Court: Anything more?

Kennedy: There is nothing further.

The Court: Anything more, Mr. Dinis?

Dinis: No, your Honor.

---

[37] Mentioned in a footnote above was his alleged consumption of three rum-and-cokes
at the boat slip, just before he went out to the party. Later we will see in depth why
he felt free to testify about one quarter a of beer, knowing he would not be
contradicted by Stanley Moore, or Ross Richards. Suffice it to say, he had
foreknowledge. Foreknowledge provided illegally in a direct act of obstruction of
justice by a member of the Massachusetts State Police. Most important, this answer
was not in response to a question, this was Kennedy being given the opportunity to
inform the record with information that he wanted on the record.

The Court: All right, you are excused subject to further recall. Off the record.

(Discussion off the record.)

The Court: All right, your next witness, Mr. Dinis.

9

JUDGEMENT
PASSED (OVER)

At the conclusion of the two-day Inquest, Judge Boyle withdrew to make his Decision on the matter. He had the power and the legal obligation to either make a formal charge himself or make recommendations to the District Attorney if he found that laws had been violated.[1] He didn't order an arrest warrant, or make any recommendations to the District Attorney. The Inquest was convened on January 5, 1970 and he issued his Report, which follows, on February 18, 1970. One week before the report was issued he retired from the bench, went golfing and became incommunicado.

Though we have already covered much of the material contained in the Report, it is important to reproduce from the public record the very words of Judge Boyle in this open forum. In all of the literature written on Chappaquiddick, the account that follows is easily the most complete and composite chronological history of the facts. To his full credit, this proves that Judge Boyle was able to read the stenographer's notes.

---

[1] In fact, by statute and based on his *own* conclusions, Judge Boyle was bound to order and sign an arrest warrant, he simply did not.

* * * *

COMMONWEALTH OF MASSACHUSETTS

Dukes County, ss   District Court
                                        Inquest re Mary Jo Kopechne

Docket No. 15220

REPORT
James A. Boyle, Justice

I, James A. Boyle, Justice of the District Court for the County of Dukes County, in performance of the duty required of me by Section 12 of Chapter 38 of the General Laws of Massachusetts, in the matter of the Inquest into the death of Mary Jo Kopechne, holden at Edgartown January 5, 1970 to January 8, 1970 inclusive, herewith submit my report.

There are 763 pages of transcript and 33 numbered exhibits. Although most testimony was given orally, some was accepted by affidavit and included as exhibits.

It is believed that, to aid in understanding this report, certain names and places should first be relatively located and some measurements shown;

1. The Town of Edgartown, which is one of six towns on Martha's Vineyard, includes a small, sparsely settled Island named **Chappaquiddick.** (Map, Exhibit 32)

2. The **mainland** of Edgartown is separated from Chappaquiddick by Edgartown harbor, the distance between being approximately five hundred feet, and transportation of vehicles and persons is provided by a small motor ferry which plies between two ferry slips or landings. The ferry slip on the Edgartown side is near the center of town. (Exhibit 19)

3. Chappaquiddick has few roads. At the ferry slip, begins a macadam paved road called Chappaquiddick Road, the main road of the Island, with a white center line which is partly obliterated at the Curve. The road is approximately twenty feet wide, running in a general easterly direction for two and one-half miles, whence it Curves south and continues in that direction past the Cottage to the southeast corner of the Island. Chappaquiddick Road is sometimes referred to in the testimony as Main Street and, after it curves, as School Road or Schoolhouse Road, because a schoolhouse formerly stood on that portion of it. (Exhibits 16, 19)

4. At the Curve, and continuing easterly, begins Dyke Road, a dirt and sand road, seventeen to nineteen feet wide, which runs a distance of seven-tenths miles to Dyke Bridge, shortly beyond which is the ocean beach. (Exhibits 15, 16, 17)

5. Dyke Bridge is a wooden structure, ten feet six inches wide, has timber curbs on each side four inches high by ten inches wide, no other guard rails, and runs at an angle of twenty-seven degrees to the left of the road. There are no signs or artificial lights on the bridge or its approach. It spans Poucha Pond. (Exhibits 7, 8, 9, 10)

6. The Kennedy Oldsmobile is eighteen feet long and eighty inches wide. (Exhibits 1, 33)

7. Poucha Pond is a salt water tidal pond, and has a strong current where it narrows at Dyke Bridge. (Exhibits 10, 18)

8. Cemetery Road is a single car-width private dirt road, which runs northerly from the junction of Chappaquiddick and Dyke Roads. (Exhibits 16, 22)

9. The Lawrence Cottage (herein called Cottage) is one-half mile from the junction of Chappaquiddick and

Dyke Roads and approximately three miles from the ferry slip. (Exhibit 20)

10. Proceeding northerly from the Cottage, on the east side of Chappaquiddick Road, a distance of one-tenth mile before the Curve, is a metal sign with an arrow pointing toward the ferry landing.

11. Katama Shores Motor Inn (called Katama Shores) is located approximately two miles from the Edgartown ferry slip.

12. Shiretown Inn (called Shiretown) is a very short distance from the Edgartown ferry slip, approximately one block.

Although the testimony is not wholly consistent, a general summary of the material circumstances is this: A group of twelve persons, by invitation of Edward M. Kennedy, a United States Senator from Massachusetts, were gathered together at Edgartown to attend the annual sailing regatta held on Friday and Saturday, July 18 and 19, 1969. They were:

John B. Crimmins	Rosemary Keough
Joseph Gargan	Mary Jo Kopechne
Edward M. Kennedy	Ann (also called Nance) Lyons
Raymond S. LaRosa	Mary Ellen Lyons
Paul F. Markham	Esther Newberg
Charles S. Tretter	Susan Tannenbaum

(All hereafter referred to by surnames).

The six young women, in their twenties, had been associated together in Washington D.C. and were quite close friends. Kopechne shared a Washington apartment with Nance Lyons. Reservations had been made for them to stay at Katama Shores, in three double rooms. Kopechne roomed with Newberg. Crimmins, chauffeur for Kennedy when he was in Massachusetts, drove Kennedy's black Oldsmobile sedan from Boston to Martha's Vineyard on Wednesday, July 16. He brought a supply of liquor with him and stayed at the Cottage. Tretter, who brought some of the young women, arrived late Thursday and stayed at Shiretown. LaRosa, who brought his Mercury car, came Thursday and shared the room with Tretter. Gargan and Markham sailed Kennedy's boat to Edgartown on Thursday and roomed together at Shiretown. Kennedy arrived by plane on Friday, July 18, was met by Crimmins at the airport, and was driven to the Cottage. Kennedy shared a room at Shiretown with Gargan. The Lyons' sisters arrived Friday morning and were driven by Gargan to Katama Shores. Markham, who stayed at Shiretown Thursday night, moved to the Cottage to stay with Crimmins for Friday and Saturday nights.[2] Kennedy, with Gargan, was entered to sail his boat in the regatta on Friday and Saturday.

The Cottage became headquarters for the group and a cook-out was planned for Friday night. Three cars were available for general transportation; LaRosa's Mercury, Kennedy's Oldsmobile 88, and a rented white Valiant.

Thursday night, those present, included Kopechne, visited the Cottage; Friday morning, they, including Kopechne, traveled over Dyke Bridge to the beach to swim; Friday evening, they, including Kopechne, traveled to the Cottage for the cook-out. Kennedy, who arrived at 1:00 P.M. Friday and was driven by Crimmins to the Cottage, was then driven by Crimmins over Dyke Road and Dyke Bridge to the beach to swim; he was driven back to the Cottage to change, to the ferry to sail in the race and, after the race, was driven back to the Cottage. There were other trips between Edgartown and the Cottage but not including Kopechne or Kennedy. These are set forth to indicate the use of, and increasing familiarity with, the roads on Chappaquiddick.

The Cottage is small, contains a combination kitchen-living room, two bedrooms and bath, has an open yard, no telephone, and is near to and visible from Chappaquiddick Road, which

---

2   Unlikely. Prosecutor Walter Steele walked back with Markham to the Shiretown Saturday morning, and Markham's clothing was scattered around the room, indicating he was not planning to stay out there Friday and Saturday.

had little traffic. The entire group of twelve had assembled there by approximately 8:30 P.M. on Friday. Two cars were available for transportation on Chappaquiddick, the Oldsmobile and Valiant. LaRosa's Mercury was at the Shiretown. Activities consisted of cooking, eating, drinking, conversation, singing and dancing. Available alcoholic beverages consisted of vodka, rum, scotch and beer. There was not much drinking and no one admitted to more than three drinks; most only to two or less.

During the evening, Tretter, with Keough, drove to Edgartown in the Oldsmobile to borrow a radio. Keough left her pocketbook in the vehicle on that trip.

Only Crimmins and Markham planned to stay the night at the Cottage. The others intended to return to their respective hotels in Edgartown. It was known that the last ferry trip was about midnight, but that a special arrangement for a later trip could be made.

Between 11:15 and 11:30 P.M. Kennedy told Crimmins (but no other person) that he was tired, wanted to return to Shiretown to bed, that Kopechne did not feel well (some conflict here — see pages 32 and 346) and he was taking her back to Katama Shores, requested and obtained the car keys to the Oldsmobile, and both he and Kopechne departed. Kopechne told no one, other than Kennedy, that she was leaving. Kopechne left her pocketbook at the Cottage.[3]

Kennedy stated he drove down Chappaquiddick Road toward the ferry, that when he reached the junction of Dyke Road, instead of bearing left on the curve to continue on Chappaquiddick Road, he mistakenly turned right onto Dyke Road, realized at some point he was on a dirt road, but thought nothing of it, was proceeding at about twenty miles per hour when suddenly Dyke Bridge was upon him. He braked, but the car went off the bridge into Poucha Pond and

---

[3]   He does not mention that her motel key, cash and airline tickets were in the purse.

landed on its roof.[4] The driver's window was open and he managed to reach the surface and swim to shore. It was extremely dark, there was a strong current, and repeated efforts by him to extricate Kopechne from the car were unsuccessful. Exhausted, he went to shore and, when recovered, walked back to the Cottage, not noticing any lights or houses on the way. He summoned Gargan and Markham, without notifying the others, and they returned in the Valiant to the bridge, where Gargan and Markham unsuccessfully attempted to recover Kopechne.

The three drove back to the ferry landing. After much discussion, it was decided that Kennedy would return to Edgartown (no mention how) to telephone David Burke, his administrative assistant, and Burke Marshall, an attorney, and then report the accident to the police. Kennedy advised Gargan and Markham to return to the Cottage, but not to tell the others of the accident. Suddenly and unexpectedly, Kennedy left the car, dove into the harbor and swam across to Edgartown. Gargan and Markham finally returned to the Cottage, but did not then tell the others what had occurred.[5]

After Kennedy and Kopechne had left the Cottage, their purported destination unknown to anyone except Crimmins, the social activities gradually diminished. The absence of Kennedy and Kopechne was noticed but it was presumed they had returned to Edgartown. Some persons went walking. Only LaRosa saw Kennedy return at about 12:30 A.M. and he, at Kennedy's request, summoned Gargan and Markham, who went to Kennedy, seated outside in the rear seat of the Valiant, and they took off. When Gargan and Markham returned about 2:00 A.M., some were sleeping and the others, realizing they would not return to Edgartown that night, then slept or tried to. There not being sufficient beds, some slept on the floor.

[4] If this is the case, then how do we explain the extreme depth of the dents all along the passenger side of the car? (See Photo Section.)

[5] Fails to mention testimony that they also jumped in the water after Kennedy, and stopped to let Kennedy continue swimming.

In the morning, those in the Cottage returned to Edgartown at different times. The young women eventually reached Katama Shores and were then told what had happened, although some of them had been made aware that Kopechne was missing.

Kennedy, after swimming across to Edgartown, went to his room, took off his wet clothes, lay on the bed, then dressed, went outside and complained to someone (later identified as the innkeeper, Russell Peachey) of noise and to inquire the time. He was told it was 2:24 A.M. He returned to his room and remained there until 7:30 A.M. when he went outside,[6] met Richards, a sailing competitor; chatted with him for one-half hour, when Gargan and Markham appeared and the three retired to Kennedy's room. When Kennedy informed them he had failed to report the accident, they all went to Chappaquiddick to use the public telephone near the ferry slip and Kennedy called David Burke, his administrative assistant, in Washington. (But Exhibit 4, list of calls charged to Kennedy, does not show this call.)[7] Gargan returned to the Cottage to tell those there about the accident. Kennedy and Markham went to the Edgartown Police Station, and were later joined by Gargan.

At about 8:20 A.M. Police Chief Arena, receiving notice of a submerged car at Dyke Bridge, hurried to the scene, changed into swim trunks, and made several futile attempts to enter the Oldsmobile. Farrar, a scuba diver, was summoned, found and recovered the body of Kopechne from the car, and also found in the car the pocketbook of Keough. The car was later towed to shore.

Dr. Donald R. Mills of Edgartown, Associate Medical Examiner, was summoned and arrived about 9:15 A.M.; examined the body and pronounced death by drowning; turned

---

[6] Fails to mention a totally calm, unconcerned Kennedy borrowing a dime from the desk clerk to make a call, and ordering newspapers.

[7] This is an important point, because as we will see in Chapter 13, there have been a number of subterfuges in relation to the actual telephone calls made by Kennedy and his associates after the accident.

it over to Eugene Frieh, a mortician, who took the body to his establishment at Vineyard Haven. The clothing and a sample of blood from the body were turned over to the State Police for analysis. No autopsy was performed and the body was embalmed and flown to Pennsylvania on Sunday for burial.

When Kennedy and Markham arrived at the Police Station, Chief Arena was at Dyke Bridge. He returned to the Station at Kennedy's request. Kennedy stated he was the operator of the car and dictated a statement of the accident as Markham wrote it down. Chief Arena then typed the statement which Kennedy said was correct but did not sign. (Exhibit 2)

On July 25, 1969, Kennedy pleaded guilty in this Court to, and was sentenced on, a criminal charge of "leaving the scene of an accident after causing personal injury, without making himself known." That same night, Kennedy made a television statement to the voters of Massachusetts. (Exhibit 3)

A petition by District Attorney Edmund Dinis in the Court of Common Pleas for Luzerne County, Pennsylvania, for exhumation and autopsy on the body of Kopechne, was denied after Hearing. Expert evidence was introduced that chemical analysis of the blouse worn by Kopechne showed blood stains, but medical evidence proved this was not inconsistent with death by drowning. (Exhibit 31)

Christopher F. Look, Jr., a deputy sheriff then living on Chappaquiddick, was driving easterly on Chappaquiddick Road to his home about 12:45 A.M. on July 19. As he approached the junction of Dyke Road, a car crossed in front of him and entered Cemetery Road, stopped, back up, and drove easterly on Dyke Road. He saw two persons in the front seat, a shadow on the shelf back of the rear seat which he thought could have been a bag, article of clothing, or a third person. The car was dark colored with Massachusetts registration plate L7-7. He was unable to remember any other numbers or how many there were intervening. Later that morning, he saw the Kennedy Oldsmobile when it was towed to shore, **but he cannot**

positively identify it as the same car he saw at 12:45 A.M.[8]
During the Inquest, a preliminary investigation was initiated
through the Registry of Motor Vehicles to determine whether
a tracking of the location on July 18 and 19, 1969, of all dark
colored cars bearing the Massachusetts plates with any and all
combinations of numbers beginning with L7 and ending in 7,
would be practicable. The attempt disclosed that it would not
be feasible[9] to do this since there would be no assurance that
the end result would be helpful and, in any event, the elimination of all other cars within that registration group (**although
it would seriously affect the credibility of some of the witnesses**) would not alter the findings in this report. [Emphasis
Added.]

A short distance before Dyke Bridge, there is a small house
called "Dyke House," then occupied by a Mrs. Malm and her
daughter. (Exhibit 18) Both heard a car sometime before
midnight but are not sure of its direction. The daughter turned
off her light at midnight. (p. 593 et seq.)

Drs. Watt and Brougham examined Kennedy on July 19
and 22. Diagnostic opinion was "concussions, contusions and
abrasions of the scalp, acute cervical strain. Impairment of
judgement and confused behavior are consistent with this type
of injury." (Exhibit 27)

Eugene D. Jones, a professional engineer, testified by
affidavit as to the condition of Dyke Road and Dyke Bridge
and concluded that the site is well below approved engineering
standards and particularly hazardous at night. (Exhibits 29, 30)

Donald L. Sullivan, an employee of Arthur D. Little, Inc.,
testified by affidavit as to a road test conducted on or about
October 10, 1969 describing the factors involved in a motor

---

8   Look did at the scene; it was Judge Boyle's badgering questions and a questionable
interpretation which brought this conclusion.

9   The Judge himself stopped this computer check. The D.A.'s office followed the
procedure and found that there were no other cars matching that description in that
part of the state, but Dinis did not press the judge to get this into the record.

vehicle, on high beam light, approaching Dyke Bridge at night, with film showing the results of such test. (Exhibit 28)

State Police Chemist McHugh, who analyzed the blood sample taken from the body of Kopechne, testified the alcoholic content was .09 percent, the equivalent of three and one-half to five ounces of eighty to ninety proof liquor consumed by a person, weighing about one hundred ten pounds, within an hour prior to death, or a larger amount if consumed within a longer period.[10]

This concludes in substance, the material circumstances as testified to by the witnesses.

The failure of Kennedy to seek additional assistance in searching for Kopechne, whether excused by his condition, or whether or not it would have been of any material help, has not been pursued because such failure, even when shown, does not constitute criminal conduct.

Since there was no evidence that any air remained in the immersed car, testimony was not sought or allowed concerning how long Kopechne might have lived, had such a condition existed, as this could only be conjecture and purely speculative.[11]

As previously stated, there are inconsistencies and contradictions in the testimony, which a comparison of individual testimony will show. It is not feasible to attempt to indicate each one.

I list my findings as follows:

[10] Quite a few drinks for a known near-teetotaler.

[11] The Judge struck John Farrar's testimony from the record regarding air bubbles that came from the car after it was overturned to tow it back to the shore. Through no fault of the Judge; Jon Ahlbum, the tow truck operator was waiting at the Inquest to be called to testify about air bubbles; Dinis didn't call him.

I. The decedent is Mary Jo Kopechne, 28 years of age, last resident in Washington D.C.

II. Death probably occurred between 11:30 P.M. on July 18, 1969 and 1:00 A.M. on July 19, 1969. [Emphasis Added.]

III. Death was caused **by drowning** in Poucha Pond at Dyke Bridge on Chappaquiddick Island in the Town of Edgartown, Massachusetts when a motor vehicle in which the decedent was a passenger, went off Dyke Bridge, overturned and was immersed in Poucha Pond. The motor vehicle was owned and operated by Edward M. Kennedy, Massachusetts. [Emphasis Added.]

The statute states that I must report the name of any person whose unlawful act or negligence **appears** to have contributed to Kopechne's death. As I stated at the commencement of the Hearing, the Massachusetts Supreme Court said in its decision concerning the conduct of this Inquest "the Inquest serves as an aid in the achievement of justice by obtaining information as to whether a crime has been committed." in *LaChappelle vs. United Shore Machinery Corporation*, 318 Mass. 166, decided in 1945, the same Court said "It is designed merely to ascertain facts for the purpose of subsequent prosecution" and "... the investigating judge **may himself**[12] issue process against a person whose **probable guilt** is disclosed. [Emphasis Added.]

Therefore, in guiding myself as to the proof herein required of the commission of any unlawful act, I **reject** the cardinal principle of **"proof beyond a reasonable doubt"** applied in criminal trials but use as a standard the principle of **"probable guilt."** [Emphasis Added.]

---

[12] The "may" he refers to is found in only one case, and was mentioned only once in passing. The requirement is *must*.

I have also used the rule, applicable to trials,[13] which permits me to draw inferences, known as presumption of facts, from the testimony. There are several definitions and I quote from the case of *Commonwealth vs. Green*, 295 Pa. 573: "A presumption of fact is an inference which a reasonable man would draw from certain facts which have been proven. The basis is in logic and its source is probability." Volume 29 American Jurisprudence 2nd Evidence Section 161 states in part, "A presumption of fact or an inference is nothing more than a probable or natural explanation of facts . . . and arises from the commonly accepted experiences of mankind and the inferences which reasonable men would draw from experiences."

I find these facts:

A. Kennedy was the host and mainly responsible for the assembly of the group at Edgartown.

B. Kennedy was rooming at Shiretown with Gargan, his cousin and close friend of many years.

C. Kennedy had employed Crimmins as chauffeur for nine years and rarely drove himself. Crimmins drove Kennedy on all other occasions herein set forth, and was available at the time of the fatal trip.

D. Kennedy told **only** Crimmins that he was leaving for Shiretown and requested the car key.

E. The young women were close friends, were on Martha's Vineyard for a common purpose as a cohesive group, and staying together at Katama Shores.

---

[13] Here he uses the rule "applicable to trials" but rejects the cardinal principle "applied in criminal trials" which he used in the preceding sentence.

F. Kopechne roomed with Newberg, the latter having in her possession the key to their room.

G. Kopechne told **no one**, other than Kennedy that she was leaving for Katama Shores and did not ask Newberg for the room key.

H. Kopechne left her pocketbook at the Cottage when she drove off with Kennedy.

I. It was known that the ferry ceased operation about midnight and special arrangements must be made for a later trip. No such arrangements were made.[14]

J. Ten of the persons at the cook-out did **not** intend to remain at the Cottage overnight.

K. Only the Oldsmobile and the Valiant were available for transportation of those ten, the Valiant being the smaller car.

L. LaRosa's Mercury was parked at Shiretown and was available for use.

I infer a reasonable and probable explanation of the totality of the above facts is that Kennedy and Kopechne did **not** intend to return to Edgartown at that time; that Kennedy did **not** intend to drive to the ferry slip and his turn onto Dyke Road was intentional.[15] Having reached this conclusion, the question then arises as to whether there was anything criminal in his operation of the motor vehicle. [Emphasis Added.]

From two personal views, which corroborate the Engineer's statement (Exhibit 29), and other evidence, I am fully convinced that Dyke Bridge constitutes a traffic hazard, particular-

---

[14] The ferry was *always* on call. Jared Grant's home phone number was posted at the ferry, specifically for late trips.

[15] Apparently perjury was not on the Judge's mind.

ly so at night, and must be approached with extreme caution. **A speed of even twenty miles per hour, as Kennedy testified to, operating a car as large as this Oldsmobile, would at least be negligent and, possibly, reckless. If Kennedy knew of this hazard, his operation of the vehicle constituted criminal conduct.** [Emphasis Added.]

Earlier on July 18, he had been driven over Chappaquid-dick Road three times, and over **Dyke Road and Dyke Bridge twice.** Kopechne had been driven over Chappaquiddick Road five times and over Dyke Road and Dyke Bridge twice. [Emphasis Added.]

I believe it probable that **Kennedy knew of the hazard** that lay ahead of him on Dyke Road but that, for some reason not apparent from the testimony, he failed to exercise due care as he approached the bridge. [Emphasis Added.]

IV. I therefore, find there is probable cause to believe that Edward M. Kennedy operated his motor vehicle **negligently on a way or in a place to which the public have a right of access and that such operation appears to have contributed to the death of Mary Jo Kopechne.** [Emphasis Added.]

February 18, 1970

JAMES A. BOYLE
JUSTICE

The Judge had spoken. After reading the foregoing, let us take a creative leap; it is not too unrealistic to imagine the following monologue taking place in Judge Boyle's mind as he wrote his report and contemplated actions:

I'm going to say he was guilty, and I'm going to retire. I don't want my pension — my life — interfered with. You prosecute him — I'll say he was guilty — that satisfies my conscience — I'm not a prosecutor — I'm a court clerk that was made a small town judge — I worked hard all my life — I want to finish it playing golf. Period. Leave me alone!

With respect to Judge Boyle, who went along to get along, the fact is that he did publish an in-depth reporting of the alleged facts. This chronological account, as above, is in fact a direct result of the testimony and facts that Senator Kennedy's lawyers controlled and wanted placed in the public record. Certain other evidence was either not allowed or stricken. Despite these shortcomings and frankly human behavior on the part of Judge Boyle, and even though he didn't *do* anything, we must remember the very importance of his findings. They were significant to the point that on the very day they were announced Senator Kennedy spoke out from Washington, stating that he "rejected...." the Judge's findings.

Frankly it is hoped here that the Senator might so "reject" the findings of this book that he summon it to court. The legal process allowing for discovery and depositions would prove enlightening. Furthermore, a judge outside of the Massachusetts jurisdiction might allow certain questions, as raised herein, to be asked under oath of parties who certainly have answers that we have not heretofore seen publicly.

Digressions aside, regardless of the fact that neither the Judge nor his minions followed up with formal criminal charges based on the Judge's findings, Judge Boyle said it all, and without bringing formal charges by his own writ, he strongly indicted the Senator by stating that he was guilty of negligence, and (as we have had a cram course on certain Massachusetts law herein), we know that because he left the scene a charge of manslaughter would have been appropriately and legitimately brought forward. In fact, certain statutes were violated by the responsible parties, i.e., the Judge and local prosecutors, in not bringing forward the criminal charges based on the finding of negligence. This was not to be, but in the Court of Public Opinion, the last words here belong to Judge Boyle:

"A speed of even twenty miles per hour, as Kennedy testified to, operating a car as large as this Oldsmobile, would at least be negligent and, possibly, reckless. If Kennedy knew of this hazard, his operation of the vehicle constituted criminal conduct."

and, to repeat:

"I therefore, find there is probable cause to believe that Edward M. Kennedy operated his motor vehicle negligently on a way or in a place to which the public have a right of access and that such operation appears to have contributed to the death of Mary Jo Kopechne."

PART TWO

THE HIDDEN FACTS

For the greatest enemy of the truth is very often not the lie — deliberate, contrived, and dishonest — but the myth — persistent, persuasive, and unrealistic.

John Fitzgerald Kennedy, June 11, 1962

10

THE KEY

In the preceding nine chapters, the public record has been presented in some detail. In this chapter the focus will tighten on two factors which are crucial to understanding what really happened and, therefore, why this tragedy won't go away. Indeed, *what* was hidden away and *why* the truth hasn't surfaced before. The first important factor is the previously mentioned but unexplained blood found on Mary Jo's blouse. The second salient factor is that Mary Jo's body *did not sink* after its alleged drowning. In order to shed light on Senator Kennedy's allegation that he, in fact, drove the car into the water and that he and his associates dove to the car attempting to save Mary Jo, it is essential to analyze in detail the facts surrounding the bloodstains and the body's buoyancy.

A thorough reading of the germane testimony at the Hearing for Exhumation and Autopsy clearly shows that not one of the individuals who viewed or handled Mary Jo's clothing at the scene observed any bloodstains. Yet, the testimony of Melvin Topjian, chemist, who testified (presented above) at that Hearing indicated a positive identification of blood found on Mary Jo's blouse.

Topjian's boss, Dr. John J. McHugh, Supervisor of the Laboratory of the Department of Public Safety, Commonwealth of Massachusetts, also indicated that blood was present on the back of her blouse. In testimony at the Inquest, Dr. McHugh stated:

Mr. Fernandes: What tests did you perform on these clothings?

Dr. McHugh: There were a series of tests. First of all I was not present in the laboratory when the clothing first was received, so Mr. Topjian had run a series of preliminary benzidine tests on this material.

Q. Would you instruct the Court as to what is this benzidine test?

A. A test that indicates the presence of blood on the material. This test had shown positive over certain areas of the submitted white shirt.

Q. Could you tell us, and if you would examine the shirt and point to those areas so the Court is informed where on the shirt?

A. Yes, sir.

The Court: I think for the record you ought to state where it is, such as the back of the neck or the inside or something of that kind.

Witness: If I might, I have it noted here. Let's see. Yes, sir. To continue on gross examination of this item under visible and ultraviolet light disclosed the presence of reddish brown and brown washed-out stains principally on the back and left sleeve surfaces. Most of these stains gave positive benzidine reaction indicating the presence of residual traces of blood.

Q. Would you point to those areas now?

A. This would be the back of the shirt, this whole area in here gave positive benzidine tests. (Indicating.) To continue, the back of both sleeves and the back of the right sleeve of the submitted shirt reacted positive, right sleeve in particular reacted positive to the benzidine test. It is the back of these two sleeves extending down here. (Indicating.) Unusually strong benzidine tests were obtained on the outside rear collar areas of this shirt. That would be along this area right in here. (Indicating.)

Examine the artist's interpretation of McHugh's testimony in the illustration of Mary Jo's blouse in the Photo Section.

There has been speculation, notably in Thomas and Richard Tedrow's book *Death At Chappaquiddick,* that these residual stains could have indicated a substance other than blood. In fact, the benzidine test can be used to determine the presence of many substances: citrus fruits, some non-citrus fruits, many vegetables, some chemicals, oxidants, paints, green leaves and *ordinary grass.* However, the Tedrows' titillating conclusion that the stains were from, "...lying or leaning back onto grass or other greenery...." ignores two crucial specifics in the methodology of the laboratory experts.

The observation of "reddish-brown" stains under ultraviolet light is not observation of *greenish-brown* as it would be with stains set by a chlorophyll-based substance, "grass or other greenery." The Tedrows' licentiously ignore this aspect of the evidence in their attempt to paint the Senator and Mary Jo into some ignoble glen, some trysting place.

In this case there simply is no *evidence* that Ted Kennedy and Mary Jo Kopechne ever got past a handshake. Their ultimate intentions that night are subject to some speculation in that Mary Jo left her purse, which contained her motel key, cash, credit cards and airplane ticket back at the cottage. Surely, if this well-organized person had intended to go back to her hotel, she would have taken her purse. Now, if she were drunk, she might have forgotten the purse. An invitation for a drive with the Senator would certainly not have been refused. Finally, it is not at all unlikely that he might have merely wished to confidentially discuss political or family business with her away from the party. It was Mary Jo that Bobby Kennedy and Ted Sorensen summoned to Hickory Hill the night that Bobby's famous out-of-Vietnam speech was written. She was more than a typist. She was a professional election specialist.

The second specific factor regarding the discovered blood stains relates to the method in which the benzidine test is applied. Professor Paul Kirk is the author of *Crime Investigation,*

Physical Evidence and the Police Laboratory, a book which is widely used by police departments and the courts. According to the Tedrows, Kirk's book makes it clear that "such testing requires close attention to the **speed of color reaction development,** color clarity, local or spotty results and any abnormalities in color reaction experience." (Emphasis added.) The point is, that it takes experience working with benzidine to make correct interpretation.

Attorney Joseph Flanagan, representing the Kopechne family at the Hearing, closely cross-examined Mr. Topjian in the apparent hope of impeaching his credibility as an expert witness and, therefore, his testimony. One wonders why this high-priced attorney, contacted initially by Kennedy people on behalf of the Kopechnes, was so well prepared concerning the technical aspects of blood determination. The answer comes immediately: an autopsy was to be avoided at all cost. As we saw in Chapter 6, it was ultimately Kennedy money that brought Flanagan to this Hearing. Unfortunately for Attorney Flanagan, but fortuitous for the discovery of the truth, the answers he received did not impeach the witness. On the contrary, Topjian demonstrated conclusively that he was aware of all the technical requirements in benzidine testing and that he had performed the tests in such a way as to positively indicate blood.

FLANAGAN: Then it is not a conclusive test to determine whether blood is present.

TOPJIAN: In my opinion it can be used as a conclusive test as whether blood is present or not, sir.

Q. Isn't it true that there are other substances that would give the same reaction to the benzidine test?

A. Not under the circumstances in which the test can be performed.

Q. In what manner would other agents react differently to the test?

A. There's a time element involved in the test, sir. The blood reacts much more rapidly than those interfering agents, sir.

Q. What is the time element?

A. The blood will react within a few seconds, the interfering agents will take a longer period of time.

Q. What were your test results with respect to the time period?

A. They were rapid, sir.

Q. Will not potato juice react as rapidly?

A. Not in the same period of time, sir, no.

A few moments later, in redirect examination by Assistant District Attorney Fernandes, the point was nailed down. Fernandes drew out from Topjian that the manner and method in which the tests were conducted "would identify the presence or absence of interfering substances, sir." In other words the chemist had used a methodology that clearly and specifically indicated bloodstains and not "interfering substances."

The fact that we have established beyond a reasonable doubt that there was blood on Mary Jo's blouse is crucial, and in fact the key to unlocking the mystery of what really happened at Chappaquiddick.

Where did the blood come from? It is extremely unlikely that she exuded sufficient amounts of blood (from her mouth and nostrils) to cause the aggregate stains that were found. (See illustration, Photo Section.) There is little doubt that the tide-moved waters swirling in the car would have simply washed any foam (assuming the logic of the medical experts from the exhumation and autopsy Hearing) away before it could have flowed down the back of her blouse and coagulated in the form

of discernable blood stains. Her body was found upright. Therefore, just as likely, blood which came from her mouth or nose
would have been found on the *front* of her blouse. The blood
stains were confined to the back of her blouse!

In order for the blood stains to set, there would have to
have been a significant flow of blood, not merely foam. Mary Jo
could possibly have been cut on the car's entry/impact to the
water. Yet, simultaneously, the water poured rapidly into the car.
Consequently, any blood from a cut at the time of impact would
have quickly washed away — it would not have had time to set
in the blouse. Further, any cuts on her back or her neck would
have been noticed by Dr. Mills, or the undertakers when they
washed her body to prepare it for embalming. The point here is
to show by logical deduction that the blood *could only* have
been introduced before the car entered the water.

However, if Mary Jo had received an accidental blow to the
back of the head *before* the car entered the water, that would
explain everything. The physical laceration of such a blow could
have easily been missed in the tangle of wet hair. Because of
her *rigor mortis* set forearms which stuck out at a right angle to
her body, Dr. Mills could not turn the body completely over, and
did not examine the back of her head in his eight-to-ten minute
examination. He only rolled the body on its side and ran his
"fingers through her hair." The salt water in which she was
immersed would have closed a wound that was, further, covered
by her hair. The undertakers washed her hair but made no
remarks in testimony that indicated whether or not they examined her head. That was not their job. That would have been
part of the job of an autopsy which, under the circumstances,
should have been performed and which might have resolved this
mystery.

So here we see that an exhumation and autopsy, which the
Senator's people fought so hard (and so successfully) to prevent,
could well have revealed a fractured skull or a recently closed
head wound. When we look at this hypothesis in light of the
blood found on her blouse, it becomes obvious why the Sen-

ator's people, including Cardinal Cushing, were enlisted to make certain that Mary Jo rested in peace.

However, there is more to this aspect of blood. The following testimonies are highly significant when read in relation to the inference made above. Senator Kennedy himself was the only direct participant to voluntarily introduce testimony regarding blood into the Inquest. Highly suspect is the fact that Kennedy introduced Joe Gargan's alleged free-flowing blood into the car. The following question was asked by D.A. Dinis of the Senator:

Dinis: And were they (Markham and Gargan) unsuc-
            cessful in entering the car?

Kennedy: Well, Mr. Gargan got halfway in the car. When
            he came out he was scraped all the way from
            his elbow, underneath his arm was all bruised
            and **bloodied**, and *this one time* he was able to
            gain entrance into the car itself. [Emphasis
            Added.]

It is worth calling attention to the fact that moments after this gratuitous volunteering of bloody detail by the Senator, literally four benign questions later the Senator became agitated, angry and in fact sarcastic; stating, *"Well, Mr. District Attorney...."*

It is not common for a witness (especially a United States Senator) to take this tone with a D.A., who in this case had in fact already changed the subject from the *"bloodied"* Joe Gargan and was merely asking some innocuous questions relating to the length of time Mary Jo had been in the car. In fact, as we have seen, the Inquest recessed briefly at this point, and the Senator was removed from the courtroom by his attorneys for a few minutes, presumably so he could regain his composure. The conclusion drawn is that it was, in fact, Kennedy's testimony regarding free-flowing blood that upset him to the point that he reacted emotionally to the District Attorney's questioning.

Joe Gargan is Ted Kennedy's cousin. Joe's mother was Rose Kennedy's sister, and the two boys spent many of their summers together, with Gargan acting as older brother and gate keeper. Joe's parents died when he was very young. Gargan is one of those "Kennedys" who have different last names. It is entirely appropriate to seriously consider and speculate on why Kennedy felt the need to gratuitously mention Gargan's being "bloodied," and then to, specifically testify that the "bloodied arm" had been inside the car.[1]

Gargan's remarks under oath when asked by D.A. Dinis "What injuries did you sustain?" did not mention blood at all. He replied, "My chest, my arm and my back was badly scraped."

He was well-educated at Notre Dame, and an attorney by training. He was the vice-president of a local Hyannis Port bank at the time of the tragedy. Gargan knew full well that others observed his unmarked arms after the accident. More important, he did not state under oath that he had been bleeding. It was Kennedy who spoke of Joe Gargan's "bloodied" arm. What Senator Kennedy had to do was something he couldn't really ask anyone else to do. He got free-flowing blood into the car!

Yet, in all fairness to the record and the Kennedy people, this theory as put forth here has recently been contradicted. Leo Damore claims that Gargan told him that David Burke, Kennedy's administrative assistant at the time and now President of CBS News, suggested that Gargan have the "deep scratches on his chest and upper arms" photographed as "evidence" that he had attempted to get into the car.[2] Gargan said that he dispensed with the idea in that he was merely a witness.

Paul Markham, the other alleged diver, who was questioned by both Dinis and Fernandes, was never asked about injuries to Gargan, but he did allow that he himself had banged up an old injury and that his leg was "throbbing" too badly for him to attempt to swim over to Edgartown around 2:00 A.M. to see whether the Senator had managed to swim safely across and

---

[1]   Gargan in his 1983 *mea culpa* interview with Leo Damore stated that he was cut on the way out of the car. Kennedy's implication had been clearly that Gargan was cut and bled *in the car*.

[2]   Damore, p. 111.

report the accident. Curiously, only a few "nearly sleepless" hours later, and after "sleeping" in the small cramped Valiant, by 8:30 A.M. Markham had no limp at all. Markham allegedly talked to Edward Harrington who talked to Damore, January 11, 1984. Damore reported:[3]

> In pain, unable to sleep, Markham walked out into the sultry darkness. He came back inside to sit in a rocking chair in front of the fireplace. He went outside again, stretching out on the back seat of the Valiant to try to get some sleep. It was dawn when Markham came back into the cottage.

Clearly even at this late date ('84) Markham continues to provide an alibi as to why he didn't spend the entire night inside the cottage. It is of more than passing interest that in twenty years this is all that he has ever said on the incident; and his actions are crucial to what follows.

Most damning to Kennedy regarding his reference to the "bloodied" Joe Gargan is the following testimony taken from the Inquest. Interestingly, in all cases the questioner regarding the "bloodied" Gargan was Armand Fernandes, the Assistant District Attorney. For some reason D.A. Dinis was either too deep in the trees to see the point or, worse, didn't want to know about blood at this late date. Pertinent individuals who were not asked about Gargan's alleged wounds were those examined exclusively by Dinis.

ARMAND FERNANDES, Assistant District Attorney:
Q. All right now, we are back at the Police Station. Now, when you saw Mr. Markham and Mr. Gargan were there. Did you have occasion to observe these two men?

GEORGE KENNEDY, Supervisor of the Registry of Motor Vehicles:
A. I did.

3 Damore, p. 86.

Q. Were you in close proximity to Mr. Gargan?

A. I was.

Q. Would you tell us what he was wearing as you remember?

A. He was wearing a chino pair of pants and a short t-shirt, sport shirt.

Q. Did you have occasion to see his arms?.

A. I did.

Q. Did you observe any marks?

A. **I did not.** [Emphasis Added.]

Q. Did you have occasion to watch them walk and move around?

A. I did.

Q. Did you make any observations as to limping or any sign of injury on anyone?

A. No limping on anybody.

.....

FERNANDES:
Q. In your observation of Mr. Kennedy did you make note of any injuries or bruises?

JIM ARENA, Chief of Police:
A. No injuries. He just appeared to be very depressed mentally, but I noticed no physical injuries.

Q. To Mr. Markham?

A. No Sir.

Q. To Mr. Gargan?

A. No Sir.

.....

FERNANDES:
Q. During any of the time that you have mentioned [in the morning following the accident] did you observe any injuries that he [Gargan] had received?

ESTHER NEWBERG, [party participant]:
A. No.

Q. Was there any mention by anyone that he had received injuries in any manner at that time?

A. No.

.....

FERNANDES:
Q. Did you make any observations with reference to injuries?

ANN LYONS, [party participant]:
A. When Mr. Markham came to pick us up?

Q. At any time.

A. Well, it was fairly obvious when he came to pick us up in the morning that something had transpired by the expression on his face.

Q. Of injuries to him?

A. No Sir.

Q. In your observations of Mr. Markham that morning and Mr. Gargan that morning and on the day that you discovered Mary Jo's death, did you observe any injuries to Mr. Gargan?

A. No Sir.

There it is! It seems that Kennedy was lying, or these other individuals are blind. In the case of George Kennedy, it must be noted that he was on the scene for the express purpose of investigating the accident, and he clearly noted that Gargan did not have any observable bruises, scrapes or cuts.

The question is simple: Why did Kennedy introduce the idea of blood? The answer is just as simple. He felt the need to explain the presence of free-flowing blood in that automobile. Why? This writer is convinced it is because he knew that there was blood in the automobile before it entered the water.

Kennedy reacted predictably to this specter of blood. He commented, "I would say to those who tend to look for things in this case are going to be disappointed."[4] His office got on the record in this story by stating that a pathologist had said that when Mary Jo was pulled out of the car she could have been scraped (just like bloody Joe Gargan), and this "could have caused an oozing of blood." Of course they forget that no one saw this "oozing of blood." Even attorney Flanagan got into the act. He "suggested blood might have resulted from slivers of shattered glass puncturing the skin during the accident."[5]

Even at that late date, a real investigation by real investigators might have discovered blood on the car seats as well as on Mary Jo's blouse. The state laboratory experts could have applied the benzidine test to the car seats in the interval between the Hearing for Exhumation and Autopsy and the Inquest. Kennedy had no knowledge as to whether that had happened, but he was not about to be surprised by the introduction

---

4   *New Bedford Standard Times*, 9-19-69.
5   Damore, p. 306.

of bloody seats at the Inquest. Thus, by placing blood in the record before it was mentioned by anyone else, he explained its presence in advance. He knew there had been blood in the car. He and his lawyers could reasonably surmise that the State medical investigators might also find it. A trial attorney wants no surprises. Ultimately, they did find some blood. McHugh spoke to Damore on September 7, 1983, telling him, "The trouble was, everyone had been in that car; they'd stripped everything off. Somebody had taken the radio, *somebody else had cut himself.* There was **fresh blood** on the backseat. Obviously, there wouldn't be blood after the car was immersed." [Emphasis Added.]

How careless of someone to have accidentally cut themselves, placing fresh blood on the backseat. Fresh blood, would have created havoc, perhaps even impeached the validity of a benzidine test applied to the seats!

While none of the previously published works have delved so deeply, dealt with the specifics and ramifications of this blood business, the closer we look in this area, the more we realize that the white-wash, the cover-up, was designed to cover a very small amount of blood that in this case carries the force of a blood bath.

In Chapter 6, the record regarding the question of drowning was presented at length. Conclusions will be drawn below.

Various experts testified on the record. Additional remarks and opinions have also been presented in numerous publications. At the Hearing for Exhumation and Autopsy, the Kennedy-Kopechne legal team and their expert witnesses attempted to show that an autopsy would not be essential to a definitive determination of death by drowning. Given the expert witnesses then presented by Dinis *et al.*, the ensuing debate by opposing expert witnesses could leave the lay-person thoroughly confused. Final conclusions and considered determinations now become subject to interpretation of newly emerging facts.

So what is the answer? How can we reach the seemingly contradicted, even obscured truth? The conclusive answer can only be found off the record. It is clear that the automobile exuded air bubbles when it was turned over to tow it out of the water. The air bubbles of course prove that air had been trapped in the car. Jon Ahlbum, the owner of the Edgartown Depot Garage who supervised the removal of the auto from the water, was present and prepared to testify at the Inquest that he had observed the escaping air bubbles. His observations were significant, crucial even. He was at the courthouse waiting to be called at the Inquest. He was never called.

Judge Boyle's final report on the Inquest stated, "there is no evidence that any air remained in the immersed car." Farrar stated to investigator Robert Cutler in 1971 that "the stenographer's tape was torn up when Boyle ordered most of the testimony [Farrar's] about bubbles bursting around the car stricken from the record...." Boyle eliminated from the record, testimony he didn't want to have heard and didn't have to hear (thanks to Dinis not calling Ahlbum) testimony he was able to avoid. But then Boyle's inexplicable conduct has already been discussed.

Let the air bubbles disintegrate.

Let go of Gene Frieh's (the undertaker) remark under oath regarding the water in Miss Kopechne's body "I did raise my eyebrows, sir, in the sense that I expected much more moisture."

Let the fact go that Chief Arena did not have to pull on the rope to bring her to the surface. As John Farrar has stated, she virtually floated when she came to the surface with him. That, therefore, she could not have been full of water.

Let go of John Farrar's comments to Ron Rosenbaum, an ESQUIRE magazine writer:[6]

> "She didn't drown. That's the point. She died of suffocation in her own air void. Gene Frieh, the undertaker, has said to me and said to others that he feels she did not drown but died of suffocation in her own air void. He's done twenty-four embalmings of drown victims and in every case they've been filled with water. Full of water from their asshole to their appetites

6   Sherrill, p. 97.

as Gene Frieh puts it. But Gene found about a half a teacup
in her. Half a teacup, that's all. She suffocated to death. But it
took her at least three or four hours to die. I could have had
her out of that car twenty-five minutes after I got the call. But
he didn't call."

Let all of these statements and facts go. They are significant,
they *point to the truth*; that Mary Jo did not drown, but they do
not *prove* she didn't drown.

In fact, an autopsy would not necessarily have *proved* whether she did or did not drown because expert witnesses can always
be produced to state under oath that the same facts can lead to
a different interpretation, a different conclusion or even that
other factors might have caused death. But here we get closer to
the point. If she had been dead *before* the car entered the
water, her body could not have filled with water as is consistent
with "normal" drowning. If she had already been dead, her lungs
would not have filled with water in the involuntary cycle of
pulling in oxygen.

She was not dead before the car entered the water. Proof of
that is the macabre, *rigor-mortised* condition (clawed hands,
tightly gripping the edge of the back seat which aided her in
holding her head up in the now upside-down foot-well of the
auto) of her arms, and the fact that her body was found in the
uppermost portion of the upside-down automobile. This fact
leads us precisely to the truth. She lived and breathed in that
airpocket, and she positioned her body and head in such a way
as to maximize her access to the air that remained trapped in
the car. Finally, she did live for a time in the car, and then
succumbed to asphyxiation by breathing her own expelled carbon
dioxide after her air pocket ran out of oxygen. Consequently,
her body did not fill up with water as in a normal drowning.

Undertaker Frieh testified at the autopsy Hearing that "I did
raise my eyebrows, sir, in the sense that I expected much more
moisture." He had applied pressure to her abdominal area with
a device called a "body block" and he said, "From our abdominal
compression on this body block there was this slight bit of

moisture, but very slight, and a slight bit of froth about the nasal area and it was of a pinkish hue."

The final conclusion regarding drowning can and should be drawn from John Farrar, who brought Mary Jo's body out of the car and to the surface.

He claims he brought her body "down (from the top of the car) and out," — and at that point it "virtually floated" upward to the surface. It is a well-known fact that bodies that drown, *sink for 72 to 100 hours before becoming buoyant.* Water intake is measured in quarts and gallons from a person who has drowned and then sunk, not "*half a teacup.*"

Mary Jo's body did not sink to the bottom of the car. Mary Jo did not drown! Mary Jo's blouse had blood stains that could have only set *before* the car entered the water!

The question becomes, if she had the presence of mind to position herself in an airpocket, why didn't she reach out to the window (only 18 inches away, the length of her forearm) pull herself out and swim to the surface? The fact that her clawed hands clutched the seat proves that she positioned herself — she didn't simply float into this position. She moved, she acted.

It is posited here that she was unable to react because she was unconscious when the car plunged into the water, and her reactions came from the deep instinct for survival. Her body with its natural buoyancy, floated upward to the air pocket. The shock of rushing water may have brought her to a semi-conscious state, and then instinctively, to survive, to keep herself in that air pocket, she used her hands and arms to hold herself in the position in which she was found. The sheer panic she must have been under might have limited her cognitive abilities (i.e., figuring out how to escape) and kept her reactions to primal, instinctual ones — therefore the fixed and undoubtedly terrified position she was found in. The following chapter will show that prior to the time that the car entered the water she had sustained an accidental blow to the back of her head. The blow rendered her unconscious, put her into a coma and was also the cause of the blood which was later found on her blouse.

After the car entered the water, she remained alive. Instinct alone caused her to hold herself in the top of the overturned car. She was left alone; no attempts were made to rescue her. Not fully conscious, she was not able to save herself. In spite of stories about rescue efforts, she was left alone. If these rescue efforts had been real, and Mr. Gargan had made it "halfway" into the car, and "scraped his back and chest" and "bloodied" his arm; how is it that he did not find her body which, according to the skindiver, was only eighteen inches in the interior of the car? That's indeed where Farrar found the body the next morning!

11

THE PLUNGE

In order to prove that the automobile was not driven into the water as claimed by Senator Kennedy, its essential to quote, once again, from Judge Boyle's Report:

> Christopher F. Look, Jr., a deputy sheriff then living on Chappaquiddick, was driving easterly on Chappaquiddick Road to his home about 12:45 A.M. on July 19. As he approached the junction of Dyke Road, a car crossed in front of him and entered Cemetery Road, stopped, backed up, and drove easterly on Dyke Road. He saw two persons in the front seat, a shadow on the shelf back of the rear seat which he thought could have been a bag, article of clothing, or a third person. The car was dark colored with Massachusetts registration plate L7-7. He was unable to remember any other numbers or how many there were intervening. Later that morning, he saw the Kennedy Oldsmobile when it was towed to shore, but he cannot positively identify it as the same car he saw at 12:45 A.M. During the Inquest, a preliminary investigation was initiated through the Registry of Motor Vehicles to determine whether a tracking of the location on July 18 and 19, 1969, of all dark colored cars bearing the Massachusetts plates with any and all combinations of numbers beginning with L7 and ending in 7, would be practicable. The attempt disclosed that it would not be feasible to do this since there would be no assurance that the end result would be helpful and, in any event, the elimination of all other cars within that registration group (although it would seriously affect the credibility of some of the witnesses) would not alter the findings in this report."

Judge Boyle gave short shrift to Deputy Sheriff Look's observations and testimony. In fact, Boyle took over the questioning from the prosecutor and judging from the tone of the questions [below], it appears that he successfully railroaded the sincere and strictly honest Deputy Sheriff Look. At the very least, Judge Boyle's conduct carries the appearance of judicial misconduct in that he aggressively *limited* testimony to certain information that he had seemingly predetermined to be essential to the record, if he was to carry out his personal agenda on the case. It is the duty and function of the lower court to attempt to build as complete a record of the facts as possible.

It is Deputy Sheriff Look's sighting of the Kennedy Oldsmobile at approximately 12:45 A.M. that is the most damning evidence in invalidating the Kennedy timetable for the events that night and early in the morning.

Now we will look closely at Deputy Sheriff Christopher (Huck) Look. In 1969, good-natured Huck Look was 41 years of age. He had an impressive background in both law enforcement and the military. He had served for fifteen years as a Deputy Sheriff for Dukes County. He was, at the time, a special officer for Chief Jim Arena, a special officer for the Edgartown Park Department and had formerly been a Lieutenant in the Edgartown Fire Department. He had resigned from the Fire Department only because his private fuel oil business began selling fuel to the Department. He wouldn't involve himself in a situation which had so much as the appearance of a conflict of interest.

Descendants of the famous Captain John Paul Jones, his ancestors had lived on the Island for more than 300 years. In the military he had served in Korea as a Sergeant First Class. Politically, he was a long-time Democrat and was known to be an admirer of the Kennedy family. He was a big man, standing 6'2" and weighing 235 pounds. He was a good student in high school on Martha's Vineyard and a star basketball player. His jersey had carried the number 7, and he considered that his good luck number, which is why he was angry that the Judge implied that he could have been wrong about the two 7's he remembered from the license plate he saw that night.

After the tragedy at Chappaquiddick, where he and his family kept a summer cottage (their home was in Edgartown proper), the people of Martha's Vineyard voted him Sheriff. He holds that job to this day. The votes of the locals were obviously a testament to his credibility. In other words, we can easily say that the public Deputy Sheriff Look was a good man and known to be scrupulously honest in deed and intent. Edward Hanify hoped that Look wasn't so respectable, and hired a private detective agency to check him out.

"Investigators for Kennedy were knocking on doors all over Edgartown asking old ladies if I get drunk or run around with women. Well, everybody knows that I don't. But even if I did, that wouldn't change what I saw."[1]

On the night of the accident he had been working as a private security guard, wearing the shirt of his Deputy Sheriff's uniform, at the Edgartown Yacht Club Regatta party. It was his presence alone that generally kept order at these annual soirees. This year the Friday-night welcoming party had been unusually sedate, and in fact ended a few minutes before 12:30 A.M.

The manager of the Yacht Club gave Look a ride over to the Chappaquiddick side at approximately 12:31 A.M., in the Yacht Club's launch. Look entered his car at about 12:39 and began the ten-minute drive to his summer cottage where his wife awaited him. As he drove down Main Street a series of unusual events occurred; we'll hear about them from Sheriff Look, in his own words from his testimony at the Hearing for Exhumation and Autopsy in Pennsylvania:

Dinis: Now at some time on your way back to your home, was your attention diverted?

Look: Yes, sir.

Q. Will you tell the court what you saw?

---

[1]   *Boston Globe*, 10-29-74.

A. I saw the headlights of an automobile approaching me on Chappaquiddick Road, and knowing the road, I slowed down, because there is a sharp corner back to the ferry and usually people will turn and cut the corner too close. I wanted to make sure this didn't happen to me. So I came almost to a complete stop, and the car passed right in front of me, about 25 or 30 feet away — a black car.

Q. Did you observe how many persons were in that automobile?

A. There was a man driving, a woman in the front seat, and either another person or some clothing, a sweater or a pocketbook or something in the back seat; what appeared to be a shadow of some kind.

Q. Did you see anything further when this car approached?

A. Yes, sir.

Q. What?

A. It passed in front of me and went into what we call Cemetery Road, maybe 10 or 15 feet. By this time I had proceeded around the corner a little bit and was approximately 30 feet away. I saw through my rear window that the car was backing up. I thought they wanted information, or were lost or something. I got out of my automobile and started to walk towards them. As I got to approximately 25 or 30 feet away; the car backing up towards me and the tail lights showing all over my uniform, I started to ask, but the car took off towards Dyke Bridge.

Q. Will you tell the court what time this happened to you?

A. It was approximately 12:40 to 12:45 A.M.

Q. Did you make any observations as to the registration of that car?

A. Well, I did make a sort of photographic thing in my mind that it had a seven.

Q. What did you do then, after the car drove down the Dyke Road?

A. I walked back and got into my car and proceeded towards my home. I met three people, two women and a man. One woman was tall and there was another shorter woman and the man was short, with curly hair. I stopped and asked if they would like a little lift. The tall girl said, "Shove off, buddy. We aren't pick-ups."

At the Inquest, some two months later, Assistant District Attorney Fernandes questioned Look, while Dinis remained silent:

Fernandes: Tell us exactly what you did. You stopped your car and you got out?

Look: I didn't stop it at first. I almost came to a stop and I saw the lights coming from the right-hand side which would be in the direction of the Fire Station, coming towards me, and I practically came to a complete stop because the automobiles when they make that large corner usually cut it very close and I was afraid I might run into him and the car passed directly in front of me about 35 feet away from my car, my headlights were on this car, and right across and then stopped. I continued around the corner and stopped and I noticed the car lights were backing up, and I said to myself, Well, they probably want some information; so I stopped my car and got out and started to walk back to them on Cemetery Road. I got about 25 or 30 feet when the car was backing up and backed towards the ferry landing on the macadamized road, and then it drove down the Dyke Road.

Q. Now at your closest point to this car how far were you from it, at it's closest point?"

A. Twenty-five or thirty feet.[2]

---

[2] A few moments later, Judge Boyle took over the questioning of Deputy Sheriff Look and the following exchange took place, which clearly indicates Judge Boyle's intimidating methods on the bench

The Court: I want to ask you about the car that came out of the water. You said, I think, that the night before you saw a dark colored car?

Witness: Yes.

The Court: You said as I understand it, that this car went by you and it was a dark colored car?

Witness: Yes, sir.

The Court: Could you be any more definite about its color other than it was a dark color?

Witness: No, sir, that it was either black or deep blue or dark -

The Court: Or a dark green, any dark color?

Witness: Yes, sir.

The Court: **You couldn't, then, identify it as being the same color?**

Witness: No, sir.

The Court: **Definitely as the car that you saw taken out of the water?**

Witness: No, sir.

The Court: And you recognized or you saw a letter, a seven, and then another seven at the end?

Witness: Yes, sir.

The Court: Do you remember how many numbers, letters and number there were on the plate?

Witness: Since that time —

The Court: No, no, I mean then.

Witness: No, sir.

The Court: Whether it was four numbers, five numbers, six numbers?

Witness: No, sir.

The Court: So that when you saw this number on this car that came out of the water, **you can't identify that as being the same identical number that you saw the previous night?**

Witness: No, sir.

The Court: **Well, you are unable to positively identify this car taken out of the water as the identical same car you saw the previous night?**

Witness: **In my opinion —**

The Court: No, I'm talking about the positive identification.

Witness: No, I can't.

The Court: You can't identify the exact color?

Witness: No, sir.

The Court: Or the exact number plate?

Witness: No, sir.

The Court: Now, I am speculating a bit, but it looks as though this car in the rear has, as many cars do, sort of a little shelf?

Witness: Yes, sir.

The Court: And I take it it was on that shelf where you saw what you thought might be a person or a bag or some clothing?

Witness: Clothing on that side of the car, yes, sir.

The Court: A sweater or clothing or a bag upon the seat, you wouldn't be able to see?

Witness: No, sir.

The Court: All right.

Fernandes: If your Honor please, I have no further questions of Mr. Look.

The Court: Thank you, Mr. Look. You are excused.

Witness: May I be excused?

The Court: Yes.

Witness: Thank you very much.

The Court: You are not to repeat your testimony to anybody until the case finally becomes public.

Witness: Yes, sir. [Emphasis Added Above.]

So, we can see the power of the Court bench controlling the proceedings and exacting the testimony it wants on the record. Let's go back in time to just after Look had spotted the car and the three individuals on the road. Sheriff Look continued on his way to his home and, when queried by his wife he said, "No, I'm not late," studying his watch, "it's only a couple of minutes to one." That sets the time clearly and involves a third party, his wife, who had nothing to do with the ensuing case.

The next morning he heard, through the local grapevine, about a car being in the water, and he arrived at the Bridge around 10:20 A.M. According to author Jack Olsen, Deputy

Sheriff Look was on the scene as the car emerged from the water, and the following dialogue transpired:[3]

"Holy Jesus!" said Look, and went over to Edgartown Patrolman Robert Bruguiere. "Gee, Bob," he said, "I saw that car last night."

"You did?" the summertime policeman said.

"Yes."

"Who was in it?"

"A man and a woman in the front seat and another person or some kind of object sticking up in the back."

Soon after this exchange Chief Arena arrived back at the scene and the patrolman reported Look's comments which led to a conversation between Look and Arena:

"The one you said that a man was driving?" Arena demanded.

"That's right," the deputy sheriff said. "It was about quarter to one in the morning."

Arena emitted a soft exclamation and climbed out of the car.

"Huck," he said, "do you know who the man was?"

"No," Look said, "I haven't the slightest idea."

"It was Ted Kennedy."

The deputy's first reaction was disbelief, but he knew Jim Arena well, and he could see that the chief was serious. "Holy Jesus," Look said facetiously. "I didn't see a thing!"

"Huck," the chief said, "how sure are you that this is the same car?"

"How sure am I? Look repeated. "**I'm positive. That's how sure I am.**" [Emphasis Added.]

[3] Olsen, p. 149-50.

Robert Sherrill's book went a little deeper into what went on at the time, with regard to the need of the Kennedy team to discredit Sheriff Look:[4]

"On the last day of the Inquest, Deputy Sheriff Look, the man who, by revealing that he had seen Kennedy's car about 12:45, heavily damaged Kennedy's claim to have left the party at 11:15, told newsmen, that Kennedy had spent thousands of dollars trying to discredit him. Look claimed that Kennedy had hired investigators who telephoned Look's friends and professional acquaintances all over the country to ask if he had to get married and whether his children used narcotics. Kennedy's staff denied the harassment."

This material above held up against Judge Boyle's terse evaluation of the Look testimony indicates that the Judge made a real effort to impeach Look's testimony — the only testimony with an alternative time sequence for the night — a time sequence that does in effect destroy the Kennedy version.

The automobile, a black, four-door, 1967 Oldsmobile 88, was registered to Edward M. Kennedy, whose address was listed as: 3 Charles River Square, Boston, Massachusetts. The license number was L78-207. This car, which had been of such concern to Senator Kennedy who hadn't wanted it *towed through town,* did become a matter of great interest. We shall see that the actual damage done to this car proves that the accident did not happen in the way the Senator claimed. According to Olsen:[5]

The wrecked Oldsmobile 88 had been towed to the Depot Corner Service Station, a few blocks from the center of Edgartown, and the workers at the station had spent the weekend chasing vandals. By late Monday afternoon an inspection showed what had been stolen: the gas cap, the chrome stripping, the Oldsmobile medallion, door locks and handles,

---

4   Sherrill, p. 149.
5   Olsen, p. 190.

armrests, dashboard knobs, windshield wipers, heater cowling, gas pedal pad, and the windshield visor.[6] There was a four-inch-wide gash in the windshield where souvenir hunters had nicked away at the glass. Jon Ahlbum surveyed the damage and ordered a tarpaulin put over the car. He lettered a sign:

TO PREVENT ANY FURTHER
VANDALISM TO THIS CAR WE
DECIDED TO COVER IT

WARNING

ANY FURTHER VANDALISM WILL
RESULT IN COURT ACTION

During the Inquest the press had been barred from the proceedings by the Massachusetts Supreme Court exclusion order, the "Kennedy Rule." With little else to go on, at one point the focus of the press swung briefly to the automobile. The *Boston Herald Tribune* reported on January 7, 1970, that the Massachusetts State Department of Public Safety Laboratory had brought, through the back entrance of the Courthouse, two doors from the Kennedy car. Both the State Police and the Arthur D. Little Company of Cambridge, Massachusetts had put the car through various tests. While these two doors had been produced, they were never mentioned in the Inquest transcript.

Zad Rust, author of *Teddy Bare,* revealed more information about the car door(s):[7]

The only interesting sight to which the newspaper men gathered at the doors of the Edgartown courthouse were treated, besides the corporate smile of the five eligible young girls, was the detached door of a car which could not have been anything

6   They fail to mention the driver's side rear-view mirror which also disappeared right away.
7   Rust, p. 218.

else than the left front door of the Kennedy Oldsmobile, brought there, presumably, as an important exhibit. It was, however, finally decided not to introduce the door into evidence in Court, and the opportunity was thereby lost to answer not for the Senator only, but also for the Court and millions of the Senator's fellow-citizens, the nagging question: Could the Senator, given his corpulence and the circumstances, have gotten out of the submerged car by the only exit available to him, this door's window?

According to the *New York Times*, in their 1980 series on Chappaquiddick, it was Assistant District Attorney Fernandes who had the door(s) brought to the Inquest, though they were never presented as evidence.

How fast was the car traveling when it plunged over the side of the bridge? It flew thirty-five feet in the air, made a rolling turn, seriously damaged the windshield and pancaked the roof. This damage was consistent with the car's actual entry into the water. What is not explained by the car's entry into *flat* water are the deep dents which run from top to bottom on both passenger-side doors, and the dents on both the front and rear quarter panels. A casual examination of the relevant photos (See Photo Section) indicates damage more likely to have been caused by hitting trees. This damage will be analyzed after we look closely at the speed of the car.

According to the Tedrows:[8]

The Registry of Motor Vehicles of Massachusetts offered evidence at the Inquest to show that the car was going 35 to 40 miles per hour at the time, but Judge Boyle would not accept it. The proceedings were stopped, the parties went off the record, and the Judge stated he would not allow evidence of speed more than 20 or 22 miles per hour. The Registry witness [George Kennedy] gave evidence on that basis. The Judge not only ruled against evidence of a higher (more

---

[8]   Tedrow p. 188.

truthful) speed but actually had the references physically expunged from the record.

The Registry prepared its 35 to 40 mile per hour speed case after an exhaustive study of all physical aspects and measurements; skid marks, heights, depths, distances, weight, trajectories, and so forth. These figures are still available if you are interested. See Figure 7 in the compilation *You, The Jury* by R.B. Cutler, 1969 and 1973 (privately printed), and give them to your expert.

In a February, 1980 feature article, *Readers' Digest* commissioned and presented the results of exhaustive research regarding the accident. The *Digest* commissioned Raymond R. McHenry, a well-known automobile accident analyst. Using standards accepted by the U.S. Department of Transportation, McHenry fed all the pertinent data into a computer. Using this scientific approach, he was able to reconstruct the accident based on the computer's conclusions:

1. Driving on the wrong (left) side of the road, Kennedy approached the bridge at approximately 34 m.p.h. (Abiding by rigorous scientific standards, McHenry stipulates that his speed computation could be in error by plus or minus 4 m.p.h. Thus the car was traveling at a minimum of 30 m.p.h.; it could have been going as fast as 38 m.p.h.)

2. Kennedy saw the bridge when he was at least 50 feet away from it, probably from farther away. At least 17 feet from the bridge, he slammed the brakes down hard "panic braking," which locked the front wheels. Propelled by the high speed, the car skidded 17 feet along the road, about another 25 feet up the bridge, jumped a 5 ½-inch-high rub rail and hurtled approximately 35 more feet into the water. Despite Kennedy's braking effort, the car was still traveling between 22 m.p.h. and 28 m.p.h. when it shot out over the pond.

So here we clearly have two independent, expert sources who based on evidence at the scene, and (using computers) in the later reference, prove scientifically that the car was going faster than Kennedy claimed. Judge Boyle had indicated that speed in excess of 20 m.p.h. on that road, under the existing conditions, would clearly indicate negligent driving. Proof of negligent driving would demand that *someone* make a formal indictment. However, an indictment was never made.

Nevertheless, to thoroughly debunk the notion that speed was responsible for the accident, again we turn to our expert at the scene, Jack Olsen[9]:

> And how did he manage to go off in a straight line, plunging up and over the side of the angled bridge almost as though the car were on a track, as though **the steering wheel had been frozen into position**? Accident experts who investigated the scene later could not even be positive that the brakes had been jammed on. Light scuff marks showed where the car had continued steady on course and off the right side of the bridge, but the wood had been damp and easily scored. No rubber residue had been visible in the sandy approach. The accident could not be explained by speed. [Emphasis Added.]

In fact the accident is never going to be explained by speed. Kennedy's testimony, his version of the events that night, doesn't come near to the real facts, the real events.[10]

A press insiders' report that received little or no fanfare was filed by Hal Bruno, the News Editor of *Newsweek* who spent some time on the scene. Author Jack Olsen[11] mentioned this item twice in his book, and Robert Sherrill also saw fit to print it:[12]

> "Two weeks later the growing suspicions that the three men had been in a collusion of silence to prevent discovery of

---

[9] Olsen, p. 257.

[10] Chief Arena himself had made an inspection of the scene before anyone else had arrived that morning and he could not find "any skid marks on the bridge or dirt road prior to reaching the bridge." Leo Damore interview, 2-14-1969.

[11] Olsen, pp. 222 and 269.

[12] Sherrill, p. 118.

Kennedy's condition that night came together in the *Newsweek* report that a guest at the party told friends that Kennedy had "four or five drinks before leaving the cottage - and that he was so stunned and incoherent when he returned that Gargan and Markham first believed that his car had merely **run off the road somewhere and that Mary Jo was simply sitting in it.**" [Emphasis Added.]

With this point we finally arrive at this author's opinion of what must be the ultimate truth behind this bizarre story — the crucial point which lies behind the actions which took Mary Jo's life. The car *was* sitting off the road when Kennedy stumbled back to the cottage. It was not sitting in the water; not yet!

A close examination of photographs[13] of the car's passenger side proves that the plunge into the water, as described by Kennedy, could not possibly have done the damage which was clearly evident as the car was pulled from the water. Inspect the photos closely, the dents on the car's doors are vertical in nature, and could not have been caused by the car's impact with *flat* water. The vertical nature of these dents on the passenger side doors indicates impact with trees or poles. Once you realize that these severe vertical dents could not have come from the car's impact with the water, the facts begin to fall into place. And, we must remember, that this is a car which according to Mr. Kennedy's Inquest testimony, had been in good shape: "*Mr. Crimmins takes very good care of the car.*" This is the unpretentious black, four-door sedan that a United States Senator uses when he is in his home state.

Yet, this is the same car that Mr. Burton Hersh, in his authorized, very friendly, upbeat, go-go, stream-of-consciousness, 1972 biography of Teddy, described as, "Edward Kennedy's *scraped-up, knock-around* 1967 Oldsmobile 88...."[14] Ultimately, the car is either taken "good care of...." or, it is "scraped-up, knock-around...."

---

13 See Photo Section.
14 Hersh, p. 489.

The photographs in the Photo Section are worth thousands of words apiece. These photos bear witness to the statements put forward here. How is it possible for this car to have received a pancaked roof at the same time that it received such extensive damage to the passenger side doors? By evaluating the photographs we can see that something is obviously amiss. The car couldn't have been smashed on its roof *and* side door panels simultaneously. What is more, the two highly placed dents on the rear quarter panel aren't explained at all by Kennedy's version of the accident. They could be explained by an accident which occurred prior to the car entering the water, an accident in which the car slid off the road hitting trees, thereby denting the doors in the vertical fashion shown in the photographs.

On viewing these photos in November of 1988, Sheriff Look said, "I find it astonishing that dents of this depth were overlooked at the time of the accident."[15] Indeed!

A photo of equal interest, the one which ultimately leads to the hypothesis presented herein is the photo which shows the driver's side of the auto as it emerges from the water. By viewing the photos in which the driver's side is visible, we can see that the entire left side of the car is untouched, almost pristine.

Except, that is, for the outside rear-view mirror, which is askew, literally hanging from its back portion. General Motors' outside rear-view mirrors were all fastened to the doors in the same way. Front and rear bolts fix the base flange to the steel door, with a chrome cover cosmetically masking this flange. The post which holds the mirror itself, is part of this ensemble. By studying the photos, it becomes clear that the entire chrome cover and assembly has been wrenched from the flange which is still bolted to the door. What is clear is that some powerful force pulled this assembly from its flange. How could the mirror assembly be hanging off the flange when all of the significant damage from the alleged accident is on the top and passenger (opposite) sides of the car?

[15] Author interview, November 23, 1988.

In order to attempt to arrive at an answer to this question it is important to bear in mind that it is common practice in the towing industry to tie the steering wheel to the outside rear-view mirror in order to insure straight tracking when a car is towed from the rear. It is suggested here that in order to *push a vehicle along a straight line*, it is equally important to tie the steering wheel to the outside rear-view mirror. How else to explain how the mirror assembly was pulled off of the bolted flange, when in fact the left (passenger) side of the car has no other mark on it?

As quoted above, author Jack Olsen may have hit on what really happened[16]:

And how did he manage to go off in a straight line, plunging up and over the side of the angled bridge almost as though the car were on a track, as though **the steering wheel had been frozen into position?**

[16] Olsen, Ibid.

12

EARLY MORNING
FLIGHTS

After the incident there were rumors of airplane flights that went to the mainland in the wee hours of the morning, before Mary Jo's body was discovered. It has been alleged that the purpose of these flights was to remove individuals who had been at the party from the scene, and therefore from any involvement. The Grand Jury that ever so gently probed the incident after the Inquest, called at least one witness who might have had some information regarding the alleged flights, but he claimed to have no knowledge of any such flights.

It is a "judgment call" to present material that is based merely upon rumors. However, this author has confirmed three independent sources for this material and believes that on that basis it is proper and fitting to present the evidence. This material, also shows that that there may have been others present at the party, others who were never named as being there. Joan Kennedy made allusion to the fact that others were at the party; however they were never named. Mrs Kennedy was interviewed by Susan James and reportedly said, "and some guests who dropped in at the party, sailing friends of the Senator's, weren't even called as witnesses."[17]

17 *McCall's*, interview, August, 1970.

Quite by accident, the author stumbled upon information regarding these flights from an unorthodox source, who was unwitting of the author's intent to write on this subject. In that the source had no knowledge or idea that the author was researching Chappaquiddick, it would be inappropriate, even unethical, to divulge his name.

An interview with Sheriff Look was the second source, and he confirmed that he was aware of flights.

Finally, in Damore's book, Lieutenant Killen told of an anonymous caller who claimed that he saw Kennedy himself at Hyannis in the early morning hours:[18]

> One call, however, "sounded like the genuine article," a witness who reported seeing Senator Kennedy "around 2 A.M. on Saturday morning in the back seat of a blue Ford LTD sedan on Cape Cod. The caller "knew where the car was going," but refused to say. He suggested Senator Kennedy could have flown off Martha's Vineyard without being seen. "Nobody's at the control tower at Edgartown airport late at night," the caller said. "You sit on the runway. You open your radio and ask: 'Is there anyone out there?' When there's no answer, you take off."
>
> The man refused to give his name, "because I don't want any trouble. The Kennedys can trace this information directly to me." Killen kept him talking as long as he could, but couldn't break him. From what he'd been told Killen deduced the caller might have seen the car en route to the Kennedy compound. Killen asked Barnstable Police Chief Albert Hinckley to question the roster of "specials" assigned driveway duty and other security posts at Hyannis Port on the night of the accident. Killen started checking air charter services on Martha's Vineyard to find out if any planes had left the Island late Saturday night or early Sunday morning. Of three airports, two were private grass facilities — one of them operated by Steve Gentle, the real estate agent who rented the Chappaquiddick cottage to Joe Gargan. Gentle denied knowledge of such a

18 Damore, p. 282.

flight. Killen could find no others from his inquiries on the Island. Nor were the landing records at Barnstable county airport in Hyannis any help. Records were kept from 6 A.M. to 10 P.M., when tower personnel left. It was, however, "possible" for a plane to land at the field after hours.... After hours of hard police work, Killen was forced to conclude the telephone tipster was a "phony."

Regarding the author's first-mentioned source of information, the individual in question was involved in Boston area legal activities in the late 1960's. He was questioned innocently, as to whether or not he had been in the Boston area around the time of Chappaquiddick. The stunning exchange is presented below:

Q. Were you in Boston around the time of Chappaquiddick?
A. Sure was, what was that, around June, '69?

Q. No, it was July, 1969.
A. That's right. Yeah. That was a crazy night, driving people around on the mainland in the early morning hours.

Q. On the mainland?
A. Yeah, people who were out there, people who were never known to be out there.

Q. People — you mean, Paul Markham?
A. How'd you know that?

At this point he brought himself up short. But, it was too late.

"How'd you know that?"

He hadn't intended to give up anything, but the totally innocent circumstances had caused the inadvertent slip. I responded that I had done some research into Chappaquiddick and it followed that if there had been any early-morning flights it was logical Paul Markham would have been aboard. He refused to discuss the matter any further, and walked away. Future attempts to question him were unsuccessful.

In fact, this has been the situation with all direct participants at the party. With the exception of several interviews granted by Esther Newberg a few days after the party, no one has spoken for the record.

When I initially met Sheriff Look in Edgartown in 1982, I explained to him that I had personal knowledge of a flight from Chappaquiddick, probably to Hyannis Port, that took people off the Island in the wee morning hours. By the time of this first interview, Look was the duly elected Sheriff of Dukes County. The local people had voted him into office, therefore establishing their opinion of his integrity. We had little time to talk that morning because the Sheriff had a pressing court case.

When I told him of my knowledge of the flight, he took me into a private office and explained, "All right, if you've come that far I'll give you some more. Flights, sure there were flights, two flights early on, they flew him over and back."[19]

"Were they taking people off?"

Look replied, "Yeah, taking people off."

"People from the party?"

"Right, I even know who flew the plane"

"Who flew the plane? Carroll?"

"No, not then," said the Sheriff. "Let's put it this way, I don't have the name of the pilot, but I do know they flew people out."

That's all there is at this point. It is admittedly not the strongest material. But often in an investigation material comes inadvertently, from sources not thought to have knowledge. Ask any detective or investigator: at some point intuition leads. The picture emerges before the individual pieces are all in place.

The material presented above has certainly convinced this writer that there were flights. The logical motivations were two-

[19] Authors interview, May 1982.

fold: to get certain, perhaps important, people off the Island and away from involvement. With all due respect, those that were left behind were in fact minions, functionaries. The second reason to get over to Hyannis Port and back was to get to secure telephones, to activate a damage control headquarters, and begin to build a professional cover-up. And they did an excellent job!

13

TELEPHONE
MYSTERIES

One area that has received some serious investigation in the press regards the alleged missing telephone calls that were made by, or on behalf of, the Senator in the early morning hours after the car went into the water. The point is simple. The Senator declared that he fully intended to report the accident, but, because of his state of anxiety, a direct result he claims of nearly being pulled out to sea in his swim to Edgartown, he was unable to bring himself to do so. Was the Senator in fact in a state of diminished capacities? Should we believe him? Ultimately you are the jury.

As has been amply demonstrated above, and firmly believed by John Farrar, the skindiver who brought her body out of the car, it is possible that Mary Jo Kopechne might be alive today if she had been brought out of the water sooner, even up to an hour or more after the car entered the water.

In this chapter it will be shown that, contrary to the Senator's claims, several phone calls were made prior to 8:00 A.M., the time he alleges to have made the first call to the outside world. And therefore, while he might have suffered from diminished capacity, it is opinion here that he was very actively involved in a conspiracy to obstruct justice in order to avoid an indictment for the crime of manslaughter.

If in fact this is true, it is understandable. After certain action was set in motion, it was really to late to turn back. Nobody wants to go to prison. Nobody wants to self-incriminate.

It is the job of the state to prove guilt. Of course if by exten-
sion, and as a result of real and perceived power, you *are the
State*, your job is much easier.

Calls were made on Senator Kennedy's credit card account
from several locations, at times when, according to the Kennedy
story, no calls were made. The news of these calls was originally
reported by Jack Anderson. Anderson's column stated, "These
calls uphold my story that Kennedy wasn't stumbling around in
confusion but was trying to extricate himself."

Human Events magazine also carried a story by Arthur Egan,
regarding these phone calls.

When the Senator was running for the presidency in 1980,
the *New York Times*, 3-11-80, produced the most complete
account to date regarding the telephone calls in a story head-
lined: "Gaps Found In Chappaquiddick Phone Data." According
to the *Times,* a bevy of characters, unsavory as well as respectable, had claimed over the years to have either seen or to have
been temporarily in possession of relevant phone records from
the New England Telephone Company. It is not essential here
to track the specifics by naming either the individuals who saw
these records or those individuals that were allegedly called by
the Kennedy people.

The most significant fact to be considered, the fact that
looms over all of this reportage about the telephone calls, is that
the esteemed counselor, Edward B. Hanify, Kennedy's publicly
acknowledged chief attorney, was in fact a director of the New
England Telephone Company. Perhaps he was chosen as lead
attorney in part because of this position, but it clearly must be
remembered that he, as a Director of the phone company, was
certainly in a position to influence the conduct of the New
England Telephone Company regarding the presentation of the
relevant phone records.

In fact, what happened was a sham, an obstruction of justice.
Deputy District Attorney Armand Fernandes had subpoenaed
the complete records from the phone company to be presented
at the Inquest. When he later discovered that calls were likely to

have been made by others, using Kennedy's credit card number, he expanded the scope of his subpoena.

The records were prepared and brought to the Inquest. In fact, according to the *Times,* The New England Telephone Company prepared four lists of telephone calls. The individual sent to the Inquest on behalf of the New England Telephone Company offered a single list (one of the four prepared lists) of sixteen calls that had been selected by the telephone company to be "helpful" for presentation to the court in response to the subpoena. The Senator, in comments he made to the *New York Times,* did confirm that he himself had made several calls. None of the calls that Senator Kennedy said he made were on the list of sixteen.

Because he was not pressed at the time he gave his testimony, the individual from the phone company did not tell the court, or the prosecutors, that he also had three more lists in his pocket; he just said that the list he was offering would be "helpful" to the court. The prosecutors, not aware of other lists, assumed that the Telephone Company was complying in full with their subpoena for "all" calls made on the Senator's various credit card accounts during the weekend. Clearly an actionable case of subterfuge and deceit, and not responsive to the subpoena that had been issued.

The phone company, as you may have guessed, has subsequently "routinely" destroyed all records relating to any calls charged to the Kennedy telephone accounts during that period. As you might also suspect, the Park Avenue Agency, which is the Kennedy family business office, destroyed all records of phone calls placed by the Senator and his associates during that period of time. Catch 22.

But these actions give us what we are looking for, ancillary covert acts which go beyond the appearance of cover-up. When you receive a large telephone bill, you determine where the calls were placed and who placed them. A business, the Park Avenue Agency, which is a trust for the Kennedy fortune, has a legal mandate that looms still larger. That mandate is more than the moral or fiduciary responsibility to the beneficiaries of the trust. The legal charge is to be certain that monies that belong to all the beneficiaries of that trust are not squandered. The records were destroyed. Recalling the words of Mr. Steven Smith, who directs the Park Avenue Agency, is instructive:

> Our prime concern was whether or not the guy survived the thing, whether he rode out the still possible charge of manslaughter.

He followed his "prime concern" but, by following that mandate and destroying the telephone records, one wonders whether or not he might have been justifiably included in a charge of conspiracy to obstruct justice.

If these missing records corroborated the Senator's version of the facts, you can well imagine that the records would not only exist, they would be displayed in a gold frame for all to see at the Kennedy Center in Washington D.C.

Assistant District Attorney Fernandes made it clear to the *Times* that these phone records were the very "foundation for assessing testimony by Senator Kennedy."

We've seen that the Massachusetts Supreme Court acted as the legal team for Kennedy and now it's obvious that the phone company was deeply involved in the maneuvers as well.

We will look at only one phone call. At 10:57 A.M., at the time that the Senator was at the Police Station, a call was placed from Vineyard Haven, the township down the road from Edgartown, to Jacqueline Kennedy Onassis's home at the Kennedy Hyannis Port compound. Her home was used, as we have seen before, as the damage-control center when the clan gathered to mastermind the situation. The final three paragraphs in the *Times* piece, 3-11-80, are most interesting with regard to our attempts to tie up these loose ends:

It seems likely, from the Inquest record, that the caller was Mr. Gargan, the Senator's cousin. Mr. Gargan refuses to be interviewed.

Also unknown is the identity of the person who took this call. According to the Kennedy friends and aides who began arriving at the Hyannis compound later that day, Mrs. Onassis and her children were away and the house was unoccupied.

It is unclear who would have known, as early as 11 A.M., to go to Mrs. Onassis's house. Later that week the house was used as a command center by those who gathered to plan strategy for Senator Kennedy's appearances in court and, afterward, on television. Mr. Kennedy said today that he did not know who would have received the call at Mrs. Onassis's home.

We cannot be certain, but based on a crescendo of circumstantial but publicly reported evidence, it is obvious that David Hackett was around somewhere.[1]

Burton Hersh, in his friendly biography, *The Education of Edward Kennedy*, referred to Mr. Hackett several times:

> Bobby, who had played Milton's blocking back in a single wing to Dave Hackett's tailback, was remembered for his ability to capitalize on **Hackett's set-up fakes**.... (p. 109.) [Emphasis Added.]

> On a family vacation cruise off the Maine coast, Ted and Dave Hackett, rowing ashore in a dinghy for supplies, passed a large yacht. A man hung over the rail and advised them to row a little faster; Ted yelled back suggesting that he mind his own business. "Come back here and say that again," the man on the yacht suggested.

---

[1] The *New York Times*, the *Chicago Daily News*, the *Boston Globe* and the *Boston Herald Traveler* all had reported that David Hackett attended the party; that, in fact, it had been held in his honor. He is also mentioned as being among the individuals who gathered at the Kennedy compound immediately following the tragedy.

"Teddy spun the dinghy around so fast I almost fell out of it," Hackett told someone [Red Fay] later. "The next thing I knew, Teddy was on the yacht and the man was being thrown overboard and all the women were screaming and running below to hide in the cabins. Their husbands were running with them, to see that they were safely tucked away, I guess. By this time, I'm on the yacht with Teddy. The men start to come back up on the deck to deal with us, but it's a narrow hatchway and they have to come up through it one at a time. As each guy appears, I grab him and spin him around and throw him to Teddy, and Teddy throws him overboard. In no time, all of the men — there were about eight of them — were in the water, I never saw anything like it." (p. 119.)

...within Dave Hackett's overall responsibility, of the intelligence operation.... (p. 412.)

At the urging of Dave Hackett and his cousin Joey, always one to fret, Kennedy tried to show some gratitude to the girls who held up so uncomplainingly throughout their months in the boiler room at Twentieth and L streets. (p. 423-33.)

David Hackett — Bob's intimate, the head Kennedy intelligence technician since 1960, the man who perfected the system that required three reliable sources to have passed word along to the appropriate boiler-room people before the Kennedys would confirm a delegate commitment. (p. 444.)

Certainly he'd [Ted] made a considerable effort earlier: in January, when Dun Gifford and Dave Hackett had gotten together and given a party for the boiler-room group. Teddy had made it a special point to come by and liven up the proceedings for as long as could manage to stay. "The drill that night, the joke," Hackett remembers, "was that we invited two eligible guys for each of the girls. There wasn't any hanky-panky at all, and no permanent relationships came out of the evening, but everyone who was there agrees that it was one of those great times, really memorable." (p. 497.)

If Mr. Hackett was not at Chappaquiddick for the party, or not at the Onassis home to receive the 10:57 A.M. phone call, that the *Times'* posits was placed by Joe Gargan, we hope that he will let us know where he was, and what time he did arrive at the compound. There is so much evidence in the complete record regrading his participation at the party, that the request for answers to these questions is legitimate.

14

ABORTED
GRAND JURY

The final nail — the one that allowed for the cover-up and, therefore the avoidance of justice — was driven by the alleged fail-safe factor in our judicial system. The very procedure designed and charged with the responsibility to make findings of fact and recommend prosecution was unceremoniously sacked. The Grand Jury process is a time-honored element in United States jurisprudence. There are those today who claim with self-righteous zeal, and often with the facts on their side, that the Grand Jury process has been used politically by the Federal government as well as state and local district attorneys to harass and persecute, let alone prosecute, suspected members of the radical and violent left and more recently, the reactionary and violent right.

Grand juries are a tools used by government prosecutors to formally bring forward facts and seek indictments in criminal matters. In their book, *Death at Chappaquiddick,* Richard and Thomas Tedrow wrote effectively on the role of grand juries. With respect for the redoubtable legal background of Richard Tedrow, we look now at his words:[1]

The judicial body known as a Grand Jury dates back many centuries into early English history, its origins now lost in

[1] Tedrow, p. 162.

obscurity. The Grand Jury came into being to protect the subjects, the common people, from oppression and injustice perpetrated by the Crown, the Establishment if you prefer. It has been a bulwark against abuses of power by the sovereign for hundreds of years. There is nothing mysterious or complicated about a Grand Jury; it is one of the cornerstones of our society.

The Grand Jury guards the rights and liberties of the public and protects its morals and social order. In the fearless exercise of its powers, and the necessary incidents thereto, the Grand Jury is not to be limited or circumscribed by any judicial or executive officer. Nor is it to be subjected to outside influence of any kind; neither judges, nor governors nor presidents.

The Grand Jury calls for such witnesses and evidence as required in fulfilling its duties. No court or person has any right to interfere in its functions. Any such interference is a violation of law.

The aforementioned facts are considered by the legal profession to be "Hornbook Law" elementary basic legal principles. In this case, Judge Paquet destroyed the Grand Jury and everything it stood for.

Some of the proceedings in the Massachusetts courts and/or by Massachusetts judges are hard to follow and harder to agree with. If the handling of the present case is considered to be standard, then one can only say with heartfelt sincerity that the Good Lord please help the parties litigant in cases pending in the courts of Massachusetts. It seems obvious that they aren't going to obtain justice by anything short of Divine Intervention.

The above section is a strong and ironic essay, written by the former Chief Commissioner of the U.S. Court of Military Appeals, Richard Tedrow. He is also the author of *Digest Opinions of the U.S. Court of Military Appeals,* which has been the basic reference guide for U.S. military court-martials. After writing the bible for military court-martial procedures, Tedrow then sat for 17 years as the final authority on the U.S. Military Appeals bench. We are fortunate to witness the prodigious career of a legal scholar of such thoroughness and staying power.

Leslie Leland is a local Martha's Vineyard drugstore owner and operator. At the time of the tragedy he was the foreman of the local Grand Jury. The jury was impaneled, according to Leland,[2] by drawing names from all Martha's Vineyard registered voters. Leland became a central figure after the Inquest had run its course.

It has been reported that Leland had attempted early on to encourage D.A. Dinis to hold a Grand Jury session, and that Leland was allegedly rebuffed by Dinis. To forestall Leland's attempts to hold a Grand Jury session, and to regain control of the case, Dinis came up with the tactic of convening an Inquest.

There is some controversy as to how Leland forced the issue about holding a Grand Jury session after the Inquest was held. According to the Tedrows, Leland formally requested that the Grand Jury be convened in this matter "particularly to look over the transcript of the Inquest proceedings." This request was in the form of a registered letter to the Chief Justice of the Massachusetts Supreme Court, who denied he had received it. Leland produced his receipt of mailing for the benefit of the press and immediately an order was issued to convene the Grand Jury on April 6, 1970. Leland felt that justice could now be served. He was 29 years old, and was acting as the bellwether for the general opinion of the people of Martha's Vineyard. The consensus was that one of those "rich, arrogant" Kennedys had perpetrated a great scandal resulting in death on their Island. These year-around permanent residents are staunchly conservative New Englanders, and frankly resentful of Hyannis Port types.

Robert Sherrill quoted Leland:[3]

---

2 Author's interview, May, 1982.
3 Sherrill, p. 162

Everyone feels that a great injustice has been done to the democratic process. That there's been a whitewash, a cover-up, and that things have been swept under the rug. I just feel we have certain duties and responsibilities as jury members to fulfill. A great deal of time has passed since the girl died, and it's time the public found out what happened.

Just being picked for the Grand Jury made me think, gee, this is a new experience. It is really doing something for your country, taking part in an important process of the American way of life. Now, there are pressures, phone calls, mail. Oh, I mean all the calls from reporters and all the letters from the public. I've gotten sixty or seventy letters so far, all in favor of this investigation, all commending me for this action. People have written me saying they are glad someone has the courage to stand up for American rights and American justice.

Leland was on his way, at age 29, to discover some of the harsher realities of public life. And, frankly, as the screws turned, he realized that the exertion of certain pressures can cause an individual with something to lose, in his case: his drugstore, to renounce "... the courage to stand up for American rights and American justice."

In 1982 Leland told the author that pressure was applied to him via his business. Apparently the Massachusetts Pharmaceutical Licensing Board didn't inform him that his license was due to expire. He received a call from a clerk telling him that his drug store was going to be closed by State Troopers because he had not mailed in his $25.00 license fee. He paid the money, but admitted to being chilled by the experience. In 1982 he would only agree to a "strictly off the record" interview, but now that he has gained the courage to tell this story publicly to *Newsweek* it is hoped that he doesn't object to its mention here.

The jury was convened under the authority of Judge Wilfred J. Paquet of the Massachusetts Superior Court. The *New York Times,* April 6, 1970 wrote tellingly about the relationship of Paquet with the Kennedy team:

About 10 years ago, Judge Wilfred J. Paquet of the Massachusetts Superior Court sentenced two convicted bookies to 10 years in jail. Two weeks later he ordered them released and explained that he had decided the sentences were too severe. "I am big enough to admit I made a mistake," he said. The District Attorney in the case sought to nullify Judge Paquet's action, and the issue was finally resolved in the Supreme Judicial Court of Massachusetts. A Boston lawyer named Edward B. Hanify, arguing in behalf of Judge Paquet, said that the judge's "honor and integrity have won the respect of his colleagues on the bench, members of the bar and the general community." Judge Paquet was upheld.

Mr. Hanify and Judge Paquet will meet again today in Edgartown, Massachusetts, where a special Grand Jury session investigating what has become known as the Kopechne case opens its proceedings. Mr. Hanify is representing Senator Edward M. Kennedy; Judge Paquet is presiding over the Hearings.

Judge Paquet turned the Grand Jury proceedings into a circus. First of all he opened the session with an unorthodox charge, that lasted for some 90 minutes; reporters present claimed that this length of time constituted a new record. This portion of the proceedings was open to the public and the press. He had a priest sit with him at the bench. You might say, what!?! A priest. Highly unusual, but it seems that Paquet was out to summon forth the Highest Wisdom and hopefully demand a little Faith and Adherence. The Reverend Donald Cousa, pastor of St. Elizabeth Roman Catholic Church, stood up in full regalia and requested that "prejudice was to be set aside and replaced by charity."

In 1959, it had often been said, and believed by some, that if John Kennedy became President, then the United States would be run from Rome. The President's youngest brother proved that wrong. If anything, in light of Cardinal Cushing's visit to Mary Jo's parents, and the display at the Grand Jury, the

Roman Catholic Diocese of Boston was at the service of the Kennedys.

Judge Paquet's restrictions to the jury were highly unusual and, some have suggested, illegal. The jury could call any witnesses that could give "useful information," but could not call for questioning any witness *who had appeared at the Inquest.* In other words the very persons who had direct knowledge of the incident could not be called to testify. As if that were not enough of a restriction, the Grand Jury was *not allowed* even to see the Inquest transcript, and therefore they could have no idea of what had been testified to by the potentially complicit parties.

It has been alleged that the Judge said, "It would be violative of your oath under God if you reveal one single thing that happens in the jury room — your lips are sealed, and I don't mean for today, I mean forever." This was clearly meant, "one single thing," to warn them that they could not repeat what District Attorney Dinis told them in the private session.

To keep this circus going, it was confided by a juror who of necessity spoke without attribution, that Dinis had told them in the closed session that he (Dinis) had read the Inquest record, and that, because there wasn't anything to it, they should disband. Forget about it!

Crucially, the Judge told them behind closed doors, with Dinis' collaboration, that they could not call any witnesses who had testified at the Inquest. And that meant that effectively their hands were tied. How could they determine if they should hand up an indictment, if in fact they could not examine under oath the very individuals whose conduct was at issue? And perhaps worse, they would not be allowed to peruse the Inquest transcript. They could do nothing, and *would risk jail* if they even dared to tell the world that their hands had been tied.

As Les Leland said, "Believe me, I'd love to comment. The people have a right to know. They wouldn't allow me to call Kennedy, Markham or Gargan. Dinis told me in the jury room that I couldn't call them. It turns out that I could have — but I didn't know it then."

In fact that last statement sums up the whole matter. It is arguable that Judge Paquet's prior involvement with Hanify was significant enough to have caused him to recuse (withdraw from a case because of potential conflict of interest) himself. Was the Judge himself, then, guilty of conspiracy to obstruct justice?

The Grand Jury session lasted only for some forty minutes. They called but four witnesses. Nina L. Trott, the desk clerk from the Shiretown Inn, and local resident Benjamin Hall, testified that they had not seen Kennedy soaking wet before dawn, because they had been asleep. Stephen C. Gentle, owner of the Katama Air Park, a private landing strip, testified that he knew nothing regarding early morning flights. The testimony of Robert J. Carroll, an active Democrat and long-time Kennedy family supporter, is not known; suffice it to say that it lasted for but a few moments. And so the Dukes County Grand Jury, with 23 members all from Martha's Vineyard, disbanded on April 7, 1970, without making any waves.

The action was effectively over. This was further proved by the diminishing ability of this case to make news; only 50 newsmen attended the Grand Jury session, a significantly lower figure than the 340 who had shown up for the Inquest that they could not even attend because the press was barred except from the sidewalks of Edgartown, Martha's Vineyard, Massachusetts.

At the conclusion of the Grand Jury session, Dinis stated, to the assembled news reporters:[4]

> The case is closed. I will file the appropriate certificate required by the Court to notify the clerk there is no proposed prosecution in this matter. That should clear the way for releasing Inquest transcript and the judge's report. This is the end of the investigation into the death of Mary Jo Kopechne.

An unidentified, and by necessity, anonymous Grand Juror in obvious frustration told the *Manchester Union Leader*:

---

[4]   Rust, p. 171.

The District Attorney offered us no help at all in our investigation. In fact Dinis did everything he could to discourage our probe in the case. I wish we could have had an unbiased district attorney leading us, and we might have accomplished something. The district attorney had all the facts and evidence before him long before the Inquest. He could have acted, but instead he played politics with the whole situation.

Les Leland the Grand Jury foreman told the *Manchester Union Leader*:

We are supposed to have freedom of speech in this country, and yet by the judge's ruling I cannot ever speak my own personal opinion on the subject. To me this is a scare tactic. If I say one word about what transpired in the Grand Jury room, I can go to jail for two years .... I don't believe justice was served here .... One day some member of the Grand Jury will defy Judge Paquet's order and tell all.

Who, pray tell, and when? The media rushed into print with *pro forma* outrage, now slightly tempered with the passage of time (the tragedy had happened six months before), the *Chicago Tribune* reported:

This remarkable ruling, depriving the Grand Jury of access to the record, amounted to a directive to the district attorney to pledge that there would be no prosecution of Senator Kennedy. The Senator has been given special benefits and kid glove treatment from every court before which he has been represented. His only court appearance was to enter a plea of guilty to leaving the scene of the accident. He was let off with a two-month suspended sentence. From the start, events in the case have been inexplicable.... Those events, with a certain amount of assistance from courts and public officials, have certainly conspired to protect Senator Kennedy at every turn of this strange sequence. Now the sudden abandonment of the Grand Jury investigation indicates what has been a virtual certainty from the beginning: that the true facts of the episode will forever remain veiled.

That sentiment, "... forever remain veiled" is not necessarily true. As stated at the outset, the goal herein is to lift the veil.

15

THE ANSWER

What did happen that night? There are so many facts at odds with the Senator's version. In attempting to square and account for the facts raised above, this author offers the following *opinion* as a hypothesis as to what might have happened.

Senator Kennedy and Mary Jo Kopechne leave the cottage for a reason of their own; it might well have been that they wished to discuss political or Kennedy family business. Mary Jo was very close, professionally, to Robert Kennedy; she was becoming a trusted associate, not merely a secretary or "boiler-room girl"; people brought coffee to *her*. Ted Sorensen and Bobby ran phrases by her when she stayed up all night at Hickory Hill, typing and assisting in the revision of Bobby's speech when he finally came out against the Vietnam War. Ted and Mary Jo would have had many things to discuss, and the party may have been too loose and free-flowing for a serious discussion about things that may have been sensitive, or, required privacy. Although extremely unlikely they might even have been headed back to Edgartown, as Kennedy has insisted. It is a moot point.

While an up side can be posited; plenty of others have attributed carnal motives to their leaving together. The problem was Ted Kennedy's drinking and driving. His own staff was known to be deeply worried about his propensity for high-speed driving, especially when he'd had a couple of drinks. After the tragedy of Bobby's death, the pressure-cooker environment had dramatically increased, and young Ted was known to use the bottle to let off steam.

It's not hard to imagine: on a narrow, windy, unlit, sandy-dirt road on Chappaquiddick, he loses control and the car slides off the narrow road, smashing into the trees. This would explain the deep dents on the passenger side of the car. The car skids into the trees and stops abruptly. Mary Jo bangs the back of her head, very hard. She's knocked unconscious, Kennedy can't revive her, and she's bleeding down the back of her blouse. He panics; disoriented, nearly hysterical, he stumbles back to the cottage for help. He retrieves Markham and Gargan. Perhaps one other person, certainly not Ray LaRosa, he was known as a "Kennedy man," but not an intimate. They return to the scene. Three, maybe four, rapidly sobering but panic-stricken men, who are not doctors, fail to find a pulse in the deeply unconscious still bleeding woman.

What to do? What the goddamned hell to do? Look at her, he couldn't get a pulse, she must be gone. They can't bring her back to life! What can they do? They can't save her, she's gone!

Possibly they can save the Senator's political career. These are attorneys, familiar with the laws of Massachusetts. If they report this accident right now! A blood test? The Senator could be look-ing at prison as a result of a mandatory manslaughter indictment. Driving under the influence, which results in death. Prison? It's impossible! Not after what his brothers have done for this nation. Is there a curse? Too much sacrifice. It isn't right! It isn't fair!

What the goddamned hell to do?

There is a way — they can't bring back the woman, she's gone but, maybe, just maybe they can rig it up — to buy the time. Come up with an alternative accident — an accident that won't be discovered for hours, and will enable the booze, the confusion, the hysteria to leave the Senator. Anything's possible with some time, just a little goddamned time!

These men are sailors all, for years; they know rigging and lines and knots, and well, by God they're convinced they can work this out — for the good of all. After all, it was just an accident, the real crime would be to let such a good young man go to prison for just an accident!

So, a plan develops, and is followed and probably improvised on. But, there is a hitch; the goddamned deputy sheriff! He gets so close he can almost look right into the car. They're driving toward the Dyke Bridge, the driver of the Olds panics; the Valiant has gone ahead to scout things out, or has already been used to retrieve a heavier car from the cabin or from the ferry slip. But, that sheriff, he had his goddamned uniform shirt on, almost looked right in the car. Jesus! No time for indecision, the god-damned sheriff could come back anytime. Line up the car with the bridge.

Tie off the steering wheel to the outside rear-view mirror, done all the time when they tow a car. Hurry up! Jesus, quiet, those houses are right there. All right. The car's straight with the bridge. The nylon line is tight on the steering wheel. How'd you get the line? Christ we're sailors on a Regatta weekend, we've got enough line to hang ourselves if we don't hurry up.

The car in the water? Two ways. Push it. Use the Valiant, use the Mercury, use the car the other guy brought, just do it. Or, maybe, we're sailors, we can rig a wedge on the gas pedal, we can do it, Christ sake, hurry up! What if it doesn't go in? Don't worry, if the car gets anywhere near the water, or the bridge, it'll go in, there's nothing to stop it. Give it all the speed you can, hurry up!

There she goes!

All right, hurry up, go ahead, get in the water, cut that rope off, get that stuff out of there.

The rear-view mirrors' what? Bent? Forget it, we'll take care of that later, can't do anything now. Don't worry about it, let's just get the hell out of here.

All right, what now? Go back to the cottage, keep everybody there, make a little noise. You stay there with 'em, nobody leaves. You too, make a little noise, make sure you're seen, bang into Esther, she's smart — and she never forgets, and then slip out, and we'll get the hell back to Edgartown and figure what to do.

OK, here's a boat, steady as she goes, out to the Victura, OK. Jesus, that guy over there on that boat is looking right at us. That's Ballou,[1] he won't do anything, it's Regatta night. Forget about it!
It's the goddamned sheriff — he's our problem. All right. Quiet, all these sounds carry on the water. OK.
Get below. What are we gonna do? Well, we've got a couple of skiffs now. Let's get you over to the Shiretown Inn, be seen. Get that time down.
You say you swam the channel, turned out to be the goddamned Hellsgate, nearly pulled you out to sea. Blew you apart, struggled up to your room, get seen, you know, get a time check, and then you fell apart in your room, made you incoherent, crazy. Good, we may need that. Christ, I feel crazy, I'm gonna be sick. Not Yet!

OK, that's done. What now? We've got to get to phones, we need some cool heads, we're in too deep to figure this out. But we can't do it here. They'll have the records of any calls we make

---

[1]   Rust, p. 83. "At about 2:00 A.M., Mr. [Remington] Ballou and his family (from the vantage point of their yacht in the harbor) saw a 15-17 foot motor boat in the Edgartown harbor approaching a small sailboat nearby. Its lights were then immediately doused and its engine switched off. Mr. Ballou and his passengers saw three persons in the motor boat." This in fact could have been a sighting of the boat which Gargan allegedly mentioned to Mary Ellen Lyons, that they had "been looking for."

Damore, op. cit., Page 263, drawing from the New Bedford *Standard-Times,* also mentions Ballou's sighting:

A little before 2 A.M on July 19, Ballou overheard a hushed conversation from "the forms of three person" passing by in a boat that doused its lights and outboard motor. Then, a larger boat with a powerful engine left Edgartown, crossing the channel to a beach near the Chappaquiddick landing, and also shut off lights and motor, Ballou related. "At this point the small boat was drifting, pointed towards the beach and the larger boat. It seemed to be waiting, like somebody casing the area to see all was quiet." Five minutes later the small boat's motor started up again, lights were turned on, and it moved out of the Harbor.

here. Gotta get back to the mainland, to Hyannis. I'll make a call,
I've got some people over there.

Here he comes, back from the phone. I called my guy over
there, a plane'll be here in thirty minutes. Christ sake, what time
is it? It's 3:05, don't worry, were on top of it now.
But that goddamned sheriff! Forget it, he's just a local stiff.
Who's gonna believe him? We've just got to hang tough on him.
We'll get something. Christ nobody's really clean.
Easy for you to say, you work in politics. Hey, no time for
jokes. Let's go!

How ya doing! Thanks a lot, just stand by here if you don't
mind, we'll need a lift back to the airport.
What now? Quiet, don't wake anybody up in the main house.
Jesus, Jackie would kill me. Quiet! Just get on the goddamned
phone, and get some help — figure this out.

All right. You guys get back over. I'm too dirty, I touched
everything over there when push came to shove. I'll stay right here,
besides, people know me, I'll do fine on the phone, it'll be all
together. Don't worry. Good luck back there. It'll be okay.
Yeah, but that goddamned sheriff.
Jesus, just go will ya. Come on, I need some help. Get him
back to the Shiretown. In the morning, get to a secure phone,
maybe back by the ferry slip. I understand, you think that Joey'll
go along, say that she was driving, or even take the rap even if he
said he wouldn't. Just try to relax, let's talk to some people, he
might not hold up. Let's think about that. Don't worry, we'll work
it out. Just get to a secure line first thing in the morning, and get
the number to me. Then I'll call you there, and we'll run the
communications out of here. Everything's gonna be all right.
Yeah, but that goddamned sheriff. Jesus, just go on back, it's
the only way. It'll be all right! I lost your brothers, I'm not gonna
*lose you. Christ, you'd think somebody owes us **one**!*

PART THREE

FINAL STATEMENTS

"Here the ways of men part: if you wish to strive for peace of soul and pleasure, then believe; if you wish to be a devotee of truth, then inquire."

Nietzsche, 6-11-1865

16

SUMMATION: EDWARD M. KENNEDY

And now in the final chapters, in the manner and method of closing arguments, we present, first, the Senator from Massachusetts (in his own words) with the few statements he has made since claiming that he did not agree with Judge Boyle's conclusions, and in fact he "rejected them."

"Nickel and dime stuff," he said uncomfortably. "They haven't come up with anything new." Interview by Carl Bernstein, *All the President's Men,* p. 275.

"The real story has been told. They're not going to find other kinds of facts because they just don't exist." *Newsweek,* November 11, 1974.

"These charges are ugly, untrue and grossly unfair. .... It is regrettable, in the atmosphere of doubt and suspicion which enshrouds us as a people, that the truth cannot compete with the unnamed sources, the groundless suggestions and the speculations which are nurtured by articles of sensationalism." Ted Kennedy's response to the *Boston Globe,* Fall 1974 series on Chappaquiddick.

"I haven't really been asked a new question in a period of ten years. There hasn't been a new fact that has questioned the position that I stated at the time of the tragedy, and there will not be and there cannot be because that happens to be the way it was." Interview Roger Mudd, ABC, 1980.

"I wish I had seen the cottages (on the gravel road) and knocked on the door and called for assistance. I wish I had, you know, reported the accident. I wish I had done many other things which I think in hindsight would have been much wiser. I think that the judicial process worked, I think that I was fairly treated by the judicial process in that state." The *L.A. Times*, 12/24/79.

"No, I think that there is one essential element in the whole tragedy. I mean, I feel, and that's the loss of life, for which I bear the responsibility for and which I will live with for the rest of my life. And that's the essential tragedy as far as I'm concerned about it, and this is a continuing factor. It doesn't alter − it's one that I feel deeply about − the sense of − the sense of loss for the Kopechne family and the sense of tragedy, which is very real for their family and for my family and that's something that I will live with for the rest of my life. I mean, the other factors are much less important as far as I'm personally concerned about. And I suppose that in response to the questions, it turns out to be a rather cold process of talking about this fact or that fact or this question or that question and it loses the human dimension and the human element and I suppose that that's certainly something that I find troublesome. But, I'm very much aware that, you know, this issue would be explored, being a candidate for the President of the United States. It would make absolutely no sense for me to be a candidate were there to be other facts that could come out that would challenge the statements that I have made. And there won't be, because there aren't other facts that would challenge those statements. But I realize that *I'll be asked about this matter over the period that I remain in public life* and I'll always feel the sense of loss of a person and I face up to *the reality of responding to the questions*." The *L.A. Times*, 12/23/79. [Emphasis Added.]

At some point one feels that a given individual has suffered enough. But how much is enough? The present writer believes it depends to some extent on whether or not the person seeks the public trust. Beyond that, history demands the truth.

17

SUMMATION:
THE PROSECUTION

Mary Jo's father, Joe Kopechne said, "I can understand shock, but I cannot understand Mr. Gargan and Mr. Markham. They weren't in shock. Why didn't they get help? That's where my questions start."[1]

"How do I know she was alive that long?" John Farrar, the skindiver, asked. "Because of the fact that the trunk was still filled with air and still dry, because of the fact that the trunk was the main source of air release. And, because Jon Ahlbum whose winch lifted the car up, saw air bubbles coming from *inside* the car...."[2]

Joan Kennedy was interviewed in *McCall's*, August 1979. She spoke of (but did not name) people who had been at the party, but hadn't been reported as having being there. She ought to have known, she was in Hyannis Port at their home on Squaw Island, adjacent to the Kennedy compound, undoubtedly some word of the party reached her at some point.

In his column, September 26, 1969, Jack Anderson wrote that, "The Senator's two loyal friends hustled him by boat off the scene of the accident. It now appears that Markham remained at the inn with the Senator and Gargan returned to the Chappaquiddick cottage."

---

1   *TIME*, interview, August 22, 1969.
2   *ESQUIRE*, interview, February, 1972.

We don't know how Jack Anderson got this information, but he has been known for decades for penetrating to the truth with his investigations. We do know that his reportage substantiates the contention, that the new evidence provided herein points the way to understanding how and why this tragedy happened. His finding that Markham stayed with the Senator during the night fits in exactly with the scenario proposed above, and that perhaps Markham, Kennedy and others, flew to Hyannis and returned before dawn. This could explain what Markham may have been really doing when he said that he was attempting to sleep in the Valiant in front of the cottage.

Senator Kennedy's purported time table for the accident is a lie, or else Sheriff Look is blind and a liar. The following is submitted as this author's *opinion* as a reasonable hypothesis based on the physical facts and new evidence presented here and in other books and publications as to what might have been the real time table of events that tragic night. While this material paints a harsh picture the author firmly believes that this material is based on the truth and are conclusions that a reasonable individual might determine to have been the course of actions.

11:15 P.M.

Edward Kennedy and Mary Jo Kopechne leave the cottage, drive around Chappaquiddick and have an accident which severely damages the right-hand side of Kennedy's Oldsmobile, and gives Kopechne a blow on the back of the head. She is bleeding and deeply unconscious.

12:00 A.M.

Kennedy returns to the cottage on foot, retrieves Gargan and Markham, and possibly a fourth individual.

12:15 A.M.

Three (or four) rapidly sobering and fumbling individuals (who are not doctors) are unable to get a pulse from Kopechne, who is in a deep coma; blood is all over the back of her blouse. They erroneously conclude that they have a dead woman on their hands![3] And, not only a possible future presidential campaign to consider, but the gruesome fact that driving under the influence of liquor in the state of Massachusetts in such cases results in a mandatory manslaughter charge. Since the young woman (apparently) cannot be saved, some mechanism must be set up to allow time to pass, to remove the possibility of the Senator's blood being tested for alcohol.

12:45 A.M.

With the rented Valiant or possibly an additional vehicle, i.e., LaRosa's large Mercury or even a previously un-cited vehicle (there were other persons, unnamed, at the party), going ahead to scout the bridge area, they drive toward the Dyke Bridge. The driver of the Oldsmobile, carrying Mary Jo's prostrate body in the back seat, spots the headlights of the Deputy Sheriff's car (which are coming straight across the Road though the Deputy Sheriff's car has not reached the corner), momentarily panics and heads into Cemetery Road. Deputy Sheriff Look let's the dark car pass in front of his car, drives around the corner, stops and walks back towards the car, which has backed out of Cemetery road. The driver, sees the Deputy Sheriff's shirt and badge reflected from the car's back-up lights, and rapidly accelerates down Dyke Road.

1:05 A.M.

The Oldsmobile is rigged by tying the steering wheel to the outside rear-view mirror. Using another vehicle to push, or a rigged wedge on the gas pedal, the car is aimed at the Dyke Bridge. Because there are virtually no physical obstructions it

---

[3] We have seen hard factual proof for all the surrounding facts; this contention is purely hypothesis, and represents the author's *opinion*. However, if true, it points to the ultimate horror in this tragedy.

will surely land in the water, whether it goes directly off the bridge (as it, in fact, ultimately did or slants off and enters the water without benefit of the bridge. They dive and remove rigging ropes.

1:20 A.M.

They drive to the ferry landing, use the telephone to arrange an airplane pickup in order to ultimately reach the "mainland" (Hyannis Port), and then "borrow" a small boat to reach the *Victura*, which has its own dinghy.

2:15 A.M.

Gargan and Markham return to the Cottage, and make noise upon their arrival. After establishing his presence, Markham leaves in the Valiant to rejoin the team at the Shiretown Inn.

2:24 A.M.

At the Shiretown Inn, Kennedy steps out on the balcony at the Shiretown Inn when he sees the night clerk in the court yard, and establishes his alibi by inquiring of the time, saying he couldn't find his watch.

3:00 A.M.

Markham arrives and they fly to Hyannis Port to set up a HQ to process the cover-up, and to make certain phone calls.

4:30 A.M.

Kennedy and Markham return to Martha's Vineyard. Markham returns the "borrowed" skiff, but inadvertently does not return it to its normal berth. He then spends the rest of the

night in the Valiant in front of the cottage on Chappaquiddick.

8:00 A.M.
After cleaning the cottage, Gargan and Markham ultimately
join Kennedy back at the Shiretown Inn; Markham, having
used the *Victura's* dinghy part-way, leaving the dinghy at the
yacht and swimming the rest of the way, arrives "soaking
wet." All dinghies are now in their approximate places.

8:30 A.M.
Kennedy, Gargan and Markham proceed to the ferry, cross
and hunker down at the pay phone.

9:15 A.M.
The accident is brought to their attention. Gargan is dis-
patched to finish cleaning up the cottage and get the girls
out of sight and off the Island. Kennedy and Markham cross
back to Edgartown and head for the Police Department.

10:57 A.M.
Gargan calls Jackie's home at Hyannis to report to the
fourth party that everything is secure, and that the girls, who
are not aware of any of the above, are going out on the next
ferry.

If Gargan and Markham had genuinely believed that the
Senator was going to report the accident when he "swam" back
to Edgartown after midnight, they certainly would have cleaned
up the empty liquor bottles at the cottage. Knowing that the
police would be arriving would be all the motivation in the
world to begin to make proper appearances.

In the absence of worry about the police arriving, the clean-up is not done until morning. One of the ladies at the party testified at the Inquest that Gargan had said on his return around 2:15 A.M., "Oh, we were looking for boats."[4] Reality intrudes in this slip of the tongue.

When Markham arrived back at the cottage after 5:00 A.M., it must have seemed logical for him to stay in the car, and not risk a light sleeper noting his second arrival. Gargan reportedly slept on the floor in the doorway of the cottage, which, if true, would insure that no one would do anything foolish.

Under oath, Kennedy testified that he had looked at the Valiant's clock to determine the time of his "swim." The rental car was found later, and did not have a clock, nor was there any evidence (such as drill holes) that it had ever had a clock.

In February, 1980 *Readers' Digest*, presented in a Feature Condensation article, the results of a study it had commissioned in November of 1979. They commissioned Bernard LeMehaute, an internationally renowned oceanographic engineer, to perform a study on tide conditions at Chappaquiddick the night and morning of July 18 and 19, 1969. They found that tidal conditions on November 9, 1979 nearly matched July 18-19, 1969. "Scrupulously following scientific methodology of proven reliability, LeMehaute determined that at the time Kennedy says the accident occurred the current was flowing at approximately .8 knots in the center of the pond, 1.2 knots at the eastern edge and probably one knot in the area where the car sank." This rate of flow was determined to not have been "an unsurmountable obstacle to a poised and experienced swimmer determined to rescue someone."

Joe Gargan, a lifelong sailor and experienced swimmer was able to get "halfway" into the car, enough to get his arm "blood-

---

[4] At the Inquest, Mary Ellen Lyons testified that on their 2:00 A.M. return to the cottage, either Markham or Gargan had said, "'Oh, don't ask us, we have been looking for boats.' It was confused."

ied," but somehow did not reach into the back seat area, where Mary Jo had positioned herself. It is contended here that he did not get halfway into the car. If he had gained any entry through the rear passenger-side window, he would have run directly into Mary Jo. John Farrar, the skindiver, did. If he entered the car from the front seat window, he could have missed Mary Jo.

Since Kennedy testified that "I believed firmly that she was dead and *in the back of the car....*" one would think that Joe Gargan would have known which window to reach into. The driver's-side (inboard to the shore of the upside-down car) rear window was closed. Both the outboard (passenger-side) windows were (blown) open. The research cited above states that at 12:20 A.M., when Gargan and Markham allegedly "dove" (an experienced sailor would never dive into dark and possibly shallow waters, one would walk in, and then swim), the tide speed would have increased to 1.5 knots; "currents of such velocity would make rescue efforts more difficult but not impossible."

The renowned columnist Max Lerner, certainly no enemy of the Kennedys, reported in his book that touched on the subject of Chappaquiddick, that Gargan and Markham knew full well that Ray LaRosa was a fireman trained in scuba diving rescue.[5] Kennedy claimed under oath to not have known this. These people are sailors, and occasionally propellers get hung by stray lines. When a friend of a sailor, a yachtsmen, is a trained scuba diver, you know it! It's a time-honored joke; they're the ones that have to dive to free the propeller! "When you're raised on the water," said Joe Gargan to the *L.A. Times,* 12/24/79, "as Ted and I were, and someone's boat tips over, you don't call the Coast Guard...."

These were the only words Joe Gargan had ever uttered publicly regarding the tragedy prior to 1983, when he talked to author Damore as noted. He was unavailable to the *New York*

---

5   Max Lerner, *Ted and the Kennedy Legend: A Study in Character and Destiny*, St. Martins, 1980, p. 112.

Times in 1980, for the series on Chappaquiddick which they ran prior to the Senator's candidacy for the Presidency.

The Senator testified that he had nearly been swept out to sea. Did Kennedy make the arduous swim to Edgartown? And, because of that hellish swim, become so mentally and emotionally incapacitated that he could not recover sufficiently to report the accident, as he alleges that he told his companions he would do, "You take care of the girls, I'll take care of the accident."[6]

Again from *Readers' Digest*, "Around 1:30 A.M., the current was weak to zero," reports LeMehaute. "After about 1:30 A.M., the current flowed southward toward Katama Bay [not out to sea, but the opposite direction] at an increasing velocity until approximately 4 A.M." At one point the Kennedy people produced expert witnesses, including the Edgartown harbor master who claimed that the tide was going out at the time that Kennedy said that it was.

However, Markham testified that he watched Kennedy swim half to three-quarters of the way across. If it *was* three-quarters of the way Kennedy would have been past the center of the channel where the tidal flow would have controlled the current. They said he was right on line to Edgartown, so they left. Under the circumstances many have indicated disbelief that they would have allowed him to swim at all. One noted Democrat has stated that either Markham or Gargan should have punched Kennedy in the jaw if necessary, anything, to stop him from diving into the water after the horrible experience he had just gone through. They claim that they let him go. But even if they did, they observed his swimming, and he was not being swept to sea, consequently, their entire testimony regarding why he didn't report the accident crumbles before the facts, before their very own words.

---

[6]   Inquest testimony.

Based on the evidence present above, it appears that Mary Jo Kopechne did not have to die. It is this author's opinion that that was the horror for Mary Jo, she was left ... and that is why she died!

18

REQUIEM

Having assumed the role of prosecutor, this writer has attempted to exercise the maximum personal control over self-indulgent editorial context in the preceding pages. However, during the writing, the ramifications that proceeded from the new hard evidence which was presented, created an emotion akin to rage at certain times. The most obvious manifestations were certain sarcasms in both footnotes and text. While these may have been off-putting to Kennedy sympathizers and even neutral individuals, it must be remembered one of the objectives of this book was to present a case for indictment on the serious charge of manslaughter.

Even though an indictment was not handed up in the real world, it was not the intent of this book to go on to the next logical prosecutor's procedure by recommending sentence. Let the reader, as jurist, vote in their own mind. In the few following pages the author finally exercises a personal prerogative — poetic philosophy, if you will — regarding the Kennedys and what they represented. The Kennedys were bound to change us. They did. It will take the long view of history to confirm that.

Up to now, we have looked at a fair amount of detail from the public record, and have seen some of the hidden facts which tell the real story of Chappaquiddick. At the outset, it was made clear that there will remain those who feel that the case has not been made, that Senator Kennedy was simply a victim of circumstances, of an accident, pure and simple. That he really did drive his car off the bridge and then, somehow, defying all logical explanation and with the physical facts to the contrary, he got out of the car and was forced to leave Mary Jo to her watery tomb. And because of his arduous swim, he was unable to report the accident. It is true that he was largely a victim of circumstances, in that, once certain courses of action were begun, there was no turning back.

It has been reported that the ladies from the party were offered large sums of money to tell their stories. They never did, never will. The reasons are simple enough.

First, they didn't have any real stories to tell. They could have spoken of others that were at the party. What would be the point? As they knew full well, that wouldn't have brought back Mary Jo. They never did know or understand the real facts in the matter. Their silence did not appear to them as a major disservice to the public's right to know. They really didn't know what happened! As we have seen, it was carefully orchestrated and controlled so that they would not know. By all intelligence standards they had no need to know.

These young women came to Washington and because they were the "best and brightest;" they worked for Bobby. The women who had been at the party were called "boiler-room girls." They wouldn't call them girls anymore, not to their faces, that is one sign of the work, the hard work of the sixties. These young women had worked for Bobby, had struggled with him and for him. How could they speak against his brother, the ideal? That is what counted, the ideal. True to their cause, they remained silent. And to that extent, to that degree, the dream is not over.

Some cynics will say that they benefited, that they profited by their silence. In view of the fact that three of these women are currently partners in Boston law firms, it appears that places have been found for them. This of course in no way takes away from their professional abilities.

Unfortunately, Edward Kennedy was never able to recover from the terrible things that happened to him. In the years after the tragedy he dutifully put on his public face, and was a father to a large, extended family. Yet he has never recovered, has never been right because of the unknown "thing" of Chappaquiddick. This "thing" has been mentioned by previous writers on the subject to mean the still-hidden truth; the knowledge; reading between the lines, — the intuition that something not right happened out there that night. And that force, that dark boding is what shows up in public-opinion polls regarding Chappaquiddick. The polls show that people have never believed the official Kennedy version of what happened that night. Yet, as pointed out above, he is first in a recent poll as the man for the Democratic Party 1992 Presidential nomination. Does this speak to moral bankruptcy, know nothingism, loss of memory, or more likely (the folk lore), that "they all do it" regarding the moral and ethical bankruptcy of some career politicians — elected representatives? So then, it appears that perhaps the public is thoroughly caught up in its role as victims in this game we often naively call democracy.

Others have written about the subject of Chappaquiddick, but the early writers went astray. The cover-up was just too good, the tracks hidden too well, and, why bother? Who cares? The reason to bother, to care, is that the truth is a foundation of democracy.

It was mentioned at the outset that the Senator sets a bad moral example because of the public's intuitive knowledge that the truth has not come out. But still he holds public office; he can't stop.

He's like that great, giant Irish tackle who gets banged in the head early in the game, too hard, and he can't remember. But because he has so much heart, he's so big, and he seems to fill the hole, and the crowd yells out his family name; the coach, beholden to the price of uniforms, doesn't — can't take him out. And that great Irish tackle can't even think in terms of taking himself out, by God he was born to play, he must play, he has no choice! And so the home team loses the game, because the tackle just can't do the job anymore. Let's not have to boo Ted Kennedy out of the game. Somebody speak to him, so that even at this late date as he leaves the field (and sets an example), we can cheer him and his fallen brothers, and get on with the game!

APPENDICES

In order to present the entire Chappaquiddick record and literature in one forum, in the following pages we will deal with the seven previously published books on the subject.[1] This is important so that informed readers can make their own judgments based on the complete literature on the subject. With the exception of Leo Damore's 1989 book, *Senatorial Privilege*, these other books are all out of print, and are not generally available in the libraries I have visited. Thus, it is important to present them in this forum.

Apologies in advance to the individuals who have put in the hundreds of hours necessary to produce a book on this subject. For obvious reasons, this author does not agree with the final conclusions of any of the other books. However, the present book could not have been written without reference to their extensive field work, and in certain cases much was gained by peering over the shoulders of Investigative giants.

Credit is given where due. By presenting synopses of their works we show where the author's ultimate conclusions led them in attempting to come up with an answer — "the solution" — to this bizarre event in our modern national history, and at the same time help to complete the Chappaquiddick record.

---

[1] Larry Ann Willis, an Oregon writer, (as is the present writer) wrote a book on Chappaquiddick in the early 1980's. I could never find distribution of the book in New York. And despite repeated calls to Oregon I was never able to obtain a copy. Reviews have said that it was a well-written book which dealt with the social implications of the tragedy, but did not propose a new solution to that dark night.

APPENDIX A

AN INSIDER'S VERSION

Jack Olsen, former *Time* Senior Editor, wrote the first book on this subject. *The Bridge at Chappaquiddick*, published by Little, Brown, was completed in December of 1969. It is a highly readable, balanced and very well investigated insider view. His work has no seeming bias or prejudicial point of view, and works as it was intended to, as good reportage.

Realizing that this was a major story in the making, Olsen rented an apartment in Edgartown and spent two months there researching his book. By doing this he was able to gain a special relationship with the local residents. Martha's Vineyard year-round residents are known to be suspicious of off-island people. Consequently, as a result his actually "moving" to town, he was able to develop personal relationships. It was his personal relationships with the local leading citizens and officials, that enabled him to be able to obtain material unavailable to later researchers. He reconstructed dialogue of the events as they were said to have occurred. None of the individuals mentioned in his narrative accounts has specifically publicly disavowed the words Olsen placed in their mouths, and Walter Steele, the Edgartown prosecutor, has verified the accuracy of those portions of dialogue that include him. He deals with the facts available at that early date. And reached a conclusion which has been adhered to by many in the aftermath.

The book consists of a Prologue and five sections or extended chapters. In the short Prologue, he describes the Kennedy family ascent and speaks of the eventual inevitability (pre-Chappaquiddick) of a Teddy Presidency. He is not kind with regard to Kennedy's intellectual gifts. He closes his book with the Chappaquiddick incident and how that incident stopped the juggernaut and forced the answers to such questions as "...who was Ted Kennedy? What was He?"

Olsen discusses the womanizing aspects in the Kennedy public reputation. With this device. Olsen signals the reader that the Edgartown Regatta weekend is indeed a time and place where Teddy was known to have been a philanderer. In January, 1980, the *New York Post* did a series which reported directly (even using names) of individuals Kennedy had affairs with at Martha's Vineyard in the two years preceding the tragedy in 1969.

According to Olsen, the climate in 1969, regarding libel suits caused Olsen's publishers to keep the juice out of this narrative. It was not established at that time that Ted Kennedy would not sue in response to what was printed about him.

The second section is a well-researched and well-written account of the weekend itself, a reconstruction made possible by publicly available information. He includes many vignettes and snippets of lore surrounding the Regatta weekend.

Section Three, "The Morning After," is a well-detailed narrative of the discovery of the automobile. This section focuses on the movements of Edgartown Police Chief Arena through the longest day in his life. Perhaps most interesting in this section is Olsen's ability to directly report the conversation between Chief Arena and Edgartown part-time prosecutor, Walter Steele. Olsen makes no bones about Steele's reluctance to sharpen his teeth to go after the most powerful man in Massachusetts.

The gathering at Hyannis Port of the Kennedy advisers is thoroughly detailed, and it appears that Olsen had very good sources.

Olsen discusses the funeral for Mary Jo. The public was still not treated to any information by Kennedy, even though newsmen were able to get within "talking distance" of him at the funeral.

In his concluding section, "The Trap," he postulates that Kennedy got out of the car after the close encounter with the uniformed Deputy Sheriff, Huck Look. According to Olsen, appearance (not being seen with a young woman after midnight), gave rise to Kennedy's rationale to send Mary Jo on alone in the car, while he crouched in the bushes. If the Deputy Sheriff had followed and discovered the two of them, something worse than a scene might have been the result, especially if there had been liquor in the car. So, according to Olsen, Mary Jo was ordered to drive the large unfamiliar car (her personal auto was a Volkswagen) and draw off the Deputy Sheriff while Kennedy hid in the bushes. Unfamiliar with the road, the foot pedals hard to reach, in a semi-intoxicated state, Mary Jo, according to Olsen, then drove herself off the bridge and drowned. However, the Senator, according to Olsen, couldn't change his story after the Police Report was filed and therefore has been forced to stick to the original.

APPENDIX B

THE ENEMY CAMP REPORTS

Zad Rust's, *Teddy Bare: The Last of the Kennedy Clan,* published in 1971, created quite a stir nine years after it was published. The fact that this book was published, although, indirectly by the John Birch Society, makes for an intensely ideological tone and extremely reactionary rhetoric. However, in no way can the sternest critic (ideologically speaking) talk away the value of Rust's earnest and painstaking research into the subject.

According to *Human Events* Magazine, September 21, 1974, the Rust book had sold over 400,000 copies. The book was receiving attention as late as 1980. The following is taken directly from the *Library Journal,* a librarian's trade magazine, April 15, 1980:

ANTI-KENNEDY BOOK PURCHASE
STIRS PROTEST IN MARYLAND

Responding to popular demand for reading materials about Presidential candidate Edward Kennedy, Maryland's Fairfax County Library bought 88 paperback copies of *Teddy Bare: the Last of the Kennedy Clan.* According to the *Washington Post,* the book, published by Western Islands, an affiliate of the ultraconservative John Birch Society, depicts Kennedy as "one of the prominent operators chosen by the Hidden Forces that are hurling the countries of Western Civilization toward the Animal Farm World of Lenin and his successors."

The large purchase of the anti-Kennedy tract stirred protest from people campaigning for Kennedy, who complained that the purchase amounts to "overkill" and the preponderance of *Teddy Bare* titles "does not indicate a fair balance." Kennedy supporters said they did not protest the purchase in and of itself, but simply the quantity of titles bought.

But, Fairfax County Library Acquisitions Librarian, Nancy Woodall defended the purchase, saying that there were specific requests for the *Teddy Bare* book. She noted that it was hard to find a favorable book about Kennedy, and there was practically nothing out in paperback except the Rust book. Cost was a deciding factor in the purchase "because of limited acquisition funds." And Woodall said that 88 copies is not an unusually large purchase; the library bought about 400 copies of Michener's *Chesapeake.*

Rust opens with a madcap devastation of the liberal flag, the "Forces of Darkness, and their front men ... of the spurious Arthurian dynasty." Finally, he settles down and describes the reasons for the Chappaquiddick party and lists the participants, as publicly known.

Rust accuses the Senator of manslaughter and concludes that the Senator was not in the car when it actually plunged into the water. His analysis is that Kennedy saved himself by "...jumping out onto the bridge before the actual plunge." Rust was not aware that the car had been travelling between 30-38 miles-per-hour. Therefore, if Kennedy had jumped at that speed he would no doubt have sustained serious injuries

In Chapter Ten, Rust speculates on the "thing" which is the secret or mystery of Chappaquiddick. He makes a case for the existence of this "thing".

Part Two, entitled The Comedy, addresses the beginnings of an attempt by District Attorney Dinis, to move towards an Inquest. Rust forgives Dinis for not acting before. It was "...only next morning, after he had heard Senator Kennedy's statement on television, could he have realized that Prosecutor Steele and Chief Arena had not told him all they knew about the case."

In this section the book explores the machinations involved in Kennedy's lawyers' battle to see to it that the Inquest be held in secret. He alludes to the monumental effort by Kennedy's lawyers to avoid any public scrutiny of under-oath testimony of Kennedy. His thesis is that the Kennedy lawyers fought for secrecy in order to avoid the possibility of anything coming out that would be destructive to the Senator's early statements, and here Rust again alludes strongly to "...the thing...." these efforts were meant to conceal.

Rust seems willing to go to any length ("...secret orders....") to show that a conspiracy exists in which the Establishment will attempt "... to perch their new Arthur in the seat of command." Unfortunately, it is difficult for the reader to analyze some of Rust's conclusions because Rust succumbs to a reactionary's need to ideologize in the extreme at the same time that he makes telling findings based on the facts he has dug out.

The third part of the book, entitled Final Hocus Pocus, includes well-drawn analysis of the lengths gone to abort any attempt by the local Grand Jury to uncover the mystery.

Dinis, drew the job of illegally instructing the Grand Jury that they could *not* call any witnesses who had testified at the Inquest. Protected by the secrecy that Judge Paquet demanded of the jurors, Dinis had no trouble burying the final ax. Rust ties this material together and closes the chapter with an apt historical reference: "One is inescapably reminded of Frederick the Great's admiring exclamation: 'There are judges in Berlin!' So are there judges in Boston."

He closes with an analysis of Deputy Sheriff Christopher Look's testimony. Rust does a thorough job here. He closely scrutinizes Judge Boyle's final report, and points out the inconsistencies to be found throughout the Inquest testimony. This author is in agreement with many of Rust's contentions. However, his final conclusion, that the Senator jumped out of the speeding car in mid-air, while endorsed by skindiver John Farrar, fails to consider how Kennedy was not seriously injured if he hit the bridge, or anything for that matter, at 34 miles-per-hour.

APPENDIX C

REDIRECT FROM THE RIGHT

Death at Chappaquiddick, is a well-written, well-thought-out report and analysis of what went on at Chappaquiddick by Richard and Thomas Tedrow (father and son). The strength of the book is in Richard L. Tedrow's background as a lawyer and specifically his experience from 1951-68 as Chief Commissioner of the U.S. Court of Military Appeals.

His son, Thomas, a 1972 Journalism graduate, was no doubt inspired by the romance of investigative journalism which swept the nation as a result of "Woodstein's" Watergate revelations. The combination of investigative zeal and solid legal expertise, youthful energy tempered by acquired wisdom has provided an excellent, highly analytical review of Chappaquiddick.

This author has benefited from the relentless and deep investigation accomplished by father and son. Credit is due to them for bringing forward certain information that might well have remained buried had it not been for their efforts. The fact that in this writer's opinion they missed the key clue regarding the blood on the blouse as determined from the benzidene test is not detrimental to their intensive efforts in as much as they have provided a well-researched analysis from the point of view of the legal profession.

The book begins with a basic statement of general known facts concerning the party: participants, estimates of length in time, and a detailed analysis of liquor brought to the party, accompanied by conjecture as to actual consumption. They conclude this section with a discussion of short vignettes of Kennedy drinking legends, and a pointed essay regarding the press's willingness to hide certain personal traits.

They move on to document Deputy Sheriff Look's sighting of the car, noting Esther Newberg's loose use of time in her various statements to the press and her Inquest testimony. They also point out and document that Kennedy was lying in his testimony regarding his presence on Chappaquiddick in previous years.

The next chapter expresses their point of view that the Senator escaped from the submerging automobile as a result of a "combination of fate, the roll of the car, and his natural urge to survive. Mary Jo's submerged tomb is a combination of fate, the roll of the car, and Kennedy's nine-hour silence."

An excellent documentation of Arthur Egan's and Jack Anderson's prior reportage regarding the missing telephone calls is included.

In Part Two, Justice Obstructed, senior Tedrow's extensive background and legal expertise show through. The writing is excellent, and informed concerning the law and its principles; yet is very easily understood by the layman. Their points are often made with paternalistic irony, such as "If your lawyer agrees with Judge Brominski, you need a new lawyer." This comes in their short denouncement of Judge Brominski's Order to deny exhumation and autopsy.

In the Tedrows' ironic, mocking style, the Massachusetts Supreme Court is reduced to a band of mere Kennedy partisans. They portray the Court as baldly supporting the Senator's presumptions and needs, while ignoring the process of justice. Their conclusion is most telling, "In other words, the Inquest record of proceedings was not to be used until it was no longer of any use."

The Tedrows make reference to the other published accounts of Chappaquiddick, mention certain rumors and conclude with the point, "that *none,* repeat *none* of the sponsors of these various theories (except for parishioners David and Honan) place any credence in the Senators testimony." It must be pointed out that David and Honan are "approved" biographers of Teddy and as true believers, they felt that the TV statement was a valid, essentially sufficient, explanation of the tragedy.

The book is most instructive in their chapter entitled simply "Credibility." Here they give a sample of known and standard instructions that judges give juries in criminal cases. Their concluding statement tells it all:

With this in mind, we the public jury are entitled to infer that they determined it was safer to suppress and to be accused of suppressing the truth than to *let the truth be known*. [Emphasis Added.]

In their conclusion, it appears they may have erred by hypothesizing, "after Kennedy escaped, the car settled into the silt, wedging the doors, preventing free egress through the windows."

No where else in the literature or the record is this "silt" to be found. The channel was freshly dredged, it seems unlikely that there was a silt buildup. The fast-moving current, a result of tide changes every six hours, kept the channel free of built-up silt. Further proof is that there was no such silt in the automobile when it was removed from the water.

Yet, all in all, the book is a welcome addition to the Chappaquiddick record.

APPENDIX D

HARD LOOK FROM THE LEFT

Robert Sherrill's book, *The Last Kennedy,* was drawn from his very powerful article for the *New York Times Magazine,* "*Chappaquiddick + 5*" July 14, 1974. The demand for reprints ran high for the published article.

He begins the book with a quotation that has stood the test of time and seems even more appropriate in that Senator Kennedy ran for the presidency in 1980, tossed his hat in the ring in 1984, withdrew it, started again in '85, and stopped again, and during all this time made jokes about his one day possibility:

> It was all very careless and confused. They were careless people ... they smashed up things and creatures and then retreated back into their money or their vast carelessness, or whatever it was that kept them together, and let other people clean up the mess they had made.
>
> F. Scott Fitzgerald
> *The Great Gatsby*

Initially, one marvels at the audacity of Sherrill. On its face, it seems incredible that the lawyers for the Dial Press had allowed certain of Sherrill's remarks to slip through into print. For instance, at the conclusion of his Introduction to his 239 page book, Sherrill states, "and when we return to Chappaquiddick, our objective...to present a case study of how a famous politician... *can kill* somebody under mysterious circumstances...." [Emphasis Added.]

How could Sherrill get away with such remarks? Why didn't Kennedy use the courts to stop publication or, failing that, sue for libel? He could have put publishers in general, on notice that no lies, no slurs, no implicating innuendo will be permitted in print. Sherrill isn't lying — he means it, and his reputation as a left-leaning, progressive journalist is clean. One can only imagine the battle he must have waged with his publisher's attorneys, regarding the quotation above. However, ultimately it is not really a mystery why he felt free to speak the truth. As Sherrill points out deeper in the book, Kennedy has clammed up. In fact, his entire strategy in avoiding serious legal problems in the matter, was simply to be silent, because of the facts in the case, there is no alternative.

However, does this mean *anyone* can say *anything* in print if it is based on truthful new evidence, in relation to Chappaquiddick? Perhaps, because if Kennedy or others were to sue; Kennedy and all the other individuals that were involved would be exposed to examination (under oath) before trial (depositions), and then be required to take the stand in an open court of law. There would be no way to guarantee that a sitting judge, outside of Massachusetts, in 1989, would not be interested in new issues, new evidence, regarding Chappaquiddick. Lawyers would certainly rise to object concerning the relevance of certain questions in relation to their bearing on an instant action of libel, yet there would never be such a tight guarantee as was given by the Massachusetts Supreme Court. A public forum was avoided at that time. There is no way to assure that a libel action brought by Kennedy, or anybody else mentioned, (all unwilling, but certifiable "public figures" to be sure), would be handled behind closed doors at the present time.

Sherrill handles this area brilliantly, and his skill as a writer and journalist shines through. He tellingly indicts the entire Massachusetts judiciary system in plain and bald language. To wit: "The law was, once again, an ass."

Sherrill shifts to an analysis of the "shaping influences" on Edward Kennedy prior to the tragedy at the Dyke Bridge. This section is particularly well-informed in presenting Senator Kennedy as a product of his particular class and heritage. It details him as a plodder, who begins to grow beyond his brothers, after they die.

In his book, Sherrill went to lengths to track down the rumor that Joe Gargan was going to take the blame for the accident. He tracks this theory to its beginnings, in print, in the *New York Times*. The story was that Kennedy acted so relaxed in his early (7:30 A.M.) meeting with Ross Richards, and his earlier calm borrowing of a dime and ordering of the newspapers, so that he could substitute Mary Jo or Gargan as the driver of the vehicle by feigning ignorance. Thus, he would had have no alternative but to play this role of almost studied nonchalance.

This concept of substituting another was old hat to Kennedy, as illustrated by the infamous cheating incident at Harvard. At that time a Kennedy look-a-like pal took his Spanish test for him. When they were discovered, they were both expelled from the university and Joe Sr. put Ted into the Army. A couple of years later when he was enrolled in law school, and while attempting to escape from local police in a high-speed automobile chase the second night in a row (this ruse having worked the night before), Kennedy pulled his car over and lay down in the front seat. This time he was apprehended and he paid a speeding ticket. It seems that his character forces him to deny, hide, disappear, or have someone else substitute for him. Simply put, Kennedy's actions have seemed like that of the denying ostrich. He denies by closing his eyes or choosing a subterfuge of concealment, hoping to make the problem go away. Chappaquiddick has never gone away.

Another theory brought out in this section relates to the possibility that Kennedy didn't know what had happened to Miss Kopechne, that in fact he wasn't in the car when it entered the water. In his police statement he had said, "I attempted to open the door and the window...." The driver's side window was in fact open (rolled down) and the two windows on the passenger side (front and back) were blown out from the impact. Some thought that this proved that he really hadn't been in the car when it went into the water.

Sherrill then goes into the theory that Mary Jo had possibly been, unannounced to anyone, asleep in the back seat of the car. Consequently, there never were any attempts to save her. This theory is favored by Kennedy insiders, apologists and certain sympathetic politicians. In this self-serving tale, Mary Jo got drunk, and passed out in the back of the car without anyone realizing it. Kennedy and Rosemary Keough (she is mentioned in this theory only because her purse was found in the car) leave in the car for some late night submarine-race watching by the ocean side, he drives over the side, they escape, and of course didn't save Mary Jo because they didn't know that she was there. This convenient theory makes him a mere philanderer, but totally innocent as far as Mary Jo's death is concerned. Some on the left like to cite this theory, as it obviously must ease their consciences' as they continue to work for or with the Senator.

Later on, he gives a very good analysis of the daily press, its seeming "hands-off" policy towards the tragedy and the lack of press analysis regarding the ramifications for Kennedy's career. By way of example, Sherrill quotes at length from *The New Republic*, accusing the magazine's editors of going "so far as to defend Kennedy's obstruction of justice." He closes his chapter on the press by applauding the *Chicago Tribune*, the *Manchester Union Leader* and the weekly news magazines for strong reporting and opinion.

Sherrill rises above his role as a Chappaquiddick investigator and publicist for the truth. As a modern historian, he puts Edward M. Kennedy into perspective *vis-a-vis* his brothers, his relation to the United States Senate, and his growing maturity and responsibility.

By ignoring Kennedy in these days (early '70's), the public missed the surfacing evidence of a dramatic transformation: he was outgrowing Jack. He was seeing the disaster of Vietnam as a family crime, and he had stopped trying to find ways to defend it.

Near the end of his book, Sherrill points out with considerable irony that when it became clear that:

Nixon might defy a Supreme Court order to surrender his Watergate tapes, Kennedy took the floor of... an almost empty chamber... the Senate, to proclaim, "If this country stands for anything, it stands for the principle that no man is above the law...."

Finally, and we must remember *The Last Kennedy* was written in 1975, Sherrill closes with the sentence, "Teddy didn't — or at least hasn't yet — asked everybody to bankroll his ego." That may have been true in 1976. In 1980 the Senator, in his bid for the Presidency, did ask us to "bankroll his ego."

Whether an individual condsiders it positive or negative, it has been argued that Ted Kennedy guaranteed Ronald Reagans election to the Presidency in 1980 by challenging the incumbent President Jimmy Carter from within his own party. This very act is unusual in American politics.

APPENDIX E

A NOVEL APPROACH

Malcolm Reybold, a retired Madison Avenue advertising executive, wrote a "historical Chappaquiddick novel," *The Inspector's Opinion*, that was published by E.P. Dutton in 1975. Reybold, who wrote without the benefit of the work of either Sherrill or the Tedrows, apparently decided to have some fun, while presenting many of the facts and known inconsistencies of the tragedy.

He reprints a good portion of relevant Inquest testimony, which underscores the material inconsistencies of the record. His rendering of the record is presented out of true chronological order; but by his grouping of inconsistencies he shows their relevance to the reader, rather than simply announcing (as the early authors did) that they exist.

Much of the novel is presented in a dear old boy, patrician tone. His hero, an heir to fabulous wealth, sets out to get to the bottom of the Chappaquiddick mystery because the TV speech hits him as less than the truth.

Reybold enlists a retired, legendary Scotland Yard detective as chief investigator and prosecutor, in a dramatized reenactment of the Inquest testimony. The eventual solution by Reybold is far-fetched and is based on the Inspector's "intuitions, deductive logic and close scrutiny of the known facts of the case."

Withholding the novel's romantic plot, we shall look ahead to the final conclusions advanced by Reybold.

As others have pointed out, the key to the mystery, according to Reybold, is Kennedy's calmness in the morning, coupled with Markham's and Gargan's attempts to show no alarm back at the cottage at 2:45 A.M. As a good investigator, he makes the strong point that Kennedy may have undone himself when he mentioned to his doctor that he had returned to the cottage for help after being unable to rescue Mary Jo. In fact that may have been the reason for mentioning Markham and Gargan in the TV speech. At that point he had to provide a cover story for his willing accomplices that allowed them as lawyers (and, therefore, Officers of the Court), to not report the accident.

In final analysis, this novel makes its case not for criminality — but for tragedy. He gives compelling emotional sentiment to the female heroine in the novel when she states: "I think he was mistaken in his choice of actions, yes; but I simply cannot bring myself to the conclusion that there was true evil involved."

Amen!

APPENDIX F

ANALYSIS FROM THE BACK BAY

R.B. Cutler, who lives just North of Boston in the affluent area known as the Back Bay, made a significant contribution to the Chappaquiddick record with his book from Bett's & Mirror Press, published originally in 1973. It is a compendium of press reports and testimonies from the legal proceedings.

This author owes a significant debt to Cutler in that he originally assembled the photographs that are the basis of the present book's theories. Without comment Cutler shared the photographs in his office in Manchester, Massachusetts in 1982. Noting certain oddities regarding these photos and supplied with a magnifying glass, it became obvious to the present author that the photos told the real story of Chappaquiddick. After this seeming "original" discovery, Cutler offered his book, which had noted the critical factors regarding damage to the car.

With respect for Cutler's prodigious research efforts into this and other national tragedies of recent U.S. history, this author feels that Cutler has veered into uncharted waters in terms of final analysis of the mystery of Chappaquiddick. He finds that there must have been foul play, foul play and deadly acts that stemmed from the actions of outside perpetrators. Cutler contends that an as yet unknown crew set-up Kennedy to stop him in attempts to reach the White House. That they forced alcohol down Mary Jo Kopechne's throat, killed her, damaged the car manually, used an individual who resembled Kennedy, and ultimately threatened Kennedy, Gargan and Markham with death if they ever told the true story of that night. Cutler and this author have agreed to disagree.

APPENDIX G

A CAREFUL INVESTIGATION

Leo Damore's best seller, *Senatorial Privilege: The Chappaquiddick Cover-Up*, is the definitive work to date on the *cover-up* staged by Kennedy and his forces after the accident occurred. As such it is an excellent companion to the present book which, purports to present what actually happened *that night*. Because Damore's book is still in the marketplace (other books have long been out-of-print) it would not be appropriate to make a dissection of this work as in the preceding Appendices. If you want to know how the Kennedy family-team wired the state of Massachusetts, buy Damore's book; you will not be disappointed.

Damore, a life-long resident of New England, originally covered the incident as a reporter in 1969. He was unable to walk away from it without digging deep. His book offers new exposure in two major areas. First, Joe Gargan, apparently at odds with Kennedy, gave Damore several interviews in 1983. The "Gargan interviews" make it clear that Kennedy wanted him to set-it-up so that it would appear that Mary Jo was driving.

Second, Damore discovered that District Attorney Dinis sent signals to the Kennedy camp. Dinis had escorted JFK to the podium to accept the Vice-Presidential nomination in 1956. According to Damore, a State Police investigator approached the Kennedy family's representatives on two occasions; passing word regarding what the D.A. would in fact present at the Inquest. The Kennedy side knew what to expect, and that there would be no surprises. Damore scrupulously documents his material.

Over several years I have been encouraged by many individuals who know who they are to finish the project, to make a footnote to history, to correct the record.

Certain individuals have offered more than moral support, and in fact helped me with direction as readers and correctors of this manuscript. Obviously the standard *mea culpa* holds here, I alone am responsible for the short-comings and the tone of the book. Special thanks to Dean Engel who was the first person to tell me that I was a writer, he then pointed out most of my mixed metaphors and grammatical problems. As the manuscript began to take shape, Dave Alsberg also pushed me to remove my most obvious Don Quixote shouts and rails against Establishment that continues to protect Edward Kennedy. Both of the above individuals made it clear that I was writing about Chappaquiddick, and should stick to the subject.

Jim Nevin, not only provided me with a place to work and with the first laser printer, he became one of the book's sternest critics, forcing me to deal with the inconsistencies that the earliest drafts contained. Ken Simondinger became my counselor in the wings, always encouraging, but more importantly, framing the issue in a mature and reflective light. What about Mary Jo?

Victor Bongiovanni showed me that ultimately I had talked the book onto paper, or so it seemed. When he finished a massive line editing (and much more) job, I was able to be proud of this work as it lays on the pages.

For those who know and care about such things, this book was written and type-set by the author using WordPerfect 5.0. Unaltered mechanicals were out-put on an H-P LaserJet Series II using Bitstream fonts.

Finally, as many good mother's do, mine struggled against this voyage into uncharted waters, after all one has to make a living, and well, "...this writing." But, after I finally had a first draft manuscript completed, and she realized that I could do this, she rallied to my support beyond my expectations.

Thank all of you.

Cutler, R.B. *YOU, THE JURY ... In Re: Chappaquiddick*, Danvers, Massachusetts: Betts & Mirror Press, 1973.

Davis, John H. *THE KENNEDYS: Dynasty and Disaster*, New York: McGraw Hill, 1984.

Damore, Leo. *SENATORIAL PRIVILEGE, The Chappaquiddick Cover-up*, Washington D.C.: Regnery Gateway, 1988.

Hersh, Burton. *THE EDUCATION OF EDWARD KENNEDY, A Family Biography*, New York: Morrow, 1972.

Honan, William H. *TED KENNEDY: Profile of a Survivor*, New York: Manor Books, 1972.

Lester, David. *TED KENNEDY: Triumphs and Tragedies*, New York: Grosset & Dunlap, 1972.

Olsen, Jack. *THE BRIDGE AT CHAPPAQUIDDICK*, Boston: Little, Brown, 1970.

Reybold, Malcolm. *THE INSPECTOR'S OPINION*, New York: Dutton, 1975.

Rust, Zad. *TEDDY BARE, The Last of The Kennedy Clan*, Belmont, Massachusetts: Western Islands, 1971.

Schlesinger, Arthur Jr. *A THOUSAND DAYS*, New York: Houghton Mifflin, 1965.

Sherrill, Robert. *THE LAST KENNEDY*, New York: Dial Press, 1976.

Sorensen, Theodore C. *KENNEDY*, New York: Harper & Row, 1965.

Tedrow, Thomas L., and Richard L. *DEATH AT CHAPPAQUIDDICK*, Ottowa, IL: Green Hill, 1976.

Whalen, Richard. *THE FOUNDING FATHER: The Story of Joseph P. Kennedy*, New York: Signet, 1966.

Boston Globe

Boston Tribune

Chicago Tribune

Chicago Daily News

Herald Tribune

Human Events

Inquiry

Library Journal

Life

Los Angeles Times

McCall's

Manchester Union Leader

The National Review

The New Republic

New West Magazine

New York Magazine

New York Daily News

New York Post

New York Times

New York Times Magazine

Politics Today

The Progressive

Providence Rhode Island Sun

Readers' Digest

Saturday Evening Post

The Nation

Time

U.S. World News & Report

Vineyard Gazette

Washingtonian

The Washington Monthly

Washington Post

A AP/Wide World
B Inquest Exhibit #19. Courtesy Philip Rollins, District Attorney
C AP/Wide World
D AP/Wide World
E AP/Wide World
F AP/Wide World
G Black Star
H AP/Wide World
I Gamma/Liason
J AP/Wide World
K AP/Wide World
L AP/Wide World
M Jack Hubbard/Black Star
N AP/Wide World
O AP/Wide World
P UPI/Bettmann
Q AP/Wide World
R UPI/Bettmann
S AP/Wide World
T AP/Wide World
U Jack Hubbard/Black Star
V Jack Hubbard/Black Star
W Jack Hubbard/Black Star
X Jack Hubbard/Black Star
Y Jack Hubbard/Black Star
Z AP/Wide World
AA Jack Hubbard/Black Star
BB Jack Hubbard/Black Star
CC AP/Wide World
DD AP/Wide World
EE Fred Ward/Black Star

Illustrations

A Inquest Exhibit 14, enhanced by R.Cutler, Courtesy Philip
   A. Rollins, District Attorney
B R.B. Cutler for Cutler Designs